# Religious Diversity in European Prisons

Irene Becci • Olivier Roy
Editors

# Religious Diversity in European Prisons

## Challenges and Implications for Rehabilitation

 Springer

*Editors*
Irene Becci
ISSRC-FTSR
University of Lausanne
Lausanne
Switzerland

Olivier Roy
Robert Schuman Centre for
Advanced Studies
European University Institute
Florence
Italy

ISBN 978-3-319-16777-0       ISBN 978-3-319-16778-7 (eBook)
DOI 10.1007/978-3-319-16778-7

Library of Congress Control Number: 2015937902

Springer Cham Heidelberg New York Dordrecht London
© Springer International Publishing Switzerland 2015

Printed on acid-free paper

Springer is part of Springer Science+Business Media (www.springer.com)

# Acknowledgments

This book is the result of a long-term collaboration of a research network that recently met at the ReligioWest workshop "The formatting of religions: religious accommodation in prisons and the military," on 11th and 12th of February 2013 at the European University Institute in Florence, organized by a team led by Kristina Stoeckl and Olivier Roy, and at the conference in Lausanne, on 21st and 22nd of May 2014, organized by a team led by Irene Becci, Jacques Besson, and Pierre-Yves Brandt at the University of Lausanne. The authors thank the organizers, the participants, and the funding institutions of the two workshops for having offered the perfect conditions to publish this work. A particular thanks go to the translator D.M. Barnes for some of the chapters, supported by the ReligioWest project funded by the European Research Council under the European Union's 7th Framework Contract Ideas, the student assistants helping to shape the texts according to the editorial lines, A. Grandjean and M. Bruttin, supported by the Interfaculty Department for Religious History and Science at the University of Lausanne (DIHSR).

# Contents

# About the Editors

**Irene Becci**   is a Professor for "Religious Plurality and new spiritualities" at the Institute of Social Sciences of Religion at the University of Lausanne. She holds a Ph.D. in political and social sciences from the European University Institute. She has worked on the topic of religion in prisons during her doctoral and on religion for ex-prisoners in her postdoctoral studies, comparing Italy, Germany, and Switzerland. She is currently enlarging her perspective to other state institutions dealing with religious diversity and spirituality. She has published widely on the subject, in particular: "Imprisoned Religion: Transformations of Religion During and After Imprisonment in Eastern Germany" (2012, Farnham: Ashgate).

**Olivier Roy**   is a Professor at the European University Institute where he heads the Mediterranean Programme at the Robert Schuman Centre for advanced studies and is a director of the program ReligioWest. He has been a senior researcher at the French National Center for Scientific Research (since 1985), Professor at the Ecole des Hautes Etudes en Sciences Sociales (since 2003), and visiting Professor at Berkeley University (2008/2009). He headed the OSCE's Mission for Tajikistan (1993–1994) and was a Consultant for the UN office of the Coordination for Afghanistan (1988). His field work includes Afghanistan, Political Islam, Middle East, Islam in the West, and comparative religions. He received an "Aggregation de Philosophie" and a Ph.D. in Political Science. He is the author of "The failure of Political Islam" (Harvard UP 1994), "Globalized Islam" (Columbia University Press 2004) and more recently of "La Sainte Ignorance" ("Holy Ignorance," Columbia University Press 2010). He is presently working on "Islamic norms in the public sphere," conversions, apostasy and comparative religions.

# Contributors

**Mohamed Ajouaou** Departement of Theology, VU University Amsterdam, Amsterdam, The Netherlands

**Farid El Asri** International University of Rabat, Rabat, Morocco

**Céline Béraud** CerreV, University of Caen, Caen, France

**Irene Becci** Institute for the Social Sciences of Contemporary Religions, University of Lausanne, Lausanne, Switzerland

**James A. Beckford** Department of Sociology, University of Warwick, Coventry, UK

**Ton Bernts** The Religion, Mind, Culture and Society Research Network, Radboud University Nijmegen, Nijmegen, The Netherlands

**Anna Clot-Garrell** Sociology Department, Universitat Autònoma de Barcelona, Barcelona, Spain

**Claire de Galembert** Ecole Normale Supérieure de Cachan, Cachan, France

**Valeria Fabretti** Department 'Scienze e Tecnologie della Formazione' (STF) and 'Centre for the Study and Documentation of Religions and Political Institutions in Postsecular Society' (CSPS), University of Rome Tor Vergata, Rome, Italy

**Mar Griera** Sociology Department, Universitat Autònoma de Barcelona, Barcelona, Spain

**Sarah J. Jahn** Center for Religious Studies—CERES, Ruhr-University Bochum, Bochum, Germany

**Khalid M. Rhazzali** Department of Philosophy, Sociology, Pedagogy and Applied Psychology-FISPPA, University of Padua, Veneto, Italy

**Frédéric Rognon** Faculty of Protestant Theology, University of Strasbourg, Strasbourg, France

**Corinne Rostaing** Centre Max Weber (CNRS), University of Lyon, Lyon, France

**Olivier Roy** Robert Schuman Centre for Advanced Studies, European University Institute, Florence, Italy

# Chapter 1
# European Research on Religious Diversity as a Factor in the Rehabilitation of Prisoners: An Introduction

**Irene Becci**

Debates about the aims and social functions of the current prison systems in Europe emerge cyclically in political arenas and the mass media. The range of opinions is extremely wide, from the criticism of prisons as inhuman and even engendering criminality and the request to abolish them, to the opposite: the claim that prisons are velveted shelters for criminals and need to be harshened. Social scientific research confirms that prisons and their aims of containment and rehabilitation are highly contested fields. Recently, the contestations have become increasingly related to religion and religious diversity. In the European context, prisons have historically implemented the modern binary conception of secularism and religion, and apart from their specific functions—to re-educate, protect, rehabilitate, punish, etc.—they play a central role in the secularization process of society. Nowadays, emerging religious and spiritual practices and discourses are transforming the secular conceptions of punishment, imprisonment and rehabilitation. In the opposite direction, secular punitive or integrative practices in institutions are transforming religious and spiritual ways of dealing with reparation and punishment.

The religious change that the correctional realms of most European countries have witnessed in recent years has concerned first of all the inmates. Compared to a couple of decades ago, their religious affiliations, discourses and practices have greatly diversified. Moreover, there has been a change in the wider discourse connecting issues of religion to prison. From the Anglo-Saxon world echoes the idea of letting religion, in particular religious communities, play an active role in the rehabilitation of criminals. As a consequence, religion—sometimes under the heading of spirituality—seems to find a new setting in the world of prisons.

This book offers insights into how these processes are developing in the prisons of Belgium, England and Wales, France, Germany, Italy, Spain, Switzerland and the

I. Becci (✉)
Institute for the Social Sciences of Contemporary Religions,
University of Lausanne, Lausanne, Switzerland
e-mail: irene.becciterrier@unil.ch

© Springer International Publishing Switzerland 2015
I. Becci, O. Roy (eds.), *Religious Diversity in European Prisons*,
DOI 10.1007/978-3-319-16778-7_1

1

Netherlands. Readers may wonder about the aim of bringing together all these case studies that follow such different historical paths with respect to religion. Here, they are indeed explored both through contrasts and continuities according to theoretical and analytical keys that are sketched out in this introduction. It is subdivided into three sections. The first section draws a picture of the work done by a European research network in this field and of the main thematic questions approached. The second section starts with some methodological reflections, and proposes a series of variables according to which an analytical framework can be created to organize comparison of national cases. Finally, in the last section, I explain the logic used to structure the book and give some hints for readers to find their way through the book according to their interests.

## 1.1 Results from National Cases

Recently, a series of publications have highlighted the changing religious profile of prisoners in Europe and the structural adjustments some prisons have made to better meet the new needs. One of the first studies on the question of religious diversity in prisons was run by James Beckford and Sophie Gilliat (1998) in the 1990s in England and Wales. There, prison chaplaincy had historically been in the hands of the Anglican Church. Only in the nineteenth century were the Roman Catholics included and these two churches remained the only ones involved in prison work until the publication of Gilliat and Beckford's study. The clear results of the study convinced the authorities to open chaplaincy first to Muslims and then to other faiths[1]. This system was in line with the larger multicultural English political model that institutionalizes differences (Todd 2012). The two English scholars started with the statement as follows (pp. 8–9):

> Religions claim to represent a level of reality which is ultimately true and irreducible to any other meaning system. Consequently, religious believers who perceive that their particular religion does not receive the same degree of respect as do others may feel seriously disadvantaged and offended. No compromise is possible when it comes to matters of absolute significance for the believers. They find it unacceptable to have to put up with what appears to be at best relative or conditional respect for their religion. Some prisoners actually become more serious about their religion precisely because they object to perceived slights against its value or integrity.

In the studies made in the prisons of England and Wales, a multi-faith spiritual care in prisons was considered a necessary and consubstantial element of the treatment offered during imprisonment. The chaplaincy model, which was traditionally led by the established churches, changed. The newly included faith communities were, hence, not the only ones to undergo adaptation. The equal treatment of all religious needs and the equal offer of spiritual care in prison were to be seen as both, the answer to increasingly diverse religious needs and the prevention of these needs becoming too "serious". Such a double aim indicates a tension—between recognition

---

[1] The details on this case are in Beckford's chapter following the introduction.

and control. This tension has inhabited the social scientific studies on religion in prison since then[2]. The issue at stake was hence not only equality—as the title of Gilliat and Beckford's book announced: *"Religion in Prison. Equal Rites in a Multi-Faith Society"*—but also the use of religion preventively against undesired consequences. What these consequences precisely entailed would become clearer only in the decades that followed, and more precisely after the terrorist attacks in New York in 2001. The English inquiry indeed gave important insights, in particular, into the practices and discourses of the chaplains and the staffs (Beckford and Gilliat 1998). The perspective of inmates was, however, not thoroughly studied.

Scholars in other European contexts took up the challenge and stepwise formed a network which was to mutually complete and strengthen knowledge on this topic.[3] Prisons were re-considered as laboratories allowing observation of the adaptation processes by the state to religious diversity and the relocation processes of religion—with its correlate spirituality—within the discursive framework of plurality, diversity and its transgression of institutional boundaries—be they religious or secular. Security arguments were well present in the negotiations for the reshaping of a multi-faith chaplaincy. As the different religious and secular actors do not have an unanimous view of the relationship between security and religion, the negotiations were tricky. The total institution "prison" is a field of power relations in which actors, and even more religious actors, move carefully—partly according to their degree of official recognition, and to their meaning for the various individuals, etc. Here, the contested nature of the concept of religious diversity pops up strikingly. In the English case, where religious diversity tends to be problematized in reference to the community, the tension lies between the positive benefits of community and the negative costs of increased segregation and rivalry between "communities".[4] Through community, religion also finds its way into a newly defined rehabilitation strategy. Community, with its mostly voluntary involvement, offers offenders—at a low cost—a link to the outside world, and prolongs the support beyond the time of imprisonment. The new question today is, however, not simply whether to integrate religion into rehabilitation, but whether to integrate religious diversity.

---

[2] See Lentin and Titley 2012 for a critical reflection on the tensions around the notion of multi-culturalism.

[3] A varying number of scientists working on this topic met regularly, starting with a workshop at the University of Warwick in 2002, then in panels organized at the conferences of the Society for the Sociology of Religion at the Social Science Research Centre in Berlin (in 2012), the European University Institute in Florence (2012), the University of Lausanne (in 2010 and 2014) and finally at the Autonomous University of Barcelona (2014). On the initiative of a research team in the latter university (Investigacions en Sociologia de la Religió), a website has been created to publicize this work: http://religionpublicinstitutions.com. One of the first publications (Becci 2011) gathering together the work of these different scholars was an issue of the *Archives de sciences sociales des religions*. More recently, the contributions to the Florence *RELIGIO* workshop have been published by Stoeckl and Roy (2014) and a selection of the Lausanne papers presenting studies on religious diversity in hospitals has been edited by Pierre-Yves Brandt and is forthcoming with the publisher Labor et Fides (Geneva).

[4] I thank Jim Beckford for having pointed out this tension in a comment on this introduction, and for his other insightful comments.

A pluralist attitude with regard to prison chaplaincy has also been adopted by the governments in Belgium and the Netherlands. Farid El Asri's article on the Belgian case offers a precise illustration of the difficulties in the political process that led to a pluralist spiritual care model. This change not only implied an adaptation of the legal framework but also a strong reorganization of the Muslim community at the national level in Belgium. Thrown from the juridical to the political levels, the processes of recognition and institutionalization are very slow and are constantly put under the pressure of pragmatic situations of urgency. In the Netherlands, as the chapter written by Mohamed Ajouaou and Ton Bernts indicates, the reshaping of the prison chaplaincy as multi-faith has had deep implications both for the minority faith communities and for the perception of religion as an individual preference. The government has opened up chaplaincy under clear secular expectations: that of gender equality, that of respect for individual rights and that of the necessity of a professionalization of spiritual care. In both cases, contrary to England and Wales, the diversification of prison chaplaincy has also implied the inclusion of secular actors claiming to pertain to the same existential field as religion, such as humanists and free-thinkers. The studies of these cases demonstrate that the integration of religious actors who are socially less recognized into prison chaplaincy provokes changes at multiple levels, having repercussions even in the religious communities which through prison chaplaincy find a way to recognition.

The contributions to this book also illustrate national cases in Europe where no such legal pluralization of spiritual care occurs. This is the case of France, Germany, Italy and Switzerland. In these countries, the presence of ministers from newly introduced religions is not completely absent, but determined by local dynamics, and therefore, occasional and contingent. The French case, presented by Corinne Rostaing, Céline Béraud and Claire de Galembert, offers a particularly interesting comparison. France is a well-known unique model of secularism offering religion a rather marginal place within prisons and weak resources to chaplaincy. Such an appreciation is mirrored in perceptions by security agents of religion as being useless in terms of prisoner rehabilitation. Nonetheless, approaching the question empirically and including the perspective of inmates highlight that even under these circumstances religion is mobilized as an individual or collective resource and becomes either a problem or a solution in the prison world. The way inmates and partly religious actors relate to religion in prison is not necessarily consonant with the normative model imagined for religion by the institution. This does not mean that it does not contribute to some sort of rehabilitation for offenders—in fact the contrary is true.

In Germany, Italy and Switzerland, the governments have kept privileged relations with the traditional main Christian churches, which have a direct impact on the organization of prison chaplaincy. Minority faiths are not directly integrated; their ministers need to be placed at a particular, different, level of intervention, with all the consequences in terms of lack of visibility, professionalism etc. that this has. Here, at the legal level there is little change. The changes in terms of religion are located at another level. In Italy, as Fabretti and Rhazzali show, the resources for religion are greater than in France in financial, legal and symbolic terms, but the model of chaplaincy remains in the hands of the Roman Catholic Church. Solutions to the new needs expressed by a religiously more diverse prison population are found locally and pragmatically. In their daily work, Catholic chaplains do in fact cohabit and work together with ministers of other faiths. Here, awareness of the new "post-secular" dimension of contemporary society needs to go through the recognition of minority religions. Such recognition is still difficult under present conditions. The chapter by Rhazzali on the organization of Muslim religious care for prisoners nicely illustrates these difficulties.

Some researchers have shifted their attention to apprehending the impact of the new religious diversity on the emerging notion of spirituality. This notion has stepped out of the theological realm and entered popular culture. Hubert Knoblauch (2009) has qualified this process as the popularization of religion. He points to the fact that some "New Age" practices, such as the use of stones or crystals, and concentration techniques focusing on "energies", etc., are so widely known nowadays that they have become an obvious part of popular culture. Bradford Verter (2003) has suggested an interesting approach that includes spirituality in the study of religion. He relies partly on Pierre Bourdieu's notion of the religious field to replace it with a more open and interrelated spiritual field. In his approach, power issues are not at stake within the boundaries of religion but across different types of fields. In contemporary society, spiritual capital can increase one's position within the artistic field, for instance, while this is not the case with the classic notion of religious capital. In the case of prisons, this implies opening up the methodological approach and not limiting the study of religion to studying chaplaincy. One of the core features of the successful new forms of contemporary spirituality is their emphasis on wellbeing achieved by focusing jointly on "body, mind and spirit". Various authors[5] have documented the ambivalent effects such links can have. On the one hand they can reinforce the so-called postmodern consumerist attitudes, and on the other offer valuable and long-lasting spiritual alternatives for persons to deal with crucial life crises, as can be experienced in prison. Religion, as well as spirituality, is interrelated with the fields of consumption and of health. Different research projects currently being carried out in Europe[6] have also illustrated the variegated links between "new" religious practices or spirituality and issues relating to improvements of one's personal condition in a holistic sense.

The two chapters that directly illustrate the importance of the realm of holistic spirituality in this context focus on the prisons of Spain, and on inmates interviewed in Switzerland, Germany and Italy. Griera and Clot look at how practices such as Yoga, reiki and meditation activities are increasingly successful in the penitentiary context in Spain. They find that holistic activities and therapies are becoming symbolic resources on which inmates rely in their vulnerable situation in prison and (re) construct their self-image, while they also work as a "peace-making mechanism"

---

[5] For instance, Höllinger and Tripold (2012).

[6] See for Great Britain www.religionandsociety.org.uk, for Switzerland www.pnr58.ch, for Sweden www.crs.uu.se and at a transnational European level www.religareproject.eu and www.eui.eu/Project/ReligioWest, last accessed on 6.1.2014

that fits in with the institutional order. My analysis of a set of self-narratives by inmates shows that they frame their change as secular, as religious, and also as spiritual. These categories are defined against each other more than in themselves.

To study religious diversity within the prison universe allows for an analysis of how the traditional notion of religion as a charitable presence, caring for the "lost souls" of prisoners, is increasingly confronted with the new notion of religion or spirituality as a useful tool in the rehabilitation of one's self. These new *problématiques*, developed in this book, go well beyond the question of equality of treatment and are finally also a critical contribution to the debate on the "post-secular"[7]. They interrogate the emergence of a political conscience and reflexivity concerning the new religious diversity and of a normative model taking religion or spirituality as a positive value.

The emergence of the notion of spirituality as opposed to religion has, however, brought religion to be defined even more narrowly. Religion is then associated with identity and becomes a category through which essential difference is perceived and expressed (Kilani 2005). One of the questions resulting from these findings is "what relation do individuals in prisons construct to this complex set of intricate notions of secularity, religion, spirituality and rehabilitation"? This book offers some first answers to this question.

To sum up, the correction facility itself is confronted with the need to adapt to religious diversity both for legal reasons but also pragmatically, to obtain the desired level of security and order. To adequately analyse these changes at their structural, practical and discursive level, they need to be approached with analytic precision. In prison, the current religious plurality emerges both inside and outside organized spiritual care and suggests new ways to deal with crime which are alternative to imprisonment. The authors of the contributions gathered here therefore rethink their methodological and conceptual toolkit in order to apprehend religion and spirituality in prisons from a more inclusive perspective, not limited to the institutional chaplaincy. They also go beyond the question of religious needs expressed and accommodated by spiritual care to reflect on how religious actors in the carceral realm think of alternatives to the current way of dealing with crime. The contributors to this volume are social and political scientists who have done first-hand research on religious diversity in prisons. In this publication, they look at their empirical material from the angle of rehabilitation, asking how this notion carries secularity into religion or vice versa.

While at a discursive level, the notion of diversity seems to imply some sort of evenness or neutrality between all the elements composing it, the contributions to this volume show that there are also differences in terms of religions' location in institutional power configurations. To what extent are different religious practices, groups or discourses considered a substantial contribution to the goals of the prison, e.g. "rehabilitation" (as a secular avatar of the historically older and more religious notion of "repentance")? The religious or spiritual experience in prison depends considerably on structural components. Most of the authors writing here

---

[7] For a sceptical critique, see Beckford (2012).

rely on Erving Goffman's (1961) conceptual framework of the total institution to highlight power dynamics around religious diversity. Goffman is not the only classic in sociology that the authors draw on: Griera and Clot reconnect to some concepts developed by Max Weber; Fabretti uses the work of Jürgen Habermas; Becci re-introduces Pierre Bourdieu.

## 1.2  A Possible Analytical Organization of the Results

Before giving some hints about the logic of the structure of this book, the larger results will be systematized in a comparative perspective. The different studies indicate a need to clarify the locations where religious diversity is present and how they can be distinguished analytically.

A first dimension for comparison refers to the persons in the institution. The religious affiliations, practices, discourses and identifications of inmates can greatly differ from those of the staff. At an individual level, all inmates and personnel have a right to religious freedom in a negative and positive sense within the framework of the particular security arrangements. The persons employed embody the institution's aims and display a variety of religious affiliations and references, too. Therefore, one of the main aims of the staff is the rehabilitation of the imprisoned. The latter, thus, undergo a learning process in prison—an adaptation to the institutional setting. In theory, they are supposed to follow the process intended for them stepwise. Although Erving Goffman (1961) draws the main line defining a total institution between staff and inmates, there is a third type of person: the *chaplains* and ministers or other religious actors occasionally intervening to offer some form of spiritual care. Strictly speaking, they are indeed a different type of personnel—since they are under a double authority, partly that of the prison and partly that of their religious community—and they often position themselves closely to inmates. Some of the chapters in this volume address the challenges the new religious diversity represents for the figure of the chaplain and the theological theme of pastoral care as they have emerged historically in the Christian context. In fact, the models available for spiritual assistance in public institutions follow a largely Christian model. Moreover, there are persons intervening in prison on religious grounds without being part of either the "staff" or the chaplaincy: this is, for instance, the case of persons offering practices considered part of holistic spirituality.

A second dimension refers to the materiality of prisons. As Sophie Gilliat-Ray (2005a, b) underlines, religion and spirituality in institutions have material, spatial and technological dimensions. Institutions are composed of buildings, places, machines and spaces. Chaplaincy occupies a particular space. Besides chaplaincy, diverse religious practices or discourses also occur in a less-regulated way in the cells, corridors, classrooms, visiting rooms, etc. Spatial and temporal arrangements are particularly important for the perception and experience of religious diversity. In terms of spaces, the chaplaincy rooms in prison as such can play an important role in symbolic terms and as a meeting opportunity for inmates. Moreover, materially, prisons are also a set of documents that frame religious diversity at a more moral-normative level (laws, regulations, contracts, etc.). At a legal level, the national cases studied here have different sets of rules about religion and religious diversity.

A third dimension is symbolic insofar as public state institutions have a discourse and self-image about their history, aim and function that contains or refers to religious diversity to various degrees. Prisons at some of these levels reproduce what Beaman and Sullivan have called "the mantra of the secular state" (2013, p. 7), which "can distract or obscure other realities". One of the most prominent thinkers in the field of the way institutions exert a certain framing effect on people's cognition was Mary Douglas (1986). Relevant studies point to an importance of institutions in the development of one's self (Mutz and Kühnlein 1992). When institutional discourses are reflected in personal narratives, the two dimensions—the symbolic and the personal—meet. The discourses accompanying or even establishing the function of prisons with regard to rehabilitation carry a certain idea of secularism and attribute a specific location to religion within this model. Religious practices need to be instrumental to the institution's aim in order to be considered part of the model. Recognition of a personal right to religious freedom in the context of prison can be considered a first step in rehabilitating the inmate as a citizen. Institutions hence have a precise understanding of their role with regard to religious diversity and spirituality. This influences the way they deal with religion, for instance when collecting information on inmates' religious preferences or affiliations.

The degree of secularism and of religious diversity can greatly vary from one dimension to another. A systematic analysis for each location allows prisons to be approached both in terms of total institutions and in terms of specific locally anchored connections. When observing the social dynamics around religious diversity in the prison setting, it is therefore, crucial to consider its organizational nature—its degree of openness or closeness, its bureaucracy, its representational discourse, its legal regulation and the actual human interactions inside it. Analysis of religious diversity in today's prisons in Europe needs to be based on a triangulation of the personal, the material and the symbolic levels. When issues of religious diversity and religious cohabitation are raised in prisons, they are regulated at different levels. While the notion of spirituality has an all-encompassing connotation, it is empirically necessary to focus on the ways in which religious lines of difference are reshaped rather than eclipsed. Religious and spiritual diversity is experienced in institutional life in relation to other markers of cultural difference. State institutions therefore, also foster processes of religious diversification and become instances of socialization about how to address tensions arising from that diversity. In order to understand the developments of these practices in one direction or the other, it is essential to take into consideration the context in which they are embedded. There are obviously huge differences from one prison to another and from one national context to another.

The authors of the following chapters have been methodologically creative in obtaining their data. They have "shadowed" personnel in everyday tasks, conducted semi-structured or narrative biographical interviews, edited questionnaires, observed rituals, decisions and negotiations and written field notes, etc. They have then analysed their data triangulations, codifications and discourses.

One of the strengths of this book is precisely that it sheds light on one topic from different viewpoints: the Italian case is analysed by Fabretti through the discourses of chaplains and institutional actors and by Rhazzali through the eyes of Muslim chaplains on their way to becoming recognized institutional actors. Inmates also have a role here, in particular in the contributions by Becci, Rostaing, Béraud and de Galembert. The French case is pictured through a social scientific analysis, and also through a philosophical reflection offered by Rognon. This latter chapter brings the reader closer to an often hidden side of chaplains' activity in prison: their involvement in the promotion of the idea of restorative justice—a very recent innovative phenomenon.

## 1.3   The Structure of the Book

The book is divided into three parts. The first part collects analyses of national cases where prison chaplaincy has recently become multi-faith: England and Wales, the Netherlands and Belgium. The chapters go into the details of the political processes involved and the sociological implications for the notion of prisoner rehabilitation. James A. Beckford's initial chapter organizes these implications within the larger frame of other—nonreligious—factors that shape prison regimes, such as political pressure to ensure security, good order, the efficient operation of prison functions and competition for scarce resources between different activity programmes. Mohammed Ajouaou—an actor involved in chaplaincy and a scientist of Islam—and Ton Bernts reflect on the effects of the introduction of religious diversity in spiritual care in Dutch correction facilities. Their focus is on the arguments brought forward to legitimize particular types of spiritual care, partly in relation to rehabilitation. The last chapter in the first section, by Farid El Asri, looks at the making of the Belgian multi-faith prison chaplaincy from the perspective of the construction of an *Islamic Council for detention*. Adopting a double perspective—as a social scientist specialized in Islam, and as a trained Muslim prison chaplain—the author shows that in this country the institutionalization of Islam stands under the reference model of the Roman Catholic church. He focuses on how professional Muslim spiritual care comes to be legitimized in the frame of a loud debate on religious radicalization in prison and the creation of a "publicly useful" Islam.

The second part presents in four chapters the results of important national studies in contexts that have not structurally changed towards multi-faith models, but which are obviously still confronted with an increasing religious diversity of the population. Here, the central theme is the notion of the state's secularity. In the chapter on France written by Corinne Rostaing, Céline Béraud and Claire de Galembert, the key notion is *laïcité*. Their analysis draws on both the sociology of religion and the sociology of the prison to understand when religion is mobilized in daily institutional life, despite the prison authorities attributing a very minor role to religion and chaplains. The authors unpack the image of chaplains as mono-dimensional actors and show the different postures they adopt: sometimes they are universalist and secular, sometimes confessional and moralizing. Sarah Jahn's chapter discusses the contradictions facing the German secular government with regard to religious diversity when it comes to neutrality and rights to religious freedom. On the basis of the constitutionally guaranteed right to corporate religious freedom, various religious groups can negotiate their intervention in prisons. However, the structural and legal conditions are such that most religious organizations in prison have a Christian background and the involvement of other religious organizations is an exception. The last two chapters in this section are dedicated to the Italian case: one from the perspective of the notion of the "post-secular", and one from the perspective of new prison Imams. Valeria Fabretti explores institutional cultures and practices linked to religious care in Italian prisons and finds that religion is still a central factor in collective life. The situation of religious monopoly in Italy is hindering cooperation and complementary learning between secular and religious actors in the public space of prison. Khalid Rhazzali completes the picture on the Italian case by focusing on Muslim actors now intervening in prisons as Imams. He discusses how they combine their competences in their recognized role as communication and intercultural mediators. They link the prison world to the community outside the prison, where a new *Imamate* is being reinvented and is on the way to European recognition, not least through arguments on gender equality.

Finally, the last section contains three chapters with further reflections on cases that—as in the second section—are not structurally multicultural: Spain, Germany, Italy, Switzerland and France. In terms of studies on religion in prison, these contributions are, however, innovative in their focus. A shift of subject area—in particular from the institutional connotation of religion to the socially emergent notion of spirituality—allows a better view of the new way that rehabilitation and religion are tied up in the prison realm. Maria del Mar Griera and Anna Clot draw on qualitative research to explore the growing success of holistic spirituality with practices such as yoga, reiki and meditation in contemporary Spanish prisons. Located at the limit of the secular, these practices appear less problematic and receive better acceptance and more rapid diffusion—particularly through prison social workers—than what is usually considered religious in the penitentiary context. I concentrate on the expectation of change at the core of the institutional idea of rehabilitation. The topic of change is reflected in the narratives of prisoners as a self-narrative. On the basis of interviews made in Italy, Germany and Switzerland, my analysis illustrates how inmates and ex-inmates alternatively draw on a secular, religious or spiritual frame to talk of expected or experienced changes. The last chapter in this section and of the book is written by Frédérich Rognon. A theologian and philosopher on the one hand, a prison chaplain on the other, Rognon gives an insight into ongoing attempts by French prison chaplains to offer alternative ways of dealing with crime in contemporary society. It nicely closes this book with a not-too-utopian reflection on the real possibilities of restorative justice being reached. The matrix of this idea is syncretic—and could be a new starting point for a diversity-inclusive reflection on rehabilitation which would contain the religion-secularity-spirituality triad.

# References

Becci, I. (Ed.). (2011). Prisons et religions en Europe. *Archives des sciences sociales des religions, 153*(1), 11–158. (Paris, EHESS).

Beckford, J. A. (2012). Public religions and the post-secular: critical reflections. *Journal for the Scientific Study of Religion, 51*(1), 1–19.

Beckford, J. A., & Gilliat, S. (1998). *Religion in prison. Equal rites in a multi-faith societ.* Cambridge: Cambridge University Press.

Douglas, M. (1986). *How institutions think.* New York: Syracuse University Press.

Gilliat-Ray, S. (2005a). The use of "sacred" space in public institutions: a case study of worship facilities at the Millennium Dome. *Culture and Religion, 6*(2), 281–302.

Gilliat-Ray, S. (2005b). 'Sacralising' sacred space in public institutions: a case study of the Prayer Space at the Millennium Dome. *Journal of Contemporary Religion, 20*(3), 357–372.

Goffman, E. (1961). *Asylums: Essays on the Social Situation of Mental Patients and Other Inmates.* New York: Doubleday.

Höllinger, F., & Tripold, T. (2012) *Ganzheitliches Leben. Das holistische Milieu zwischen neuer Spiritualität und postmoderner Wellness-Kultur.* Bielefeld: Transcript.

Kilani, M. (2005). Il faut déconfessionnaliser la laïcité. Le religieux imprègne encore les imaginaires. *Journal des Anthropologues, 100*(101), 95–110.

Knoblauch, H. (2009). *Populäre Religion. Auf dem Weg in eine spirituelle Gesellschaft.* Frankfurt a. M: Campus.

Lentin, A., & Titley, G. (2012) The crisis of 'multiculturalism' in Europe: Mediated minarets, intolerable subjects. *European Journal of Cultural Studies, 15*(2), 123–138.

Mutz, G., & Kühnlein, I. (1992). La biographie, un script? Utilisation des savoirs quotidiens et scientifiques dans la reconstruction biographique de l'évolution d'une maladie. In U. Flick (Ed.), *La perception quotidienne de la santé et de la maladie. Théories subjectives et représentations sociales.* L'Harmattan.

Stoeckl, K., & Roy, O. (Eds.). (2014). Religious pluralism in a Christian format: the 'Muslim chaplain' in European prisons. *International Journal for Politics, Society and Culture*, April 2014. ISSN: 0891–4486 (print version), ISSN: 1573–3416 (electronic version).

Sullivan, W. F., & Beaman L. G. (Eds.). (2013). *Varieties of religious establishment.* London: Ashgate.

Todd, A. (2012). Religion, security, rights, the individual and rates of exchange: religion in negotiation with British public policy in prisons and the military. *International Journal of Politics, Culture and Society.* doi: 10.1007/s10767-014-9181-z

Verter, B. (2003). Spiritual capital: Theorizing religion with bourdieu against bourdieu. *Sociological Theory, 21,* 150–174.

# Part I
# The Making and Working of Multi-faith Prison Chaplaincies

# Chapter 2
# Religious Diversity and Rehabilitation in Prisons: Management, Models and Mutations

James A. Beckford

## 2.1 Introduction

Sociological research into religious and spiritual care in prisons has developed strongly in the twenty-first century, especially in Western Europe. Since 1998, when Sophie Gilliat-Ray and I published *Religion in Prison. Equal Rites in a Multi-Faith Society*, this field of research has expanded to include numerous countries and a wide variety of perspectives on religion in prisons. For example, the work of Inger Furseth (2000, 2001) in Norway and with Lene Kühle in Denmark (Furseth and Kühle 2011) has highlighted the differences between the responses of these two Nordic countries to religious diversity in their prison populations. Irene Becci's (2011, 2012) investigations and her research with Brigitte Knobel's study in Italy, Germany and Switzerland (Becci and Knobel 2013) have added new and exciting dimensions to the comparative study of religious and spiritual care for prisoners. Also in Switzerland, Mallory Schneuwly Purdie (2011) has highlighted the strictly practical character of the questions that Muslim visitors tend to address to prisons and, with Irene Becci, the gendered character of Swiss prisons and how it shapes gendered expressions of religiosity (Becci and Schneuwly Purdie 2012). Meanwhile, Khalid Rhazzali (2009) has completed his doctoral research on the place of Muslims and Islam in Italian prisons; and Sarah Jahn's (2014) doctoral research was on "Religion in Prison in Contemporary Germany". In Spain, Maria del Mar Griera and Anna Clot (2015) have conducted empirical inquiries into the responses of Spanish prisons to the growth of religious diversity. And the team of Céline Béraud, Claire de Galembert and Corinne Rostaing (2013) has produced an exceptionally comprehensive and profound report on the situation of religion in French prisons (see also Beckford et al. 2005). At the same time, Rachel Sarg's (2013) ongoing research in the prisons of Alsace throws new light on religious diversity and conflicts. Meanwhile, fresh thinking about this field of research in the UK has

J. A. Beckford (✉)
Department of Sociology, University of Warwick, Coventry, UK
e-mail: j.a.beckford@warwick.ac.uk

© Springer International Publishing Switzerland 2015
I. Becci, O. Roy (eds.), *Religious Diversity in European Prisons,*
DOI 10.1007/978-3-319-16778-7_2

also come from Andrew Todd (2011; Todd and Tipton 2011), Sophie Gilliat-Ray et al. (2013), Stephen Hunt (2011), Peter Phillips (2014) and me (Beckford 2013).

All these sociological studies of religion in prisons are distinctive and useful for their focus on roles, identities, relationships, processes, structures, institutions, power and regulations. They reveal the social frameworks within which the provision of religious and spiritual care in prisons is shaped and delivered in different ways in different countries. Moreover, these frameworks have historical roots. They emerge from long, long chains of causes, contexts, reasons, reactions and effects. And the patterns that we observe today are only provisional: they may evolve in unexpected directions in the future.

The central argument of this chapter is that the relationship between religious diversity and the rehabilitation of prisoners varies with national frameworks for managing religion in prisons. The example of the Prison Service of England & Wales shows that the balance between religion and other interests has changed over time and that the growth of religious diversity has posed some interesting challenges to the accommodation of religion in prisons. It also shows that the growing significance of community chaplaincy is giving rise to fresh questions about equality in relation to the provision of religious and pastoral care for prisoners before and after their release.

## 2.2   History

When it comes to religion or spirituality in relation to prisons and rehabilitation, history must be the starting point. This is especially true for the UK because its modern prison regimes were heavily shaped by religious ideas two centuries ago. The very idea of "correcting" the conduct of lawbreakers rather than simply subjecting them to public humiliation, physical punishment or execution came from Christian thinkers primarily associated with Quakers and Evangelicals in the late eighteenth century and early nineteenth century.

It was George Fox and other pioneers of Quaker spirituality in the late seventeenth century in Britain and North America who were largely responsible for fashioning a set of particularly radical ideas and practices intended to control human minds and bodies by means of internalized scrutiny of the self and a vivid fear of God. Solitude and silence were two of the conditions that Quakers considered essential for the cultivation among prisoners of self-awareness that they were sinners. Many Puritan clergy of the Church of England also contributed to the development of Quaker thinking about imprisonment and its potential for inducing spiritual and self-discipline and thereby, rehabilitation.

These ideas impressed various reformers of prison systems in Western Europe and North America. The combination of a profound fear of God, a stern moral conscience and rigorous self-discipline seemed to offer a much better alternative to the chaos, hopelessness and physical degradation that had been characteristic of many prisons since medieval times. Indeed, the Quaker/Puritan alternative was so appealing that it was translated into the architectural design and daily regimes of new types of prison establishment—most notably at the Lincoln Prison in England, at the Eastern State Penitentiary in Philadelphia and at the Auburn Prison in New York State (Graber 2011).

The "separate system" at Eastern State Penitentiary kept prisoners strictly isolated from contact with each other and with members of prison staff except chaplains. The "silent system" at Auburn required prisoners to live and work together but to do so in silence. In both institutions, the aim was to rehabilitate prisoners by preventing them from thinking about anything except the need to earn repentance from a fearful God by disciplining their conscience and experiencing remorse for their sins and crimes—hence the term "penitentiary" was most appropriate for institutions where distinctively religious "technologies of the self", as Michel Foucault called them (Foucault 1977; Martin et al. 1988), could be deployed as a strategy for simultaneously punishing prisoners, reminding them of their sinful nature, eliciting a deep fear of God and encouraging them to control their mind and body by continuous reflection on Christian scripture and religious obligations.

The lengthy report that Gustave de Beaumont and Alexis de Tocqueville first published in 1833 on the Philadelphia and Auburn penitentiary systems (among others) on the basis of their 1-year investigation in the USA makes some acute observations about the differences between these two types of penitentiary. Beaumont and Tocqueville thought that the intensely religious "separate system" of Philadelphia was too harsh to produce a genuine moral reform in more than a small number of prisoners. But they considered it more likely that the combination of hard work and silence in the Auburn system would lead to the moral regeneration of many more prisoners. However, most interestingly, they placed a high value on the American penitentiaries of all types because they were likely to stop prisons from functioning as factories of crime (or schools of criminals) and to teach prisoners useful skills and habits of work. If it also proved possible to reform the morality of prisoners, this was a bonus. In short, my interpretation of their report is that they could clearly see the pragmatic advantages of placing religion at the centre of prison regimes but that they did not regard the inculcation and rigorous practice of religion as necessarily the only way to rehabilitate prisoners.[1] Their conclusion was that the prisoner leaving an American penitentiary may not be an honest person, but he or she will have picked up some honest habits.

One of the distinctive characteristics of the Beaumont and Tocqueville report on American penitentiaries is that the term "religion" refers mainly to Protestantism. The earliest prison reformers indeed represented a variety of Protestant perspectives, and most of the chaplains and other religious personnel who visited prisons

---

[1] "La necessité du travail, qui dompte son penchant à l'oisivité; l'obligation du silence, qui le fait réfléchir; l'isolement, qui le met seul en présence de son crime et de sa peine; l'instruction religieuse, qui l'éclaire et le console; l'obéissance de chaque instant à des règles inflexibles; la régularité d'une vie uniforme; en un mot, toutes les circonstances qui accompagnent ce régime sévère, sont de nature à produire sur son esprit une impression profonde... Peut-être en sortant de prison n'est-il pas un honnête homme, mais il a contracté des habitudes honnêtes." Beaumont et Tocqueville 1845, p. 150.

in the early nineteenth century also came from Protestant denominations. It was as if Beaumont and Tocqueville took it for granted that only Protestants were prison reformers. This may not have been true, but Winnifred Sullivan (2009) has argued that prison reform in early and mid-nineteenth century was particularly important for Protestants because it gave them a rare opportunity to exercise influence in the public sphere without breaching the constitutional separation of religions from the American state.

Nevertheless, it is doubtful whether large-scale Christian conversion was the result of religious regimes in penitentiaries Graber (2011, p. 6). In fact, Protestant prison reformers not only failed to generate the moral reform that they sought but they also had to concede that their teachings needed to be modified if they were to remain constitutional and/or influential. In other words, would-be prison reform actually resulted in the reform of Protestantism. As Jennifer Graber (2011, p. 12) put it, "In order to secure their prison programs, Protestant reformers increasingly articulated a religiosity of citizenship focused on lawful living and obedience to secular authority". They gradually abandoned the particularities of Quaker, Presbyterian or Methodist beliefs and practices for the sake of "a vision of the redeemed life composed of common morality and hard work".

In sum, the history of the formative period of modern penitentiaries in the USA and Britain highlights a creative tension between two forces at work in them. On the one hand, were the religious motivations of many prison reformers and, on the other hand, the political and institutional pressures towards the preservation of good order, discipline and productive work. In practice, these two forces could coexist peacefully in a dynamic balance—especially at a time when levels of religious diversity among the prison population tended to be low. However, recent controversies about the place of faith-based programmes and residential units within prisons indicate that the balance can be precarious and contentious (Burnside et al. 2005; Sullivan 2009) when religious diversity is on the increase.

## 2.3   Models of Managing Religious Diversity

National prison systems differ widely in their ways of striking a balance between the interests of religion and the other factors that shape prison regimes. These other interests include, for example, political pressure to ensure security, good order and the efficient operation of prison functions; the professional interests of prison administrators and officers; competition for the scarce resources to be distributed between different programmes of activity; access to space designated for special purposes within prisons; and so on.

My argument will be that recent increases in the level of religious diversity in prison populations pose some interesting challenges to the ways in which religion has usually been "accommodated" in prison establishments. Indeed, responses to the growth of religious diversity offer an interesting insight into not only the different ways in which prison systems make space for religions but also the variations in their understanding of questions about equality in relation to religion.

Elsewhere, I have suggested that religious diversity is an elusive and contested concept, but that, in the context of prisons, it can be reduced for sociological purposes to at least four dimensions: varieties of religious tradition; variations within traditions; differences in the salience accorded by individuals to religion; and discrimination between officially recognized and nonrecognized religions. And the key to understanding the response to the challenges posed by increases in religious diversity is to examine the variety of national models for accommodating religion in prisons (Beckford 2012, 2013). The models consist of the institutional arrangements for defining and managing what counts as religion in prisons and how it should be provided and regulated (Thomas and Zaitzow 2006). In the space available to me here, I can only sketch the model applicable to the prisons of England & Wales.

In England & Wales, the state is closely intertwined with the Church of England at various levels from the monarchy down to local authorities. In practice, many other Christian denominations and organizations representing a wide variety of faith traditions are also present in British public life. They are also engaged in partnerships with the state for the delivery of welfare services and education. Unfair discrimination on the grounds of religion or belief is outlawed, as are religiously aggravated criminal offences.

The Prison Act 1952 requires all prisons to have a chaplain from the Church of England, and such other ministers of religion as the Secretary of State may consider necessary. Governors are legally required to record the "religious denomination" of all prisoners at the point of reception and to inform the relevant chaplain. Moreover, "A member of the chaplaincy team must visit prisoners in the segregation unit daily. It is a statutory duty to visit all prisoners undergoing cellular confinement"; and "A member of the chaplaincy team must visit prisoners in the health care centre daily". In addition, many chaplains—full time, part time and sessional—are actively engaged in the work of prison committees, in discussions of prerelease planning and community reintegration as well as other aspects of the corporate life of their prisons.

The framework governing religion in the prisons of England & Wales specifies that the Prison Service "recognizes and respects the right of prisoners to register and practise their faith whilst in custody". This is a recognition of individual prisoners' rights, although much of the framework is actually concerned with the collective involvement of religious groups, chaplains and representatives of selected faith traditions. In fact, it is principally about "religious provision" or the corporate responsibility for facilitating the personal and collective practice of religions. Hence, the "Performance Standard 51. Religion"—by which the quality of each prison's arrangements for religion is regularly assessed—stipulates that all establishments should "enable prisoners to participate in corporate worship and other religious activities that encourage their spiritual and personal development whilst in custody, and in preparation for release into the community". The "required outcomes" relate to such things as the appointment of chaplains, the accurate conduct of "religious registration", opportunities for corporate worship and the provision of pastoral care. The emphasis is heavily on the official requirement to make these provisions rather than on the rights and freedoms of individual prisoners simply to practise their faith.

In this way, religion is reified, in part, as a set of collective obligations that prison establishments in England & Wales are required to facilitate.

Another distinctive aspect of the way in which religion is facilitated in the prisons of England & Wales can be seen in the policy of selecting only certain religious traditions for inclusion in the list of "faith specific provision". This selectivity also applies to the range of religious traditions from which chaplains may be appointed on the advice of the Prison Service's panel of Faith Advisers. In 2013, the traditions of Quakerism and Rastafari were added to the list, but Scientology, the Nation of Islam and Jedi Knights remain excluded. Moreover, chaplains are expected to "work as an inclusive team and meet together on a regular basis". This reinforces the impression that the provision of religious and pastoral care in the prisons of England & Wales is as much to do with the integration of approved religious practices and personnel into the corporate life of prisons as it is with the individual rights of prisoners.

## 2.4   Responses to Religious Diversity

The model of integrating religion into the corporate life of prisons in England & Wales is reflected in the fact that the Prison Service information and administrative systems collect and use data about the identification of prisoners with recognized and nonrecognized religions. Table 2.1 presents data concerning the self-designated religious affiliation of prisoners at the end of June 2013 and the general population of people over the age of 15 in England & Wales in 2011.

In terms of their religion, prisoners are significantly less likely to be Christian than is the general population of England & Wales; nearly three times more likely to be Muslim; and less likely to register any religious affiliation. Since the mid-1970s, there has been a slow increase in the proportion of prisoners with no religion; a

**Table 2.1** Population in prison establishments by religious group, England & Wales, 30 June 2013. (Sources adapted from: Ministry of Justice, Offender Management Caseload Statistics, Office of National Statistics, Census 2011, England & Wales)

|               | Number of prisoners | Percent | % of general population aged 15+ |
|---------------|---------------------|---------|----------------------------------|
| All Christian | 42,341              | 50.50   | 59.3                             |
| Muslim        | 11,426              | 13.62   | 4.8                              |
| Buddhist      | 1638                | 1.95    | 0.4                              |
| Sikh          | 799                 | 0.95    | 0.8                              |
| Hindu         | 451                 | 0.53    | 1.5                              |
| Jewish        | 268                 | 0.31    | 0.5                              |
| Other         | 1322                | 1.57    | 0.4                              |
| Not recorded  | 1113                | 1.32    | 7.2                              |
| No religion   | 24,484              | 29.20   | 25.1                             |
| **Total**     | **83,842**          | **100** | *100*                            |

**Table 2.2** Changes in percentage of selected religious registrations, HM Prisons, England & Wales, 1975–2013. (Sources adapted from: Unpublished lecture by L. Rees to the Howard League for Penal Reform, 19 June 1975. Ministry of Justice, Offender Management Caseload Statistics)

|              | 1975 (%) | 2013 (%) | % change (1975–2013) |
|--------------|----------|----------|----------------------|
| Christian    | 95       | 51       | −44                  |
| Other faiths | 3        | 19       | +16                  |
| None etc.    | 2        | 31       | +28                  |

dramatic rise in the number and proportion of Muslims; and a steady decline in the proportion of Christians (Table 2.2).

These developments have elicited three main responses from the Prison Service of England & Wales:

First, the principle of employing full-time and part-time chaplains to provide spiritual and religious care for prisoners affiliated with recognized faiths has been maintained—but modified in some important respects. Full-time chaplains in particular continue to be fully integrated into the corporate life of prison establishments. Indeed, some Muslim chaplains now occupy senior positions in the coordination of chaplaincies. And the Muslim Chaplains Association cooperates with the Prison Service in the training and professional development of Muslim chaplains.

Second, the recruitment and training of chaplains are no longer the sole preserve of the main Christian churches and denominations. Chaplains now represent a wider range of faiths. There are currently 362 chaplains working full time or part time in the 146 prisons, Immigration Removal Centres and Young Offenders Institutions of England & Wales. Roughly 140 of them are Anglicans, 90 are Muslims, 77 are Roman Catholics, 50 are from the Free Church traditions, 2 are Sikhs and 2 are Hindus. In addition, about 800 other chaplains are paid for the small number of hours that they spend each week or month visiting prisons. According to Todd and Tipton (2011, p. 9), the number of unpaid volunteers who support the work of chaplains is estimated to be about 7000.

Third, prison chaplaincies are now officially organized on a "multifaith" basis, which means that many worship spaces are shared by a number of different faith groups and that chaplaincy committees in all prisons are expected to include representatives from all the recognized faith groups having chaplains in them. In addition, the official document that specifies precisely how prisoners are permitted to practise their religion contains authoritative information about all the recognized faith traditions (Ministry of Justice 2011). It is based on extensive consultation with leading representatives of these traditions.

## 2.5  Continuity and Mutation

The system of religious chaplaincy in the prisons of England & Wales has progressively mutated since the mid-1970s when only 3% of prisoners identified themselves with faiths other than Christianity (Beckford and Gilliat 1998, p. 52). Approximately 19 % of today's prisoners fall into this category. And the proportion of prisoners registering no religious affiliation has risen sharply from 2 to 28 %. The Prison Service Chaplaincy has adapted to these changes by slightly expanding the list of "recognized" faiths and by appointing more chaplains from faiths other than Christianity (mostly Muslims). But it has not relaxed its influence or control over the ways in which chaplains provide spiritual and religious care. In essence, the model of chaplaincy that remains in force is a pragmatic adaptation of Christian principles and practices. All faiths are expected to conform to norms which were originally framed for the purposes of Christian chaplaincy. Indeed, it seems to me that the past 40 years have witnessed a process of formalization and standardization of chaplaincy norms that are supposed to apply to a growing number of different faith groups. It is as if "other" faiths have been coopted into a system that remains similar in many respects to the Christian model that prevailed long before religious diversity had increased significantly in the prison population.

This is ironic in view of the official adoption of a "multifaith" ethos for prison chaplaincy in England & Wales. For, while there is no doubt that a notion akin to the American ideal of "equal respect for all faiths" has gradually found acceptance in prisons, the basis on which chaplains from different faith traditions are expected to work in harmony has not changed significantly.[2] It remains focused on the conduct of regular collective worship, scriptural study, pastoral support and the advocacy of access to "permitted" artefacts, diets, clothing, etc. And the career trajectory of full-time Hindu, Muslim and Sikh chaplains is virtually the same as that of their Christian counterparts. In other words, the social forms of chaplaincy have not changed despite the fact that additional religions have been recognized, included and supported.

Furthermore, the increase of religious diversity among prisoners has not led to the introduction of any form of interfaith activities. Each faith group continues to operate separately from the growing number of others—albeit in a largely co-operative and collegial spirit. And, apart from the provision of physical space for chaplaincy activities, most of the resources that the Prison Service provides for chaplaincy are distributed among particular faith groups: not aimed at shared or joint activities. Moreover, prisoners are not permitted to register affiliation with more than one faith group at a time. No spiritual or religious activities are available to prisoners without reference to their registered religious affiliation. In short, the growth of religious diversity among prisoners has not weakened the boundaries that separate them into "gated" enclaves.

This raises the question of whether prison chaplaincy creates separate religious enclaves which do not reflect the fluidity and fuzziness of religious identities and practices in the outside world.[3] It is possible that prisons are among the very few

---

[2] For example, HM Inspectorate of Prisons (2012, p. 65) operates with a formal expectation that "Chaplains demonstrate religious tolerance and cooperation with one another".

[3] See Cunningham (2004) for some counterintuitive reflections on the "gated" character of today's globalized world.

places in Britain where there are no alternatives to identification with a single religion—or with none.

It is not at all surprising, then, that the hypothesis that multifaith chaplaincy might induce a "generic" type of chaplaincy has not been confirmed. My interviews with 10 Muslim, 4 Hindu and 2 Sikh chaplains serving in the prisons of England & Wales in 2010 showed that they made a clear distinction between multifaith and interfaith.[4] They insisted on recognition of the integrity of each faith tradition whilst also acknowledging that "having a multifaith chaplaincy gives everybody the opportunity to understand that religions can work together" (M7). But a Sikh chaplain complained that efforts were made to convert Sikh prisoners to other faiths.

Nevertheless, some of the chaplains whom I interviewed were sensitive to the fact that prison chapels which had previously served as places of Christian worship had been adapted or converted into multifaith spaces. They were clearly aware of the resistance that had been expressed towards these developments. A Muslim chaplain, for example, said that he "could see this fear, you know, that Muslims are taking over" (M1).

In addition, other Muslim chaplains reported that certain "hard-line" prisoners would refuse to take part in collective prayers in a multifaith space that was shared with other faiths. One of them claimed that "most [Muslim] prisoners would prefer to pray in a mosque, designated prayer area, mosque which did ... fulfil all the requirements of a mosque" (M1). Indeed, prisoners who had lived in establishments with a mosque sometimes made unfavourable comparisons with establishments that had only a multifaith centre. But the opinion of most of the Hindu, Muslim and Sikh chaplains whom I interviewed was that sharing multifaith spaces did not imply any "watering down" of the theological specificity or integrity of their practices. On the contrary, they saw the use of multifaith spaces as an opportunity to demonstrate mutual respect and mutual support. A Muslim chaplain put it in these terms: "there's no fear factor that a multi-faith chaplaincy will diminish somebody's Islam" (M9). And a Sikh chaplain added that multi-faith chaplaincy:

> just gives a good image of a different faith working together; and it should act as a model if, say, Sikhs, Christians, Muslims are working well together and, you know, work in harmony. I mean they can live in harmony so it just gives a good picture to the wider world. I think that it's a good role model (S2).

Nevertheless, a significant mutation of the time-honoured model of prison chaplaincy has been gradually taking shape in England & Wales since the 1990s. It is not strictly speaking a response to the growth of religious diversity but it could have implications for cooperative working among different faith groups. It is the rising influence of "community chaplaincy".

---

[4] Interviews were conducted on the telephone and recorded for analysis with N-Vivo 9 software. Interviewees, two of whom were women, were identified only by an index number and the letter H for Hindu, M for Muslim and S for Sikh. For further details, see Beckford (2013, p. 192). I am grateful to the Religion and Diversity project at the University of Ottawa for financial support and to Ilona Cairns for research assistance.

The concept of community chaplaincy emerged in the 1970s in Canada and was formalized in the Canadian province of New Brunswick when a prison chaplain, Pierre Allard, persuaded the Correctional Service of Canada (CSC) to support his proposal to extend the work of chaplains outside the walls of prisons (Kirkegaard 2012). His idea was that rehabilitation was most likely to be successful if the provision of religious and spiritual care inside prisons could be strengthened by links with supportive volunteers and groups on the outside. It was the period of transition from incarceration to release (often referred to as "through the gate") that struck Pierre Allard as having the greatest impact on the probability that released prisoners would reoffend. The success of community chaplaincy, according to the founding vision, depended heavily on the willingness of local religious groups to offer support and care to released prisoners, thereby creating a bridge between prisons and their localities.[5] The fact that Allard went on to become director general of chaplaincy in the CSC probably created more opportunities for the movement for community chaplaincy to flourish and helped to ensure that partnerships between CSC and local faith groups spread rapidly through many regions of Canada.[6]

Reports about community chaplaincy in Canada quickly attracted attention in the UK, especially after a presentation that Pierre Allard made on "The community of prison chaplains" at a conference of the International Prison Chaplains Association in Switzerland in 1990 (Payne 2012). The idea was then championed by an assistant chaplain general of the Prison Service of England & Wales as well as by various individuals in local faith groups with interests in criminal justice.

The timing of these developments was such that they coincided with the emergence of the New Labour government's enthusiasm for policies that aimed to intensify the engagement of voluntary and community groups in partnerships with the state (Beckford 2011). Indeed, the then minister for probation and prisons gave a speech in 1999 to the annual conference of the Prison Service Chaplaincy in which he outlined:

> other opportunities in which Chaplaincy can play a vital role in terms of reaching out to the wider Christian community in order that we can ensure that when people are released from prison or discharged back into the community, we are able to provide other intervening factors to work against recidivism and re-offending. This is namely the support of strong communities outside the prison walls for the individual released prisoner. This will mean one to one work, drop-in centers, befriending, mentoring, and a whole range of activities that I believe Christian communities and faith communities are uniquely placed to provide (Paul Boateng quoted in Payne 2012, p. 10).

Canadian experts spoke at British seminars on community chaplaincy in 2000 and 2001, and Churches together in Britain and Ireland—the country's largest ecumenical organization—sponsored a full-time community chaplaincy project officer.

The first British experiment with community chaplaincy was launched in the Welsh city of Swansea when prison chaplains and an ecumenical grouping of local clergy—led by two officers of the Salvation Army—obtained funding from the Welsh Assembly to cover the cost of running a community chaplaincy in June 2001

---

[5] See http://www.monctonchaplaincy.com/en/history.html.

[6] Pierre Allard eventually became CSC's assistant commissioner for security and regimes.

and conducting a fact-finding tour of Canada soon afterwards (Emery 2012). With further support from the European Social Fund, the project not only expanded in scope but also underwent a formal evaluation (Grayton et al. 2008); furthermore, it experienced occasional difficulties in securing continuity of funding. Subsequently, other prison chaplaincies and community groups in England & Wales have developed their own independent variations on the Canadian and Welsh models. According to a former assistant chaplain general to the Prison Service, "1354 ex-prisoners were supported through community chaplaincy teams, which had 50 paid staff and about 500 volunteers" in 2010.[7] The Community Chaplaincy Association—a national network—has been supporting and facilitating their work since 2010.[8] The network currently links 27 member projects.

The aim of each community chaplaincy project is to do two things: on the one hand, to offer spiritual, religious and practical assistance to ex-offenders after release from prison and, on the other hand, to recruit and train local volunteers to visit and mentor prisoners whilst still in detention. At the same time, the volunteers and leading members of local faith groups also work in collaboration with prison chaplains. Indeed, in some cases, prison chaplains are appointed to serve primarily as community chaplains. This amounts to a partnership between the voluntary and community sector of civil society and the state-funded providers of religious and spiritual care in prisons. Moreover, this is fully congruent with the current UK government's strategy for transforming the rehabilitation of offenders. Its recent green paper on "Transforming rehabilitation: a strategy for reform" (Ministry of Justice 2013, p. 3) embodies principles such as:

- offenders need to be supported "through the prison gate", providing consistency between custody and community;
- those released from short sentences, who currently do not get support, need rehabilitation if we are to bring their prolific reoffending under control
- the voluntary sector has an important contribution to make in mentoring and turning offenders' lives around
- nothing we do will work unless it is rooted in local partnerships and brings together the full range of support, be it in housing, employment advice, drug treatment or mental health services.

The central rationale for community chaplaincy can be summarized as follows:

- it is good for faith groups to share responsibility for helping the ex-offenders who return from prison to live in their localities;
- the support offered to released prisoners can be crucial in helping them to avoid reoffending;
- forging "pre-emptive" relations between local faith groups and prisoners is likely to enhance the latter's transition to life after release and reintegration into their communities.

---

[7] Minutes of the All-Party Penal Affairs Parliamentary Group, 24 January 2012. http://www.prisonreformtrust.org.uk/PressPolicy/Parliament/AllPartyParliamentaryPenalAffairsGroup/PrisonandcommunitychaplaincyJanuary2012.

[8] http://www.communitychaplaincy.org.uk/.

The Community Chaplaincy Association's "theory of change" posits that if a relationship of trust can be established between mentors and "mentees" before the latter's release from prison, the prospects of a successful continuation of the relationship after release will be better. The relationship of trust is expected to be the basis for various activities and outcomes ranging from discussion of alternatives to practical advocacy and long-term plans for fostering self-sufficiency and positive relationships with others. But some of the chaplaincies' websites make no reference to religious faith. For example, the Open Gate Mentoring Project, associated with the women's prison and Young Offenders Institution at Low Newton in Co. Durham, describes its aim as simply "to aid resettlement and help reduce the risks of re-offending, so building safer communities for all".[9] Moreover, the Community Chaplaincy Association reports that 40% of the prisoners and ex-prisoners who have accepted help from community chaplaincy projects have no affiliation to faith groups. By contrast, the Greater Manchester Community Chaplaincy (GMCC) attributes its success to "the cooperation between a faith-based organization, GMCC, and the statutory agencies, prison, police and probation. GMCC was developed by prison chaplains at HMP Manchester, Greater Manchester Churches Together and Greater Manchester Probation, by working together to establish the project and secure funding to enable the project to develop".[10] Some chaplaincies stress their multifaith character,[11] whereas others, such as Optim: the Onesimus Philemon Trust Immanuel Ministries,[12] appear to be focused exclusively on Christians.

The question now arises of how well community chaplaincies respond to the full range of religious diversity found among prisoners and ex-prisoners today. It is clear that the original impetus towards community chaplaincy in Canada came from Christian clergy and volunteers. Similarly, early adopters of the idea of community chaplaincy in England & Wales came predominantly from Christian groups. And, although the community chaplaincy based at the Young Offenders Institution in Feltham, West London, has had a Muslim advocate and activist from its very beginning, references to religions other than Christianity are not common on the websites of other chaplaincies. The phrase "all faiths and none" appears frequently as a description of the community chaplaincies' targets among prisoners and ex-prisoners, but evidence of the active involvement of volunteers and organizers other than Christians is unclear.

This leads to a worrying hypothesis: the "space" for faiths other than Christianity may be narrower in voluntary community chaplaincies than in statutory prison chaplaincies. There are two main reasons for this. One reason is that prisons are public authorities which are subject to the full range of laws insisting on non-discrimination and equality. This means that the presence of prison chaplains

---

[9] http://www.opengate-ne.org.uk/.

[10] http://greatermanchestercommunitychaplaincy.org/history-of-community-chaplaincy/.

[11] The West Yorkshire Community Chaplaincy Project describes itself as a multifaith organization, adding that "we do not proselytise, but see the work that we do as a practical application of faith". http://www.wyccp.org.uk/about.

[12] http://williammcfetridge.wix.com/optim.

representing a wide range of faith groups is to some extent guaranteed by law in England & Wales. The second reason is that research on volunteering and participation in civil society organizations has consistently found that members of ethnoreligious minorities are disproportionately underrepresented among activists.[13] It is also known that Hindus, Muslims and Sikhs, for example, are relatively reluctant to show public interest in the work of prison chaplains representing their particular faith communities.

For these two reasons, it would be a matter of concern if the Prison Service of England & Wales followed the example of the Correctional Service of Canada and tried to save money by boosting community chaplaincy and the use of volunteers at the expense of full-time or part-time prison chaplains. While community chaplaincies may be successful in reducing the rates of recidivism for those released prisoners who have benefited from their mentoring programmes, it remains to be seen whether prisoners and ex-prisoners from *all* faith groups enjoy equality of opportunity to participate. In this connection, it is instructive that an evaluation of the Swansea Community Chaplaincy Project found that only one Muslim and one Buddhist prisoner out of a total of 143 had participated in the programme (Grayton 2008, p. 123). And an evaluation report of a different community chaplaincy recommended that "steps are taken to develop closer links with wider faith groups" (Lewis 2006, p. 35).

In sum, community chaplaincy represents an interesting mutation of prison chaplaincy. By easing the transition for released prisoners "through the gate" and by providing support for them "on the outside", it aims to fill a gap that has long been a concern of prison chaplains and probation workers. Many prison chaplains were concerned that they had no way of knowing whether prisoners who had been involved in religious activities during their incarceration actually practised their faith after release. Community chaplaincy projects are intended to offer not only spiritual and religious care to released prisoners but also practical guidance, moral encouragement, social support and practical assistance. Research is needed, however, to examine the extent to which the use of public funds to subsidise community chaplaincy does not inadvertently put members of faiths other than Christianity at a relative disadvantage.

## 2.6  Conclusions

What makes the chaplaincy of the Prison Service of England & Wales a distinctive model is that it combines two characteristics. The first is the clear integration of chaplains into the structures and daily activities of all prisons. This represents strong continuity with the time when the Church of England enjoyed ascendancy over prison chaplaincy for more than two centuries. The second characteristic is the

---

[13] This is not to overlook the extensive involvement of Hindus, Muslims and Sikhs in their own "communal" charities such as Sewa UK, Islamic Relief UK or Khalsa Aid.

Prison Service's inclusion of chaplains from certain faiths other than mainstream Christianity on the same basis as Christian chaplains—at least in principle.

In combination, these two characteristics help to ensure that levels of satisfaction with the current state of chaplaincies tend to be relatively high. A certain amount of "permitted" religious diversity has been accommodated within a framework, which has not undergone major changes. A limited number of additional faith groups have been added to the list of recognized faiths. At the same time, "Prison Service Instruction 51. Faith and Pastoral Care for Prisoners" (Ministry of Justice 2011) has increased the level of detailed specification for what prisoners are allowed to claim and to do in the name of their registered religious affiliation.

The only significant mutation of prison chaplaincy in England & Wales is the spread of projects for community chaplaincy. They are partnerships between prisons and local groups of volunteers and community organizations, but their relations with the Prison Service Chaplaincy are ambiguous. With their focus firmly on rehabilitation, reintegration and the reduction of recidivism, community chaplaincy projects promise to extend the remit of chaplaincy beyond the prison walls. But these projects also give rise to questions about equality of opportunity for members of all faiths to participate in—and to benefit from—them.

Further questions about equality in the context of religious diversity among prisoners have been taking shape in recent decades. There are now good grounds for speculating that full implementation of the Equality Act 2010 may generate difficult problems for the Prison Service Chaplaincy. This piece of legislation not only makes it an offence to discriminate unfairly on the grounds of "religion or belief" but it also requires public authorities such as prisons to "promote" equality. This requires public authorities (a) to eliminate discrimination, harassment and victimization, (b) to advance equality of opportunity and (c) to foster good relations between people from different groups. Rastafarians, for example, recently used this legislation successfully to challenge their exclusion from the list of faiths recognized by the Prison Service.[14] Similar action is planned by prisoners demanding recognition for their faith as Jedi Knights.[15]

Her Majesty's Chief Inspector of Prisons' Annual Report for 2012–13 emphasizes that "We embrace diversity and are committed to pursuing equality of outcomes for all" (HM Chief Inspector of Prisons 2013, p. 1). The report adds that the "background, faith or religious beliefs" of prisoners should have no bearing on equality of provision or respect for their human dignity (p. 32). These claims are bold; and the Prison Service of England & Wales has certainly gone a long way towards establishing the principle of equal respect for different faiths. But doubts still linger about the range of the faiths that are recognized in British prisons and about the possibility that the spread of community chaplaincy may inadvertently constrain offenders' equality of opportunity for access to religious and spiritual care before and after release from prison.

[14] http://www.voice-online.co.uk/article/rastafarian-holy-days-now-honoured-prisons.
[15] http://www.express.co.uk/news/uk/471647/Star-Wars-Jedi-prisoners-planning-to-sue-prison-service-for-not-recognising-religion.

My doubts are not about the capacity of spiritual and religious care to increase the probability that released prisoners will be successfully rehabilitated and reintegrated. My sociological scepticism is about the suitability of the organizational framework of chaplaincy in the prisons of England & Wales to deliver that care effectively and efficiently.

# References

Becci, I. (2011). Religion's multiple locations in prison. Germany, Italy, Swiss. *Archives de Sciences Sociales des Religions, 153*, 65–84.

Becci, I. (2012). *Imprisoned religion. Transformations of religion during and after imprisonment in Eastern Germany*. Farnham: Ashgate.

Becci, I., & Knobel, B. (2013). La diversité religieuse en prison: entre modèles de régulation et émergence de zones grises (Suisse, Italie, Allemagne). In A.-S. Lamine (Ed.), *Quand le religieux fait conflit* (pp. 109–121). Rennes: Presses Universitaires de Rennes.

Becci, I., & Scheuwly Purdie, M. (2012). Gendered religion in prison? Comparing imprisoned men and women's expressed religiosity in Switzerland. *Women's Studies: An Inter-Disciplinary Journal, 41*(6), 706–727.

Beckford, J. A. (2011). Religion in prisons and in partnership with the state. In J. Barbalet, A. Possamai, & B. S. Turner (Eds.), *Religion and the state. A comparative sociology* (pp. 43–64). London: Anthem.

Beckford, J. A. (2012). Public responses to religious diversity in Britain and France. In L. G. Beaman (ed.), *Reasonable accommodation. Managing religious diversity* (pp. 109–138). Vancouver: UBC Press.

Beckford, J. A. (2013). Religious diversity in prisons: Chaplaincy and contention. *Studies in Religion/Sciences Religieuses, 42*(2), 190–205.

Beckford, J. A., & Gilliat, S. (1998). *Religion in prison. Equal rites in a multi-faith society*. Cambridge: Cambridge University Press.

Beckford, J. A., Joly, D., & Khosrokhavar, F. (2005). *Muslims in prison: Challenge and change in Britain and France*. Basingstoke: Palgrave.

Béraud, C., de Galembert, C., & Rostaing, C. (2013). *Des hommes et des dieux en prison*. Paris: Ecole Normale Supérieure Cachan.

Burnside, J., Adler, J. R., & Rose, G. (2005). *My brother's keeper. Faith-based units in prisons*. Cullompton: Willan.

Cunningham, H. (2004). Nations rebound? Crossing borders in a gated globe. *Identities, 11*(3), 329–350.

de Beaumont, G., & de Tocqueville, A. (1845). *Système pénitentiaire aux Etats-Unis et de son application en France*. Paris: Librairie de Charles Gosselin (3rd edn. First published 1833).

Emery, D. (2012). Be determined and confident. The beginning of community chaplaincy in Swansea. *International Journal of Community Chaplaincy, 1*(1), 14–19.

Foucault, M. (1977). *Discipline and punish: The birth of the prison*. London: Allen Lane.

Furseth, I. (2000). Religious diversity in prisons and in the military—the rights of Muslim immigrants in Norwegian state institutions. *MOST Journal of Multicultural Societies, 2*(1), 1–12

Furseth, I. (2001). *Muslims in Norwegian prisons and the defence*. Trondheim: Tapir Akademisk Forlag.

Furseth, I., & van der Aa Kühle L. (2011). Prison chaplaincy from a Scandinavian perspective. *Archives de Sciences Sociales des Religions, 56*(153), 123–141.

Gilliat-Ray, S., Ali, M., & Pattison, S. (2013). *Understanding Muslim chaplaincy*. Farnham: Ashgate.

Graber, J. (2011). *The furnace of affliction: Prisons and religion in Antebellum America*. Chapel Hill: University of North Carolina Press.

Grayton, L., Davey, J., Williams, A., Luscombe, C., Brook, A. (2008). *Swansea Community Chaplaincy Project. Evaluation of the Swansea Community Chaplaincy Project at HMP Swansea, October 2006—March 2008*. Canterbury: University of Kent.

Griera, M., & Clot, A. (2015). Banal is not trivial. Visibility, recognition and inequalities between religious groups in prison. *Journal of Contemporary Religion. 30*(1), 23–37.

HM Chief Inspector of Prisons for England and Wales. (2013). *Annual Report, 2012–13*. London: HM Inspectorate of Prisons.

HM Inspectorate of Prisons. (2012). *Expectations. Criteria for assessing the treatment of prisoners and conditions in prisons*. Version 4. London: HM Inspectorate of Prisons.

Hunt, S. (2011). Testing chaplaincy reforms in England and Wales. *Archives de Sciences Sociales des Religions, 153*, 43–64.

Jahn, S. (2014) Religion und Strafvollzug in der Bundesrepublik Deutschland (Prof. Dr. Hubert Seiwert), University of Leipzig.

Kirkegaard, H. (2012). The long journey home. A brief early history of community chaplaincy in Canada. *International Journal of Community Chaplaincy, 1*(1), 3–8.

Lewis, E. (2006). *An independent evaluation of the North Staffordshire Community Chaplaincy Project*. Stoke-on-Trent: Wider Impact Consultancy.

Martin, L. H., Gutman, H., & Hutton, P. H. (1988). *Technologies of the self: A seminar with Michel Foucault*. London: Tavistock.

Ministry of Justice. (2011). *Prison service instruction 51. Faith and pastoral care for prisoners*. London: Ministry of Justice, National Offender Management Service.

Ministry of Justice. (2013). *Transforming rehabilitation: A strategy for reform*. London: Ministry of Justice.

Payne, B. (2012). The history of community chaplaincy in England and Wales. *International Journal of Community Chaplaincy, 1*(1), 9–13.

Phillips, P. (2014). *Roles and identities of the Anglican chaplain: A prison ethnography*. Unpublished PhD thesis, Cardiff University.

Rhazzali, M. K. (2009). *L'slam dans la prison. Le vécu religieux des Musulmans dans les prisons italiennes*. Unpublished PhD thesis, University of Padua.

Sarg, R. (2013). La pluralité religieuse en milieu carcérale: ajustements et gestion des conflits. In A.-S. Lamine (Ed.), *Quand le religieux fait conflit* (pp. 63–76). Rennes: Presses Universitaires de Rennes.

Schneuwly Purdie, M. (2011). Silence … Nous sommes en direct avec Allah. L'émergence d'intervenants musulmans en contexte carcéral. *Archives de Sciences Sociales des Religions, 153*, 105–121.

Sullivan, W. F. (2009). *Prison religion. Faith-based reform and the constitution*. Princeton: Princeton University Press.

Thomas, J., & Zaitzow, B. H. (2006). Conning or conversion? The role of religion in prison coping. *The Prison Journal, 86*(2), 242–259.

Todd, A. (2011). Responding to diversity: Chaplaincy in a multi-faith context. In M. Threlfall-Holmes & M. Newitt (Eds.), *Being a chaplain* (pp. 89–102). London: SPCK.

Todd, A., & Tipton, L. (2011). *The role and contribution of a multi-faith prison chaplaincy to the contemporary prison service*. Cardiff: Cardiff Centre for Chaplaincy Studies.

# Chapter 3
# The Effects of Religious Diversity on Spiritual Care: Reflections from the Dutch Correction Facilities

**Mohamed Ajouaou and Ton Bernts**

## 3.1 Introduction

When we speak of religious diversity within the context of detention in a democratic constitutional state, we tend to assume that the presence of freedom of religion and belief is self-evident. After all, this right is anchored in national and international law: it is set down in Article 6 of the Dutch Constitution, Article 18 of the International Covenant on Civil and Political Rights, and in Article 9 of the European Convention on Human Rights. This constitutional protection is translated in Article 41, paragraphs 1, 2, and 3 of the Dutch Custodial Institutions Act (Penitentiaire Beginselenwet), as follows:

> The detainee has the right to believe and practice his religion or worldview, either individually or in a community with others. The director is also to ensure that there is sufficient spiritual care, in the institution, that accords as much as possible with the religion or worldview of the detainee. The director gives the detainee the opportunity to have personal contact, at times and in places set down in the house regulations, with the spiritual caregiver of the religion or worldview of his choice who is associated with the institution, … given that the detainee, in particular in secure institutions, is not able to provide spiritual, medical, and social care for himself.

What is striking in this translation of the right to freedom of religion in the Dutch detention context is that it is linked directly to the availability of spiritual care. Thus, the stipulation that the detainee must be able to "practice his religion in a community" is possible only under the supervision and guidance of a spiritual caregiver. The clause that allows the detainee to "practice his religion individually" is,

M. Ajouaou (✉)
Departement of Theology, VU University Amsterdam, Amsterdam, The Netherlands
e-mail: m2.ajouaou@vu.nl

T. Bernts
The Religion, Mind, Culture and Society Research Network, Radboud University Nijmegen, Nijmegen, The Netherlands
e-mail: t.bernts@kaski.ru.nl

© Springer International Publishing Switzerland 2015
I. Becci, O. Roy (eds.), *Religious Diversity in European Prisons,*
DOI 10.1007/978-3-319-16778-7_3

in the spirit of the article quoted above, made dependent on the extent to which individual contact with a spiritual caregiver is possible. The clause that states that "the detainee, in particular in secure institutions, is not able to provide spiritual, medical, and social care for himself" points to the fact that freedom of religion is, moreover, understood in terms of the "care" that a spiritual caregiver offers (see Beckford in this volume).

In other words, freedom of religion in detention depends on, and is shaped by, the availability and organization of spiritual care within the prisons. The reasoning behind this is simple: in the world outside, citizens may choose to attend, or not attend, a church, mosque, temple, etc. This choice is not present in the detention context, rather it is the government that brings in the services of the church, mosque, temple, etc., appoints the spiritual caregivers, and makes agreements with the send-ing institutions about the religious framework, in accordance with the principle of the separation of church and state. Thus, from a formal legal perspective, the idea that the detainee may "believe and practice his religion or worldview" is limited to what the government (and the prison) can facilitate with respect to means, person-nel, and space in the daily program.

In the last decade, prison chaplaincy in The Netherlands has been characterized by extensive religious diversity. Currently, the state recognizes seven religions that supply chaplain services to the detainees. Traditionally, these were Roman Catholic, Protestant, Jewish, and Humanist chaplains, but in the last decade they have been supplemented with spiritual caregivers from the world religions of Islam, Hindu-ism, and Buddhism. In 2010, an internal research report (Henneken-Hordijk and Mol 2010) was published, containing the number of detainees, their preferred type of spiritual care, and accordingly—that is, based on these preferences—the number of chaplains that were allowed to be supplied to the prisons. We present the results here in Tables 3.1 and 3.2.

The diversity in supply actually exceeds the diversity in demand. Not only is chaplaincy also provided, in some instances, to the substantial non-religious group, but there is also a great diversity in religious beliefs and practices, as well as differ-ences in salience among those detainees who consider themselves as belonging to one of the aforementioned religions (see also Beckford in this volume).

In some instances, there are aspects of religiosity that are not directly linked to spiritual care. Examples include some of the things we observed in the Mus-lim community: when Muslim prisoners decide to pray together during labor time (which is not allowed); when Muslim prisoners do not want to work with products containing pork; when Muslim prisoners do not shake hands with female staff and/

**Table 3.1** Number of detainees (2010)

| Detention centers | 9510 |
|---|---|
| Juvenile institutes | 675 |
| Forensic-psychiatric institutes | 1595 |
| Detention centers for illegal incomers | 1520 |
| Total | 13,300 |

**Table 3.2** Preferences of detainees for spiritual care, and staff of chaplains (2010)

|  | Preference (in %) | Number of positions for chaplain[b] |
|---|---|---|
| Roman-catholic | 29 | 46 |
| Muslim | 27 | 42 |
| Protestant | 22 | 35 |
| Humanist | 12 | 19 |
| Hindu | 3 | 6 |
| Buddhist | 3 | 5 |
| Orthodox | 2 | 0 |
| Jewish | 2 | 3 |
| Total | 100 | 156 |
| N | 10,310[a] | |

[a] 19% of detainees indicated no need for spiritual care, 3% had other preferences
[b] Distribution of staff is exact according to the preferences of the detainees

or refuse to receive orders from them; when they make statements that are associated with ideological motives such as *takbira* (loud utterance of *Allahu Akbar*); when suddenly their religiosity is highlighted through outward signs (long beard, clothes, religious attributes such as prayer rug); or, when some become interested in often orthodox and radical literature and audio material. These examples raise the question of whether the role of Muslim spiritual caregivers is to indicate which religious behavior is "honored" and accepted.

In this chapter, we will elaborate on the effects that the (increasing) religious diversity has on spiritual care, more specifically, on its legitimization and organization. We will show that this legitimization is increasingly phrased in terms of generic care (by all participants), and that the organization and coordination of this diversity brings along a standardization of practices. In our view, these processes should not be seen as forms of formatting religion, but rather, the elaboration of the dimension of care may be interpreted as a form of innovation, and the dimension of standardization as a form of professionalization of prison chaplaincy (Ajouaou and Bernts 2014). Innovation is the process of developing new goals, practices, and competences in view of changing contexts. With professionalization, we specifically mean the development of clear competences and standards for daily practice, a clear view of the goals of prison chaplaincy, an optimal organizational structure, and a system of feedback and quality control.

We will first explore the legitimation of spiritual care by the state (and the correction facilities), by the religious traditions and other (humanistic) sending organizations, and by the detainees themselves. Secondly, we will describe the organizational management of religious diversity. There are several parties involved in, and responsible for, concretizing religious freedom in the detention context: the state, and more specifically the correctional facilities on one hand, and on the other hand the sending organizations. We will examine these different roles and responsibilities.

We will demonstrate these effects at a general level, throughout prison chaplaincy, and more in detail as they occur within the Muslim chaplaincy. We have chosen this religion because it has, in the recent years, rapidly grown and is now one of the four major religions, and because it has attracted widespread public and political attention. Due to these particularities of Muslim chaplaincy, the presumed effects of religious diversity on the professionalization and innovation of prison chaplaincy are eminently visible.

## 3.2 Religious Diversity and the Legitimation of Spiritual Care

As we saw above, the legitimation of spiritual care in a constitutional state is anchored in the freedom of religion that the state should implement, at the minimum in sectors it bears direct responsibility for. For that matter, the government has, as we shall see, an interest of its own in this, it has its own agenda, and sets conditions for this collaboration with the sending organizations. The legitimation by the government, however, is not sufficient, and requires legitimation from the other actors, namely the churches and other sending organizations, and of course from the detainees themselves.

From a Christian perspective, the legitimacy of spiritual care is found in the Christian holy sources (Ganzevoort and Visser 2009: 333). In its humanistic canon, the Dutch Humanist Society refers to the sixteenth-century humanist, Dirck Volkertsz. Coornhert. Presumably, he set down the basic principles for humanistic spiritual care in his *Comedie van Lief en Leedt*. In Islam, the Quran requires that prisoners receive attention (Quran 76: 8). Al-Khalifi reports that the first prison in an Islamic context was a wing of a mosque. Prisoners could thus benefit from the religious atmosphere with respect to their wellbeing and rehabilitation. According to Al-Khalifi, in the eighth and ninth centuries, the sultans Ibn Mansur al-Mahdi and Harun al-Rashid introduced spiritual counselling for prisoners, with a view to expediting their social rehabilitation (Ajouaou 2014: 21). Similar foundations of spiritual care can be found in other religious and worldview traditions.

The legitimation of spiritual care by churches and other sending organizations is also important because of the ideological and actual separation of church and state. Within a democratic constitutional state, the state is barred, by law, from doing anything more than facilitation. In the Netherlands, the sending organizations are partners of the state, and they determine the (theological) frameworks of spiritual care with regards to content. This legitimation is not limited to the spiritual care inside the correctional facilities, but extends to other forms of (after)care. Here, one can think of the involvement of volunteers in providing spiritual care and various other forms of care for ex-detainees. The involvement of volunteers, by spiritual caregivers in the care of detainees, is an aspect of the "practice of the religion of one's community."

In general, the commitment to provide care for those who are vulnerable is the most important stimulus, although the "sending or mission mandate" (Evangelization, *dawa* in Islam) provides an extra motivation. The "mission mandate" is sometimes the most important motivation for supporting and recognizing the work of spiritual caregivers and the communities behind them. The mission mandate, however, had to be abandoned after the government took over the financial obligations of spiritual care. In the Netherlands, the decision to finance spiritual care from general funds goes back to 1824, when the government (King William II) appointed spiritual caregivers and provided adequate remuneration (Abma 1990: 103).

Legitimation, from the perspective of the detainees, is somewhat intertwined with the legitimation given by the government. Spiritual care is, on the basis of the principles of human rights, a right of the individual, and not, or no longer, the right of the church or of any religious organization to impose its religion, and even less an obligation for the individual to respond to the spiritual care offered (until the beginning of the nineteenth century, detainees were obliged to attend religious services) (Abma 1990: 102). Legitimation by the detainee is also important because his or her religiosity affects the degree and the way in which religious facilities and spiritual care is given shape to. Thus, the processes of secularization, depillarization, and deinstitutionalization (Taylor 2009:674-675) immediately invoke the question of whether detainees expect spiritual care along traditional pillars from the various religions, as is now the case, or if they need spiritual care at all. In line with this, the following question also arises: how can the dominance of the classical religions (three quarters of the spiritual caregivers at this time are either Christian or Muslim) be explained in this secularized and individualized society? Does the religious landscape in detention differ from that landscape outside the prison, and does the model of spiritual care provide "artificial protection" against the "the corrosive acids of secularization?" (Beckford 2001: 374).

It does indeed seem that the legitimation of spiritual care sketched above does stand against a crisis, when we consider its context in a strongly secularized and depillarized society like that of The Netherlands (Henneken-Hordijk and Mol 2010). There are a number of possible explanations for this. Secularization could, in light of constitutional legitimation, simply be a shift in the worldview of the perspective from which spiritual care must be provided—for example, more from the humanist or atheist viewpoint. In addition, secularization seems to be less an issue for new religions, such as Islam, than for the established religions, according to the Netherlands Institute for Social Research (SCP (Maliepaard and Gijsberts) 2012: 133). There has also been a decision to use the so-called "*behoeftepeiling*" (need gauge). Here, since 2004, the detainees have been asked what type of spiritual care they desire. Detainees apparently express their need for spiritual care in terms of the various existing religious and worldview traditions. That could be due to the intensification of the religiosity and spirituality of people in "anxious" situations. In detention, this could lead detainees into returning to their religious and worldview roots. Another explanation could be that the spiritual caregivers, including those associated with the traditional religions of the Western prison system, have expanded and adapted their care and guidance repertoire to a target group of people who are largely secularized, but have not completely deserted the old religious frameworks (Taylor 2009: 675). Detainees' appreciation of spiritual care, their statement that they desire it in its currently existing form, is a sign of the legitimacy the service enjoys. Various studies point to this. A list from the Custodial Services Agency on the actual amount of detainees in November 2012 shows that the capacity of Dutch prison detention is around 10,500, excluding the capacity in private youth detention centers and private forensic psychiatric treatment clinics. In 2005, this capacity still averaged 14,108, and a drop to an average of 8875 is expected by 2015 (Molenaar 2010). This means that one spiritual caregiver is available for every 90 detainees. About 70% of the detainees make use of spiritual care (Spruit et al. 2003: 2–5; Oliemeulen et al. 2010: 62). These 70% ask for a spiritual caregiver from one of the denominations mentioned above. Interestingly, a third of those with no religious affiliation also have a strong need for spiritual care (Spruit et al. 2003: 145). Hence, the criterion of belonging or not to a religion does not clearly determine the need and use of spiritual care. Therefore, the 30% of the detainees who do not make any use of spiritual care do not exclusively include individuals who have no religious or worldview background. This percentage only concerns those who have no need for, or make no use of, the service of spiritual care. In sum, the various religions and worldviews, including humanistic spiritual care, appear to correspond greatly with the detainees' need for spiritual care. According to a survey among detainees carried out by the Custodial Institutions Service (Mol and Henneken-Hordijk 2007: 46):

> In general, people are very satisfied with the service of spiritual care…. If that satisfaction is viewed according to the spiritual caregiver with whom the detainees have had contact, then the detainees who have had contact with a minister or a humanist are often more satisfied than those who have had contact with a rabbi (both 79% (very) satisfied versus 62% (very) satisfied). Of those who have been in contact with an imam, 72% are (very) satisfied. For the pandit and the pastor, it is 77% who are (very) satisfied.

Why are detainees satisfied with the services of the spiritual caregivers? A detainee with a Muslim background indicates one possible answer:

> Many people see you as a, as crap, as finished, you know! The [detainee for them] is not human. And then say she is finished, you know. That is how they see you … that's the image they give you. With an imam you are not part of those people [who are seen as 'crap' and who are quickly forgotten].

In general, individuals in detention view themselves as having been written off (the metaphor 'crap'). Most have no trust in anything or anyone anymore. Here, we see that the basic appreciation for spiritual care lies in the particular characteristics of the cleric, that, according to the sociology of work, is characterized by the profession's "credence goods." Spiritual care concerns itself with "the shadow sides of life, with hiding the unpleasant phenomena: doctors do that with sickness, lawyers with crime, and ministers give a place to death and sin." (Flap 2001: 41–42) The basis on which the detainee accepts and receives the services of spiritual care depends on this credence, or trust, which arises in the context of detention. This credence is not given as a matter of course, but rather must be "earned" (Flierman 2012: 161–62) by the caregiver. The "professional activity" of the spiritual caregiver concerns itself with the means of back and forth communication based on "religious communication," (Flierman 2012: 33f., 161f) and the protection of privacy by legal professional secrecy and professional privilege. The back and forth communication and "religious communication" differs according to the religion or worldview, on the basis of which the interactions occur, or based on the religious and worldview profile of the prison (Spruit 2009: 155). For instance, in a Christian context, this communication is different from that in an Islamic context. In the context of Islam, the cultural and migration background of the prisoners plays an important role. The interaction enables the prisoner to be himself (through unconditional treatment without targets, an agenda for assistance, an attentive and listening ear, remembering the prisoner's story, being treated as a human being and not as a criminal, receiving understanding, an unbiased attitude, etc.); and from that perspective, the prisoner reflects or is led to reflect on his or her crime, and how it relates to him- or herself and the environment and restoration of him- or herself, the damage done and the relationships broken (Loman and Hummelen 2009: 438–40).

In addition to the personal care of the prisoner, the spiritual caregiver also makes a contribution to a humane detention atmosphere in general, he or she advises the organization in the area of ethical questions. In addition, the Islamic spiritual caregiver also gives advice in the area of radicalization, as we saw above. The prisoner also profits from these services.

The positive appreciation of spiritual care by detainees is apparent not only in these regularly conducted surveys, but also in the inspection reports that are sent to the Dutch Parliament. In these reports, the perspective of the detainee is central in the assessment. That spiritual care is positively appreciated is also demonstrated by reported complaints about the availability, accessibility, and quality of spiritual care. A negative judgment is accompanied by recommendations for improving the care up to the desired level. To demonstrate these concerns with spiritual care in the correctional facilities, we present some passages from an inspection report (Justitiële Jeugdinrichting De Hartelborgt: 2012, p. 42–45) of the youth detention center "De Hartelborgt," with two locations in Kralingen and Spijkenisse, both near the city of Rotterdam:

> three spiritual caregivers work in De Hartelborgt: an imam, a priest, and a minister. Representatives of other religions, such as a rabbi or pandit, are available on demand. The imam conducts two services every Friday in the Spijkenisse facility and visits the Kralingen facility [semi open prison. T.B & M.A.] once a month, given that youths there can also visit a mosque in the neighborhood. The priest and the minister hold two joint services every Sunday in Spijkenisse. They visit the Kralingen facility when asked. The spiritual caregivers alternate their workdays during the week so that the meditation room is available for individual meetings with the detainees. A detainee can request to speak to a spiritual caregiver via the group leader. The spiritual caregiver then goes to the individual in question and conducts an intake interview. The detainee is informed about the work of spiritual care. Meeting the spiritual caregiver does not interfere with other activities. The spiritual caregivers can thus always organize services and individual meetings so that they fit into the daily program and the agenda. Sometimes, they have to be creative or shift appointments because of lessons the detainees need to attend, but this does not produce major problems. The spiritual caregivers and the librarian also coordinate a group of volunteers who attend the prayer services, and a group of volunteers who visit individual inmates. The institution does not register the frequency of activities such as discussion groups and church services. The spiritual caregivers benefit from the professional secret, which means they do not report on the content of their work to others. If needed, they do have contact with other officials about an inmate's state of mind. The spiritual caregivers also visit inmates who are in isolation. (…)

**Assessment** The offered spiritual care largely meets expectations. Spiritual care is well represented and has good facilities at hand to offer young people religious counselling during their detention. (…)

**Recommendation** The institution should monitor if spiritual care activities fall out.

These passages from the inspection report clearly demonstrate a positive evaluation of spiritual care. It fits without major problems in the daily routines of the institution, and offers the young detainees religious counseling as well as moral support and reflection. The professional confidentiality is respected, and at the same time they may contact others when necessary. Interestingly enough, the inspection is concerned about the fact that spiritual care activities may sometimes fall out. In this respect, they represent not only a valuable, but also a possibly vulnerable type of care. Therefore, a better monitoring of the activities of spiritual care is recommended, in case these activities start declining or disappearing.

## 3.3   Religious Diversity and the Organization of Spiritual Care

As already mentioned, two parties are responsible for, and organize, spiritual care. These are, first, the state (and its representatives, the prison directors), and second, the sending organizations.

The state's responsibility lies in the principle of neutrality and equality of the constitutional state. In detention, these principles are given shape in the legal clause quoted above: "The director is also to ensure … spiritual care in the institution that accords as much as possible with the religion or worldview of the detainee." In practice, this comes down to the government making sure that spiritual care, by the various religions and worldviews, is offered. This implies the recognition of the sending bodies as official partners of the state in making spiritual care possible, as well as appointing spiritual caregivers from all religions and worldviews as civil servants. A beginning here was made only in October 2007, when the Dutch State recognized the Islamic sending organization, appointed a head of Islamic spiritual care, and as of January 2008, appointed about 60 prison imams as civil servants. The provisional recognition of Hindu and Buddhist sending organizations followed in 2009, with the definitive recognition in 2012.

The collaboration between state and sending organizations on behalf of prison chaplaincy may be presented according to the organizational model presented in Fig. 3.1. The organizational model shows that the management of the prison chaplaincy is the common responsibility of a number of autonomous organizations (seven denominations on one side, and the state on the other), on the basis of parity and permanent deliberation. Each of the two parties has a specific responsibility. The state guarantees a pluriform supply of spiritual care by shaping necessary conditions in the correctional facilities, and the sending organizations have the task of educating and recruiting chaplains, and of defining the specific view on chaplaincy.

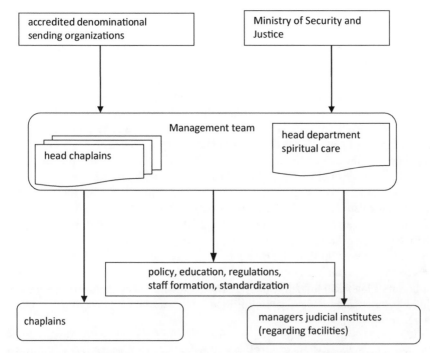

**Fig. 3.1** Simplified organizational model of prison chaplaincy in The Netherlands

The state and sending organizations worked out together a sort of standardization of services, in view of the religious diversity between and within the different traditions. The right to "believe and practice a religion or a worldview individually" takes shape primarily in the individual contact of the detainee with the spiritual caregiver. This contact arises through the request of the detainee, the request of the personnel of the institution (reference by the director, psychologist, doctor, etc.), or on the initiative of the spiritual caregiver himself. The confidentiality of the individual talks is an important aspect of this individual religiosity. The detainee sits, as it were, in the "confessional," and can tell his story with no fear that it will be reported. The spiritual caregiver, after all, is accorded professional privilege and privilege of nondisclosure (he is not allowed to testify). Moreover, individual religiosity in the context of spiritual care includes the intake interview that occurs immediately after entering the institution. In that interview, the spiritual caregiver introduces himself, asks how the detainee is doing, points to the "services" of the spiritual care, and asks if there is need for further contact. Another form of individual religiosity are the so-called "ambulant conversations," i.e., short conversations that the spiritual caregivers conduct during recreation, lunch, at work stations (if the spiritual caregivers are admitted there) or simply in the block the detainee is staying in. The talk can vary from a greeting to a short conversation. Visibility, being present, and expressions of sincere involvement by the spiritual caregiver are essential in this type of contact.

The clause that prescribes the detainee's right to "practice religion or worldview in community with others" is given shape in the form of the weekly celebrations, such as Friday service for Muslims, Sunday service for Christians, meditation sessions for Buddhists, and reflection meetings for humanists. No weekly celebrations are held for smaller religious groups because of the small number of detainees. In these cases, management and standardization occurs, for example with regard to the Sugar Feast (at the end of Ramadan) and the Feast of the Sacrifice. In the outside world, these two feasts are not celebrated on the same day, and Muslims have never succeeded in agreeing on one communal celebration. In prison, however, one day is stipulated for the celebration. The so-called Turkish method for calculating this is used here. This model uses astrological calculations with predictable dates, which fits better into the tight organization of a prison compared to the Moroccan model, in which the date of the celebration is set only on the final day. The Friday service is also held at a standard time, from 1:00 to 2:00 p.m., in all institutions throughout the whole year. The time of the service can vary in the world outside the prison. In addition, a time limit of about 15 min for the sermon is imposed, whereas these can be as long as an hour outside the prison. These forms of standardization seem to be small logistical adjustments, but there is a deep theological struggle behind this adjustment among the Islamic spiritual caregivers, and between them and their target group.

We conclude that there exists a standardization of the delivered "services", including regards toward respect of a fair distribution of workload, the possibilities to quality control, and—not in the least—to justify spiritual care inside and outside the correctional facilities.

In the *Specification of services* compiled in 2006, several of the services are summed up as follows: intake interviews, casual conversations, private conversations, discussion groups, prayer services (reflection meetings for humanistic spiritual care), especially religious gatherings (Easter, Sugar Feast, etc.), and help in crisis situations (Dienst Justitiële Inrichtingen, 2006).

The responsibility of the sending organizations is shaped by the situation of religious diversity, in the sense that they feel a shared and mutual responsibility for the spiritual care of the detainees. This is shown in several ways. In the first place, it concerns the attitude of the established major sending bodies: the Roman Catholic, Protestant, and Humanist bodies. This attitude entails that they are willing to make room for newcomers. After all, the budget for spiritual care was traditionally based on the norm of one full-time spiritual caregiver for every 90 detainees. If more imams come, for example, then the other types of chaplains have to give up a few positions. Although the government has the means to force this change, in itself it does appeal to the moral sense of the sending organizations. The latter agreed to a study on the need for spiritual care, whereby the results led to prisons bringing in a larger number of imams. In addition, the sending bodies and the state have agreed that there will always be a minimum of 10% of chaplaincy that will be reserved for small religious groups, in order to ensure religious pluriformity.

The other aspect of mutual responsibility can be illustrated primarily by the acceptance, by all religions and worldviews, of sharing the same prayer room. That has been a challenge, especially for Christian denominations, given that the prayer rooms were originally chapels with a distinctive Christian character. Here as well it is true that the government can force this change, but instead, appeals were made to the moral sense of the religious groups to work out a solution for this. The sometimes difficult negotiations have resulted in the prayer rooms now being called "silence rooms" (meditation areas), which all religions and worldviews can use, and whereby the religious symbols and attributes of one religion are only displayed if that religion is holding a service or celebration. The room is decorated as a mosque on Friday, as a church on Saturday and Sunday, and possibly as a meditation area for the Buddhist chaplain when he or she comes for meditation, or remains neutral if humanists use it.

A third aspect of mutual responsibility is a matter of working relations and can be called "professional collegiality." This aspect concerns spiritual caregivers. Examples of this collegiality is the acceptance of the newcomers as full colleagues, helping them in the organization of their care-giving activities, but also in being attentive to the needs for spiritual care by the smaller religious groups that are not always present. In the latter case, the spiritual caregivers should quickly contact the desired spiritual caregiver, and the organization also helps him or her to quickly take up contact with the detainee.

The internal responsibility of the sending organizations has many variants. Organizationally, it is desired that each religious group mirrors the religious diversity of its members in its supply of spiritual caregivers. We can take the Protestant, Jewish, and Islamic religions as examples. The Protestant sending organization sees to it that thirteen churches are represented, from orthodox to liberal. The Jewish sending organization is required to provide both orthodox and liberal rabbis. The presupposition is that this selection of chaplains does justice to the diversity within Protestantism and Judaism. The recognition of the Islamic sending organization by the Dutch state included the guarantee that spiritual care has to be provided for everyone considering him- or herself as a Muslim. In addition, the sending organization agreed that this religious diversity would be mirrored in the spiritual caregivers it would appoint. This implies that, in addition to the theological traditions, such as the Sunnis and Shiites, the different law schools (*madhahib*) in Islam are represented. A Shiite spiritual caregiver was appointed in 2008. The diversity of law schools is derived from the number of ethnic groups that are represented by the Islamic spiritual caregivers: 10 ethnic groups, from Moroccan to Indonesian and native Dutch people. The distribution follows roughly the percentage in society: 40% of Islamic caregivers have a Moroccan background, 40% are Turkish, and 20% are other. At this time, there are seven female spiritual caregivers, one of whom works at the women's prison, while the others work in a men's prison.

The Ahmadiyya movement and the Alawis, two Islamic religious minorities, are not represented neither in the board, nor among the spiritual caregivers. One reason for this is that these two groups are too far from each other religiously to include them in one organization. The Islamic sending organization has nonetheless agreed to offer spiritual care to prisoners from the Ahmadiya and Alawi movements. In actuality, this happens via the spiritual caregivers present, but if an adherent of the

Ahmadiya or the Alawi tradition wants a spiritual caregiver from his or her respective tradition, the Islamic spiritual caregiver will see to it that the request is fulfilled. This management model of religious diversity within Islam does not mean, however, that there is a separate spiritual caregiver for every theological tradition or law school. The quality policy of Islamic sending organization is that each Islamic spiritual caregiver has to develop skills to act as imam and spiritual caregiver for all Muslims, regardless of their backgrounds. This means that in practice, the spiritual caregiver's own religious tradition or law school will not have the upper hand in the contact with the prisoner. This policy requires that the spiritual caregiver has a hermeneutical and "ecumenical" approach. That is not without problems, and it demands a high degree of leadership from the spiritual caregiver to do justice to the religious diversity he or she has to deal with. Problems arise primarily in group discussions and at Friday service, when detainees come together in larger groups. Bekir (pseudonym), a spiritual caregiver whose activity has been researched, illustrates the tensions of religious diversity as follows.

Bekir has a Turkish background. The law school he follows is the Sunni, Hanafī school. He finds it justified to include some of his own tradition in his work. However, he views a law school not only as a collection of laws, but primarily as a way of interpreting and understanding. This points out that he applies autonomy and hermeneutical approaches to this area. At the same time, he does not make value judgment about other law schools. Whenever it does not do any injustice to religious diversity, Bekir does not see any objections against bringing out recognizable elements from his own religious background. This recognizability does not mean that he prefers his own tradition over or against others. He sometimes borrows from the guidelines of other law schools. Furthermore, he orients himself broadly toward all traditions. This orientation entails, on one hand, that he recognizes and studies the tradition of the individual detainee and, on the other, that he strives for consensus when these traditions converge:

> I don't want to say by this that I do not have a certain *madhhab* or direction or follow a law school. No. I do that, but those cultural aspects that have been added, that have come into the culture, those I leave aside and attempt to find the basis in which everyone can find themselves.

This "basis" leads Bekir to what he calls the "core," i.e., the most basic form of implementation in which as many detainees as possible can recognize themselves. Specific customs or traditions are not given any place in meetings. They are recognized by him, and he recommends they be followed in private, for example, in the detainee's own cell. This pattern of reduction and elimination of local forms of expression is not, therefore, a matter of principle, but rather it is a pragmatic matter. It is prescribed by the need of the target group (Ajouaou 2014: 245). His colleague Ahmed (pseudonym), who has a Moroccan background, describes his attitude as follows (Idem, p. 214):

> I feel that I am Sunni in the broad sense of the term. But if I say Sunni, then I mean the majority of Muslims, thus with all their *madhāhib* [law schools].

This broadening of the theological horizon of the Islamic spiritual caregiver by orienting him- or herself to all traditions and law schools has contributed to the exclusion of radical spiritual caregivers within this religious group. It has also contributed to meeting an important requirement for working as a cleric in detention: No evangelization (*dawa* in Islam).

Finally, we need to introduce a nuance. The picture drawn above does not indicate that religiosity among Muslim detainees is so transparent and explicit. Although studies outside the prison context show that most Muslims in The Netherlands call themselves "religious," (SCP (Maliepaard and Gijsberts) 2012: 133) and that the interest in Muslim spiritual care is great among Muslim detainees, we do not know what their religiosity consists of. Not enough research has been done on that subject. To put this in perspective, we will cite Bekir once more (Ajouaou 2014: 239–240):

> Yeah, some are Muslims, but they participate once or twice in the feast prayers (Sugar Feast ad Sacrifice Feast). They feel Muslim only during the feast and [do] very little for the rest; they have been circumcised and whatever, but for the rest they don't have very much to do [with the faith]. Another does want to participate in the Friday service, another still manages to read the Qur'an, someone else somewhat less. Thus, it can vary, for detainees also. And I am totally open to that. (…) The one is more practicing than the other. The one does nothing, the other prays …. In general that people who are on the same level do not know too much, no. In general you can say that they come more from the world of the coffee shop[1] than the mosque.

## 3.4   Conclusions: The Effects of Religious Diversity

Religious diversity has changed the legitimation and organization of prison chaplaincy. In the legitimation brought forward by the state and more specifically the correctional facilities, and also by the detainees themselves, chaplaincy is seen as a distinctive form of care; distinctive because traditions and competences outline the context of this care, and not in the least because of the special position the chaplains take in their "free space." The cooperation between the seven denominations working together with respect to prison chaplaincy, their care for a population of detainees who show a great diversity of denominations and religious, spiritual, and secular attitudes, has for effect that a shared notion of care has evolved. Of course, this is not the case for all aspects of spiritual care—for instance, the religious services are a clear exception. This development can be witnessed to an even greater extent in the chaplaincy that is found in the military and in health care organizations, where there is often only one chaplain available (Bernts et al. 2014). The questions that are raised by this tendency are interesting with respect to a more generic form of spiritual care for the sending organizations. The legitimation they receive for providing spiritual care is traditionally based on specific religious questions and needs of the detainees. In this respect, it could be a threatening development. On the other hand, a Christian head of the military chaplaincy, states that the current state and work of the chaplaincies should be evaluated by the churches as one of their common

---

[1] In The Netherlands this means a shop where legally soft drugs are sold.

practices in the parishes of tomorrow. Stated otherwise: working together in prison (and military) chaplaincy in a situation where the "clients" are often under severe pressure, and where there exists a great diversity between and within religious and humanistic traditions, means a fundamental challenge for innovation.

In an analogous and complementary way, the religious diversity has favored the management and organization of spiritual care. In our chapter, we have demonstrated the management model, as well as the standardization of services and activities. The structure of standardized services and activities is designed by the management team, for reasons of better insight in the profession and workload, the accountability to the financier (the State), quality assessment, optimal facilitation by the institutes, and better external and internal communication (to other disciplines, to the board of the correctional facilities) of the content and function of spiritual care.

Besides the aforementioned services, the chaplains have a distinct role in the organizational policy: they give advice on different topics, and they participate in meetings with personnel and staff, on subjects that include cultural differences. Of course, this is carried out on the basis of their professional code of confidentiality. It is obvious that the traditional position of the prison chaplain, consisting merely in the rendering of religious services inside detention centers, no longer reflects adequately all the aspects of the actual praxis of spiritual care.

As we have described elsewhere (Ajouaou and Bernts 2014), this professionalization process is further supported by clear descriptions of the required competences of the chaplains, and eventually to the specific requirement of an academic education: in the last two years, such an education at the Free ('Protestant') University of Amsterdam was installed for the last group of chaplains, namely the Hindu and Buddhist chaplains. The time when ordination as such was sufficient lies behind us. And an important factor in this process of professionalization was, as we have seen, religious diversity. This diversity is—in a still ongoing process—leading to a new spiritual and professional identity.

# References

Abma, J., et al. (1990). Geestelijke verzorging in penitentiaire inrichtingen. *Justitiële verkenningen, 6,* 103–124.

Ajouaou, M. (2014). *Imam behind bars. A case study of Islamic spiritual care in Dutch prisons towards the development of a professional profile* (originally a PhD, University of Tilburg). CreateSpace Independent Publishing Platform: North Charleston.

Ajouaou, M., & Bernts, T. (2014). Imams and inmates. Adaptation or contextualization of Islamic prison chaplaincy? *The International Journal of Politics, Culture of Society.* doi:10.1007/s10767-014-9182-y.

Arts, W., & Batenburg, R. (Eds.). (2001). *Een kwestie van vertrouwen. Over veranderingen op de markt voor professionele diensten en in de organisatie van vrije beroepen (A matter of trust. About changes in the market for professional services and in the organization of professions).* Amsterdam University Press: Amsterdam.

Beckford, J. (2001). Doing time: space, time, religious diversity and the sacred in prisons. *International Review of Sociology/Revue internationale de sociologie, 3,* 371–382.

Bernts, T., Ganzevoort, R., Leget, C., & Woitkowiak, J. (2014). *Omvang en verdeling van de geestelijke verzorging in de krijgsmacht vanaf 2016* (Extent and distribution of chaplaincy in the Armed Forces, from 2016). Kaski: Radboud University Nijmegen.

Dienst Justitiële Inrichtingen. (2006). *Samenvatting eindrapport 'Diensten' specificaties (Summary of Specifications of Services of Chaplains)*, Ministry of Security and Justice, The Hague.

Flap, H. (2001). *'Professies als probleem: sociaal-wetenschappelijke vraagstellingen op het terrein van vrije beroepen' (Professions as a Problem. Social-Scientific Questions in the Field of Liberal Professions)*. In: Arts et al. (Eds.), 2001, pp. 31–50.

Flierman, F. (2012). *Geestelijke verzorging in het werkveld van justitie (Spiritual Care in the Penitentiary Field)*. Eburon: Delft.

Ganzevoort, R., & Visser, J. (2009). *Zorg voor het verhaal. Achtergrond, methode en inhoud van pastorale begeleiding (Care for the story. Background, method and content of pastoral counseling)*. Meinema: Zoetermeer.

Henneken-Hordijk, I., & Mol, G. (2010). *Voorkeurspeiling Geestelijke Verzorging DJI. Resultaten metingen 2008, 2009 en 2010 (Preference Monitor Spiritual Care. Results for 2008, 2009 and 2010)*. Ministry of Security and Justice, The Hague.

Iersel, A. van, & Eerbeek, J. (Eds.). (2009). *Handboek justitiepastoraat (Guide to prison pastorate)*. Damon: Buddel.

Justitiële Jeugdinrichting De Hartelborgt: Inspectierapport, doorlichting, Inspectie Veiligheid en Justitie (2012) (*Inspection report, audit, inspection Security and Justice*). Inspectie Veiligheid en Justitie: The Hague.

Lomman, G., & Hummelen, H. (2009). *'Internationaal perspectief' (International Perspective)*. In: A. van Iersel & J. Eerbeek (Eds.), 2009, pp. 437–440.

Oliemeulen, L., et al. (2010). *Geestelijke Verzorging in detentie. Visie van ingeslotenen op behoefte en aanbod (Spiritual Care in Detention. Attitudes of Detainees on Need and Demand)*. Center for Research on Societal Cate, Radboud University: Nijmegen.

SCP (Maliepaard, M., & Gijsberts, M.). (2012). *Moslim in Nederland 2012 (Muslim in The Netherlands)*. The Hague.

Spruit, L. (2009). *'Het religieus profiel van gedetineerden, met het oog op herstelgericht pastoraat' (A religious profile of the detainee for the purpose of restorative ministry)*. In: A. van Iersel & J. Eerbeek (Eds.), 2009, pp. 155–170.

Spruit, L., Bernts, T., & Woldringh, C. (2003). *Geestelijke verzorging in justitiële inrichtingen. (Spiritual care in judicial institutes)*. Nijmegen.

Taylor, C. (2009). *Een seculiere tijd (A secular age)*. Lemniscaat: Rotterdam.

# Chapter 4
# An Outline of the Construction of the Islamic Council for Prisons in Belgium

Farid El Asri

## 4.1 Introduction

The current demand for religious care in Belgian prisons exceeds available provisions in terms of diversity. How do the institutions devoted to providing chaplains manage this ever-growing number of demands and the training of chaplains? In this chapter, I aim at presenting the slow process of developing the function of an Islamic chaplaincy in Belgium and particularly the debate on the gap between the allocation of posts and the assumed workload, particularly in view of the over-representation of Muslim prisoners. The issue of Muslim leadership, which is developing in the Belgian context, the quest for legitimacy within the Muslim community and the State, the aspects which concern training and the construction of a temporal authority for Islam will all be tackled here in a transversal manner (Dassetto et al 2001).

The organization of chaplaincies in prisons is at a crossroad involving numerous issues and expectations. Moreover, the chaplain has to deal with multiple configurations in his job. Among other things, he has to face the complexity of a community with contrasting ethno-religious and linguistic backgrounds, as well as Islamic tendencies that need to be constantly managed in a context in which traditionalism, Salafism, and even radicalism intermingle on a daily basis. Religious tendencies are an important element for the understanding of Muslim inmates in Belgian prisons.

The changing sociography of the prison environment in which a certain "popular radicalism" is expressed in multiple ways further complicates the approach. Among the poorly educated and relatively young prisoners a pronounced religiosity often manifests in simplistic practices.

F. E. Asri (✉)
International University of Rabat, Rabat, Morocco
e-mail: elasrifarid@gmail.com

© Springer International Publishing Switzerland 2015                    47
I. Becci, O. Roy (eds.), *Religious Diversity in European Prisons,*
DOI 10.1007/978-3-319-16778-7_4

There are, moreover, the expectations of religious institutions that aspire to effective mediation in unknown environments in which reports and studies that focus specifically on the Muslim faith are very rare or nonexistent. Knowledge is transmitted orally and stems from a chaplaincy know-how that has been accumulated through the practice of the profession. Finally, the pragmatism of the chaplain, which is exercised on a daily basis, and the specific tasks he is linked to, restrict his room for manoeuvre in a field that, after all, remains unpredictable. It is to be noted that chief counselors deal increasingly with the management of human resources and the guidance of chaplains in the field. The processing of cases remains urgent in a situation in which personnel face a constant overload.

The multiple forms of support in prison, where the "glocal" element interferes at the highest level, ultimately render the function more complex. This has an impact on the very nature of religious support: whether it is in discourse or in the formulation of counter discourse and theological content against a certain religious radicalism hovering in prisons. The contrasting feelings linked to imprisonment and those related to the conversion to Islam, as well as variable motives and influences, weigh upon chaplaincies' approaches and the good word is often replaced by the strength of theological arguments, aimed particularly at establishing and thus legitimizing the religious position of an "official" Islam, which is represented by the chaplains officially appointed for prisons. The status of religious discourse transmitted by officials can, therefore, be confused with the legitimacy of a function designated by the public authorities.

In most cases, the first involvement in chaplaincy occurs through volunteering, before being given the stable status of chaplain. Now this shift from occasional volunteer work to full-time positions raises several issues. Let us remember, for example, the vocational training of chaplains and the religious status that derives from this and, in particular, the issue of creating a religious authority for the prison environment. We can also mention the purpose of this religious service for prisoners.

Because of its history, its dominance of the religious institutional landscape, and the fact that it is native to the Belgian culture, the Roman Catholic Church remains an implicit or explicit reference model for institutionalized religious experiences and one which Islam draws inspiration from since its recognition in 1974. The recognition of the function of Muslim chaplaincies in Belgian prisons derives from the slow and long process of the institutionalization of Islam in Belgium. Negotiations on the status to be granted to Muslims are mainly based on the Catholic precedent.

Below the surface of this new professional category for Muslims in Belgium, a complex institutional game is going on for the legitimization of a "publicly useful Islam." The latter certainly aspires to influence public authorities in Belgium or to limit or reduce suspicions towards the Muslim religion in general and towards Islam in prisons in particular.

## 4.2   Occupancy Overload and Demand for Islamic Support in Prison

The reality of prison life in Belgium, which the recent organization of Muslim chaplaincies is confronted with, is, as we briefly summarized in the introduction, rather complex. The discomfort of imprisonment and the levels of demand for moral or spiritual guidance far exceed the manpower allocated by the Muslim Executive of Belgium (EMB). As a result of this, the systematization of individualized support becomes almost impossible and occasional community gatherings (for collective prayer, during Ramadan, the Feast of the Sacrifice, etc.) are among the few solutions to bring inmates together in the atmosphere of a communal ritual for Friday sermons or general religious counseling.

The overcrowding of prison spaces, therefore, has an impact on the function of the Muslim chaplain, and for a good reason. Total occupancy rates currently exceed 100%. The 23 so-called *maisons d'arrêt* detention centres and nine penal institutions have a joint capacity of 8133 places, but the occupancy amounts to 9873 inmates, according to an analysis of the composition of the prison population conducted by various institutions,[1] including The Human Rights League in Belgium. Between the 1980s and now there has been more than a 70% increase in the number of prisoners, with a record high in 2007 when the number crossed the symbolic threshold of more than 10,000 inmates, who had either already been sentenced or were being held in preventive custody. Depending on periods, the latter category makes up to 30% of the prison population. In addition to a greater use of preventive detention by the judicial authorities over the past 30 years, other factors, such as the extension and accumulation of sentences, as well as a more restricted access to parole conditions, justify the increase.

Regarding capacity overflow, statistics indicate a dominant population of inmates of so-called "foreign origin" (42%, including foreigners without any legal residence permits, EU foreigners, and people belonging to the migrant generations, who were born in Belgium but do not possess Belgian citizenship). Inmates of Moroccan origin represent the largest group (11.47%). On 23 October 2014, the Flemish politician Bart de Wever, one of the major winners of the parliamentary elections who had a lot of say in the recent composition of the federal government declared that the 1200 Moroccans to be found in Belgian prisons could fill up a Moroccan prison on their own. This statement to the media made headline news in the press and caused outrage on community social networks in Belgium.

In a range of a 100 nationalities, the Turks are at the bottom of the list, only making up 2.5% of foreign inmates. The works of the criminologists Fabienne Brion et al. (2001) and Charlotte Vanneste (2002) have demonstrated that this over-representation of people of foreign origin cannot be attributed to a tendency of a

---

[1] Cf. http://www.iev.be/getattachment/1b978060-8b2e-4557-9b47-ea5e4b9857fa/Prisons---silence-on-entasse-!.aspx, consulted on 18 of October 2014.

particular part of the population to violate the law. Rather, it is due to specific economic factors and a markedly more severe treatment of people of foreign origin by the penal system.

A significant percentage of these Belgian inmates of European or non-European origin is said to be of Muslim origin. It is particularly on the basis of a nationality linked to a Muslim country, but also on the basis of requests for the support of Muslim chaplaincies or by the choice of meals that are preselected, that the religious origins of the inmates are determined. In certain prisons, such as in Brussels and Liège, the supply of halal meat is sometimes on general offer in prison canteens. This sometimes gives rise to virulent reactions from militants in secular associations.[2] The criticism goes as far as to talk about an Islamization of prisons through "the table" and, already in 2009, gave rise to some questions to the Minister of Justice in the Chamber of Representatives.[3]

Women represent about 5 % of the prison population and two Muslim chaplains take care of these inmates. We have no details on the precise number of female Muslim inmates, but the investment made by chaplaincies is substantial. The duo, therefore, have to tackle a high demand for support between different detention centres spread around the whole country and in different linguistic areas.

## 4.3   Context for the Recognition of Religious Practice in Belgium: Experience of Muslim Actors

One needs to bear in mind the changes that have occurred in the importance of established religions in Belgian society, with the loss of the influence of traditional churches and the growth of new religions. From a sociological point of view, over the past 100 years, religious behaviour and convictions have deeply changed, with, among other things, the shift from a historically traditional form of Islam towards a rise in literalism. The growing number of Muslims, combined with the decline in established traditional churches, has altered the positions of different religions, including those in Belgium. The Roman Catholic Church has lost its dominant position and its "natural" involvement in politics has become more relative. In tandem with this, new religions, and Islam in particular, have become more visible in the public arena and carry more demographic weight. As a result, the national religious landscape fundamentally differs from that of the nineteenth century, when constitutional relations were established between the Church and State. Traditionally, a

---

[2] Cf. http://www.fdesouche.com/260578-belgique-70-de-repas-halal-dans-les-prisons, Consulted on 20 October 2014.

[3] Cf. http://www.lachambre.be/kvvcr/showpage.cfm?section=qrva&language=fr&cfm=qrvaXml. cfm?legislat=52&dossierID=52-b073-380-0744-2008200909338.xml, Consulted on 20 October 2014.

religious community is authorized to determine on its own how it wants to organize its representation within the Belgian State.[4]

The Constitution of 1831 accepts no State religion, but recognizes the freedom of religion.[5] At a European level, with the ratification of the European level, with the ratification of the *European Convention for the Protection of Human Rights and Fundamental Freedoms*[5] in 1955, Belgium committed its government authorities to guaranteeing the freedom of conscience and religion. The neutrality of the Belgian State in religious matters, which nevertheless differs from *French secularism*, does not revoke the right, in accordance with Article 181[6] of the Constitution, to recognize services of a public nature conducted by religious denominations and, in so doing, goes some way towards being implicated in the functioning and taking into consideration of their tasks. In other words, the State recognizes no religion, but admits "administrations entrusted with the management of the temporal (earthly) aspects of the religion."[7]

The Belgian authorities currently recognize six religions: Roman Catholic, Protestant, Jewish, Anglican, Muslim, and Orthodox. Recognition for the secular movement, on the other hand, has been inscribed in the constitution since 1993. Some of these recognitions even predate independence[8] and are, therefore, not subject to acts of the Belgian State. On the other hand, for Muslim and Orthodox denominations, the entire institutionalization process is fully Belgian and based on the amendment to the law of 4th March 1870.[9]

Since the recognition of Islam through the Law of 19th July 1974[10] to the Royal Decree of 1999 recognizing the EMB as the manager of the temporal affairs of Islam, there have been many negotiations between the authorities, on one hand, and the Muslim community, on the other. These situations are a reflection of administrative efforts, political circumstances and security issues. The process for the recognition of Islam therefore follows an unusual path, both because of its historical peculiarities and because of the debate its structural unstable institutionalization continues to fuel.

---

[4] A number of spokesmen represent an ecclesiastical and hierarchical structure. Other denominations have opted for a more democratic representation of their local communities, such as in the case of the United Protestant Church, for example, which has a synodal structure. The Muslim community prefers a direct representation of Muslim individuals, elected through a national campaign.

[5] Cf. Article 19 (previously Article 14 amended by the constitutional reforms of 1993).

[6] Old Article 117: "The salaries and pensions of religious ministers are paid by the State; the sums required to cover these are annually included in the budget."

[7] Belgium has no official religion. There is only a legal recognition of denominations, which limits itself to the "temporal" aspects of these religions, i.e. an official recognition of administrations entrusted with their organization and management.

[8] Protestant religion: Decree of 5 May 1806 concerning the accommodation of ministers and the maintenance of the temples of this religion. Catholic religion: Decree of 30 December 1809 concerning the building of churches. Jewish religion: Decree of 17 March 1808.

[9] It is to be noted that the recognition of the Anglican Church dates back to the law of 4 March 1870.

[10] It was endorsed by Royal Decree on 3 May 1978.

In the words of the researcher Lionel Panafit (1997), an analysis of the historicity of the recognition of the Muslim faith implies "three modes of differentiated objectification." The first period was determined, right up to the mid 1980s, by the pace of Belgian foreign policy. The institutional untangling of the Islamic case was then focused on diplomatic and trading relations. The debate on institutionalization was then internalized to concentrate on the integration of Muslims who had become permanent residents. Up until then they had been considered as temporary foreigners in Belgium. Finally, starting in the 1990s, a web of contacts was woven with vertical negotiations between the Muslim community and the government.

The chronology of the institutionalization of Islam partly explains the current management of Muslim affairs. Also, the reviewing of some of the key moments in this process will enable us highlight the setbacks of the Belgian Islam under development and the urgent situation and delays in most of the religion case files. The case of the chaplaincies, which seems to have been settled, today raises the issue of the ability to adapt to the reality of prison life.

Debates on the recognition of Islam started as early as 1971, with bills being submitted to the Chamber of Representatives, on one hand, and the Senate, on the other. The initial challenge was to, above all, grant Islam some symbolic recognition at a diplomatic level, particularly in exchanges with oil-exporting countries. The official recognition of Islam in 1974, coincided with the Belgian government putting a unilateral and definitive halt to immigration. The law of 19th July of that year[11] was amended with the addition of Article 19a, the article regarding the temporal aspects of religions of 1870. A Royal Decree was then enacted on 3rd May 1978[12] in order to make its implementation possible. Six days later, the *eastern pavilion* of the Cinquantenaire building, leased to Saudi Arabia until 2073, became the headquarters of the *Islamic and Cultural Centre of Brussels*.[13] This structure initially focused on defining the law of 1974.[14] In 1985, Jean Gol, who was the Minister of Justice several times, proposed a Royal Decree stipulating: "the creation of a *Supreme council of Muslims in Belgium and the organisation of committees in charge of managing the temporal aspects of recognized Islamic communities*."[15] In 1989, the government appointed a *Royal Commissariat* for immigrant policy[16] to advise the political decision makers in matters of integration and immigration. This *Commissariat* proposed the establishment of a *Supreme Council of Muslims of Belgium* on an elective and co-optive basis. Despite opposition to the use of

---

[11] Cf. *Moniteur belge*: 23.8.74.

[12] The Royal Decree applies to the organization of committees in charge of the management of the temporal aspects of Islamic communities. Cf. *Moniteur belge*: 6.5.78.

[13] Created by non-national students a few years earlier

[14] Competitors to the CIC were to emerge soon afterwards. Already in 1976 there was the establishment of the *Culture et religion islamique* association and in 1982 the Turkish government established the Turkish Religious Foundation of Belgium—*Diyanet* in Brussels.

[15] In the wake of the negative opinion of the Council of State, 3 years later, the Minister Gol attempted to submit a similar bill, but by then parliament had been dissolved as a result of the political situation and the project was stillborn.

[16] Future Centre for Equal Opportunities and the Combat against Racism.

polling from political circles and the Ministry of Justice's request for the process launched on 27th March 1990 to be blocked, the organizing committee made it happens and went to the polls.[17] The Minister of Justice created, through a designation of members, the Provisional *Council of Wise Men for the organization of the Islamic Religion* and established it in July 1990. The State then sanctioned the Islamic and Cultural Centre (CIC) by ministerial decree, and suspended it from its function of appointing Islamic religion teachers.[18] Despite these measures, on 13 January 1991, slightly more than 26,000 Muslims went to the polls and elected a *General Council* from which the *Supreme Council of Muslims of Belgium* would emerge. In 1992, the establishment of a *Technical Committee,* after lengthy negotiations, allowed for the dissolution of the *Provisional Council.* A couple of months later, a *Constituent Assembly* was born. Its role was to be limited to the setting up of a *Provisional Executive of Muslims in Belgium.* At the end of 1993, a list of members was drafted. A year later, the *Provisional Executive* inherited, among other things, the tasks of the dissolved Technical Committee and a budget of 3 million Belgian francs.[19] On 3rd July 1996, the *Provisional Executive* was renewed by Royal Decree, thus giving it an indelible seal of recognition. A year later, the *Provisional Executive* asked the Minister of Justice to establish a body to be the *Head of Religious Affairs*, a request which was positively received. The minister nevertheless requested more concrete proposals, which he received in 1998. Approval for the creation of the Head Body of Religious Affairs was immediately granted[20] and, in 1999, the 16 people comprising it were introduced to the public through a press conference. In the spring, Article 19a of the law was amended and the EMB was officially recognized by Royal Decree.

Each time the State was supposed to grant Islam just recognition, the need for a single spokesman proved to be a major obstacle. In order to overcome this problem, the Belgian government operated as follows: In 1998, it allocated the responsibility of organizing national and Muslim elections to the *Provisional Executive.* The new *Muslim Executive* was, at least partially, the product of those elections. Through an amendment of the 1870 law, the Belgian government was declared competent in respect of recognizing a representative body for Islam.[21]

---

[17] The polling stations were mostly in prayer rooms, but this would not be the case in the 1998 elections.

[18] On 16 November 1990, responsibility for teaching reverted back to the Council of the Wise. Cf. *Moniteur belge* 24.11.90.

[19] 75,000 EUR.

[20] It was adopted by Royal Decree on 24 June. On 24 September, a Ministerial Decree stipulated the supervision of the elections by a *Joint Steering Committee.* On 13 December 1998, some 48,000 voters went to the polls and, on 6 January 1999, the steering committee confirmed the votes. A *screening* was then conducted to preserve, within the Executive, the candidates deemed *desirable* by State Security and the Public Prosecutor's Office. On 8 February 1999, the chairman of the *Provisional Executive* submitted the list of candidates to the Executive. Finally, a confidential list was submitted to the Minister of Justice and this formed the basis for the creation of the actual *Executive.*

[21] The election proposal for the Head of Religious Affairs, which was revised several times, was finally accepted by the Ministers of Justice in 1998. On the whole, the public authorities actively

At the end of the 1970s, Islam in Belgium shifted from an individual presence phase to an effective recognition which symbolized its emergence from legal clandestinity. We call it the *necessary phase* in which Islam was intrinsically linked to Muslim immigration. The year 1998 marked the transition between the immigration phase and the period of confirmed institutional presence.

## 4.4    The Standardization of the Status of Muslim Chaplains in Belgium

The negotiations between the EMB and the religious authorities concerned by the allocation of chaplaincy functions to Muslims in penal establishments were conditioned by the overall task of institutionalizing Islam in Belgium (Muslim Executive of Belgium, 1998).

At present, there are no Muslim chaplains in the army. As for moral and religious assistance in hospitals, there is no data on the breakdown between religions and provisions for this purpose. There is certainly a remuneration of Muslim actors but it is impossible to quantify. Finally, we should point out that there are several "Islamic religion teachers" working in public institutions for the protection of young people Public institutions of Youth Protection (IPPJ), along with a Catholic chaplain and lay counselors.

Islamic chaplains in prisons, on the other hand, for a long time remained at minimal levels through volunteer work and authorized visits; they have limited themselves to the needs linked to detention. A brief retrospective enables us to determine that the first framework for chaplain services, which was established with the Royal Decree of 17th September 1981, and was supplanted by the Decree of 13th June 1999.[22] The latter concerns the creation of a chaplaincy service belonging to recognized religions and moral counselors in penal institutions and establishing their administrative and penal status. The coming into force of this text was initially postponed before eventually falling into disuse. On 23rd March 2001, a new Decree was adopted, repealing the administrative and pecuniary status established by the decree of 13th June 1999.[23]

In August 2000, the Minister of Justice in charge of the management of the temporal aspects of religion conducted an investigation to determine the framework, and human and financial resources to be allocated to religious denominations and nondenominational moral assistance. A stormy debate then ensued, on the basis of discussions within the EMB, regarding the reliability of the data put forward by

---

participated in the preparations and organisation of the elections by creating a Support Committee whose members play a supportive role and, where applicable, act as an intermediary. This committee was chaired by a Judge of the Constitutional Court. The Muslim electorate was then asked to elect 51 members to the Muslim Assembly. According to the procedure, there were provisions, which the government would allow, for the consultative body to then designate seven other members. In the subsequent phase, the members of the Muslim Assembly were to elect 17 members within their ranks for what was to become the official spokesbody to liaise with the Belgian public authorities, i.e. the Muslim Executive.

[22] Cf. *M.B.*, 13 June 1999. This Royal Decree incorporates the rules relating to the Decree of 1965.

[23] The Royal Decree of 23 March 2001 concerns the general rules of penal institutions.

the Ministry. The EMB made the following declaration on the subject in its press release: "The Minister of Justice has, nevertheless, not given any precise explanation for the variations in the number of representatives allocated to each religion and nondenominational moral assistance group, in relation to the figures of the most recent known projects."[24]

The representatives of the religions and nondenominational moral assistance groups, on one hand, and the Minister responsible for religions, on the other, finally reached a new agreement to determine the numeric composition of chaplains allocated to each recognized religion: 29 Catholic chaplains, 16 Muslim counselors, 4 orthodox chaplains, 2 Jewish chaplains and 2 Anglican chaplains.

This agreement, reached in January 2001, was supposed to be sanctioned by a Royal Decree in 2002. A budgetary agreement linked to this framework had therefore also been reached. In 2002, however, the budget allocated through this agreement could not be put together by the Minister. Consequently, there was a reduction in the composition of the staff to be appointed for chaplaincies. The envisaged 65 religious counselors for prisons were to be reduced to an effective full-time staff of 40. This decree, which was never adopted, was compensated by another Royal Decree in 2002, which contained temporary provisions regarding allocations to people providing religious and moral services in penal institutions.

Under Belgian law, which functions on the basis of a pillarization system, the legal framework for the status of chaplains and Islamic counselors was fixed by Royal Decree on 25th October 2005.[25] It sets the framework of its staff in penal establishments and salary scales. The breakdown of chaplains and Islamic counselors, as well as concerning recognized religions and nondenominational moral and philosophical counselors, is presented in Article 1 of the Decree. All of the proposed functions are practiced full-time for an annual salary which varies according to seniority and the status of the head chaplain. Thus, there are 24 chaplains for the Catholic religion and more than one head chaplain. The Muslim religion is in second place with 17 Islamic counselors and one head chaplain. For the nondenominational philosophy group, nine moral counselors are appointed. For the other religions, the breakdown is less: six for the Evangelical Protestant Church, four for the Orthodox, two for the Jewish and one for the Anglicans.

At the end of all these talks, Muslim chaplains first started to officially operate on 1 March 2007. The breakdown of the personnel for the 18 full-time posts allocated was carried out according to a division between 14 French-speaking chaplains and 10 Flemish-speaking ones.

Muslim chaplaincies administratively depend on the social service of the EMB, which manages the temporal aspects of Muslim worship. Within its social service one can find the management of the Feast of the Sacrifice, Ramadan activities and, among other things, the distribution of food parcels in prisons and halal ritual slaughter meat. It also includes the management of religious funeral services (in-

---

[24] Cf., consulted on 15 October 2014

[25] On the basis of the law of 12 January 2005 regarding the administration of penal establishments and the legal status of prisoners, cf. more specifically Article 72.

cluding services for deaths that have occurred in prison) and Islamic counselors and chaplains in penal institutions, hospitals, custodial institutions for young offenders, and the army. One of the missions linked to the latter tasks is to ensure the monitoring of the training and work of Islamic counselors and coordination between the head counselor and the various departments and chaplaincies.

Apart from establishing a clear working framework and the creation of a religious function remunerated by the State (in addition to the imams and Islamic religion teachers in official schools), access conditions have made it possible to create a framework for the training of chaplains and to clarify the specific tasks to be conducted, as well as a deontological framework for their function.

The EMB emphasizes this last point on its website by clearly stating its resolve to counter radical deviations from Islam: "All of this will, for example, enable us to avoid the circulation of works, which promote ideas contrary to the functioning of our Rule of Law among inmates of the Muslim faith."[26]

This last point regarding vigilance also raises the debate on the patchwork management of volunteer chaplaincy practices where works of just about any tendency are disseminated in prisons.

## 4.5   From Religious Training to Vocational Training

Within the range of religious training offered by Muslims in Belgium, there are the traditional options on offer, private academic training or one-off and vocational-training-oriented options (set up for the need to recruit candidates). With an element of pragmatism, dictated by the needs of a religion that requires day-to-day management, Muslims organized their presence with enthusiasm. The development of existing human resources somehow met the needs of the moment, particularly in supplementing the shortage of leaders with religious training.

The establishment of Islam and its demographic, organizational and educational development have since raised the issue of the training of its staff. The diversity of areas involved and the growing demand for people trained in the light of multidisciplinary requirements (humanities and social sciences, civism, languages...) sharpen the need. We note, however, that this is not an exclusively Belgian problem but one that concerns all European countries.[27]

The implementation as well as the management of higher education rest primarily on the Muslim citizens of the country, and the dynamics of Muslim associations, as well as the active moral authorities and bodies managing the temporal aspects of Muslim affairs. The separation of powers, as it is applied in Belgium, can continue to be respected, without impeding the promotion of academic structures devoted to

---

[26] {0>Cf. http://embnet.be, rubrique aumônerie, consulté le 17 octobre 2014<}0{>Cf. http://embnet.be, rubrique aumônerie, consulted on 17 October 2014<0}.

[27] On this subject see Dassetto (1999) and Maréchal (2004).

the vocational training of Muslim staff who will dedicate themselves to the tasks managed by the recognized head Muslim body of religious affairs: imams, religion teachers, Muslim counselors, etc.

Most of the training in Islamic sciences available in Belgium is organized through the private initiatives of Muslims acting individually or in groups. The Belgian experience echoes much of what is going on in neighbouring countries or on the other side of the Channel. These platforms endeavour to propose differentiated training for staff (imams, religion teachers,[28] chaplains…). They sometimes issue unofficial qualifications (unofficial certificates and unclear partnerships regarding the follow up to the process of integration in the working world).

The inadequate structures, lack of experience and resources (human, logistic and financial) only exacerbate the obvious need to address these structural deficiencies. Considering the rarity or inexistence of specific Islamic training, the few private institutes are overloaded and sometimes limit themselves to responding to pressing needs. This training tends to adapt its programmes, timetables and structure in order to be possibly recognized by a public university of the country or State. They sometimes form partnerships with universities in Muslim countries but also university teachers on Belgian soil. The latter option is still very much an exception at an official level.

The training of Muslim chaplains was directly and specifically established by the Head Body of Religious Affairs in order to propose candidates for the 18 recently earmarked posts. Training was therefore a sine qua non condition for the assignment of these posts. The EMB even organized *two types of training*: one for Islamic religion teachers and one for chaplains.

On the basis of recruitment demands in education, the executive organizes selection competitions for future Islamic religion teachers including pedagogy and Islamic sciences. The organization of the test generally stems from an urgent need for teachers or the need to create a reserve of future teachers. It is therefore very random. An application to participate in this selection must be submitted to the administration of the Executive, which will convene applicants once the selection has been set up.

In 2000, the last training of Muslim counselors for penal establishments took place (a similar form of training is being developed for hospitals). Initially the training of Muslim counselors for penal establishments was organized by the *Centre Islamique et Culturel du Cinquantenaire*. The training, lasting approximately 2 months, for the allocation of the 18 posts was able to take place in the year 2000 and was attested by a written test (in humanities) and another oral exam (in religious sciences). Out of the about 50 people who enrolled for the training, only 16 were selected. The qualification issued at the end of the training is a: "Certificate awarded for the successful training of Muslim counselors for visits to penal establishments." The latter was approved by the Minister of Justice, who only issues access autho-

---

[28] Cf. Bastenier and Dassetto (1987), Cattonar (2001), Cattonar and Maroy (2002), and more recently Maroy (2005).

**Table 4.1** Subjects taught in the training of Muslim counselors for visiting prisons

| Criminology |
| --- |
| Criminal law |
| Urban crime |
| Inmate psychology |
| Psychology of adolescence |
| Sociology of deviance |
| Sociology of immigration (identity/values) |
| Analysis of penal establishments |
| Administrative management |
| Aids |
| Intercultural mediation |
| Analysis tools |
| *Islam* |
| Knowledge of the basics of Islam |
| Spirituality |
| Jurisprudence of worship |
| Jurisprudence of the causality of revelation |
| Jurisprudence of context |
| Jurisprudence of bearing witness |

rizations to the people who have passed their training. In total 18 subjects (see Table 4.1) will be taught by teachers from professional circles (social stakeholders, members of prison managements, imams) or the country's universities.

## 4.6  Conclusion

The institutional framework of Islam in Belgium, the reality of prisons and the relatively low number of human resources until now, as well as the training pretexts created to appoint people to positions that urgently need to be filled and the reality of the tense position of Islam in prisons recalls into question the whole issue of chaplaincy and its effectiveness in terms of its impact and actual support. The usefulness of the position and the ever-growing demand for chaplaincies shows the need for this function, but fails to go beyond dealing with the mere urgency and to address the lack of training to capitalize on the framework. The diversity of the community, the specificity of inmates' profiles and the often offensive nature of religious discourse will call for a re-launching of continuous training. Moral support will also have to include theological support. But then the diversity of forms of Islam that are encountered in prisons will be able to be reduced to a binary between a form of Islam that is delegitimized by its conservatism and its risk of extremism, on one hand, and the legitimacy of a form of Islam, which is perceived as official but not always authoritative. The transformation of the reality of prisons can be an example of the slow transformation of Islam in Belgium in a situation in which its gradual institutionalization places it in a kind of new Islamic Church.

## Bibliography

Bastenier, A., & Dassetto F. (1987). *Enseignants et enseignement de l'Islam au sein de l'école officielle en Belgique*. Louvain-La-Neuve: CIACO.

Brion, F. A., Rea, C., Schaut, A., & Tixhon. (2001). *Mon délit? Mon origine. Criminalité et criminalisation de l'immigration*. Bruxelles: Éditions De Boeck-Université.

Cattonar, B. (2001). *Les identités professionnelles enseignantes. Ebauche d'un cadre d'analyse*. Louvain-la-Neuve: Cahiers de recherche du Girsef, n. 10, March.

Dassetto F. (1999). Leaders and leaderships in Islam and transplanted Islam in Europe. In E. Helander (Ed.), *Religion and social transitions* (pp. 87–103). Helsinki: Department of Practical Theology.

Dassetto F., Maréchal B., & Nielsen J. (Eds.). (2001). *Convergences musulmanes, Aspects contemporains de l'Islam dans l'Europe élargie*. Louvain-la-Neuve: Ed. Academia Brylant & L'Harmattan.

Exécutif des musulmans de Belgique. (1998). Modalités relatives à la formation d'un organe Chef de culte pour les musulmans de Belgique, Ronéo, mars 1998.

Maréchal, B. (2004). Modalities of Islamic instruction. In B. Maréchal, S. Allievi, F. Dassetto, & J. Nielsen (Eds.), *Muslim in enlarged Europe* (pp. 19–78). Leiden: Brill.

Maroy C. (2005). *Les évolutions du travail enseignant en Europe. Facteurs de changement, incidences et résistances*. Les cahiers de Recherche en Éducation et Formation, n°42

Maroy C., & Cattonar, B. (2002). *Professionalisation et déprofessionnalisation des enseignants*. Le cas de la Communauté française de Belgique, Cahiers de recherche du Girsef, n. 18, Sept.

Panafit L. (1997). Les problématiques de l'institutionnalisation de l'Islam en Belgique (1965–1996). In F. Dassetto (Ed.), *Facettes de l'Islam belge* (pp. 253–269). Louvain-la-Neuve: Academia-Bruylant.

Vanneste C. (2002). Des logiques socio-économiques à leur traduction pénale: l'exemple de la Belgique de 1830 à 1995, Sociétés et Représentations, La vie judiciaire, CREDHESS, Paris, sept. 2002, n° 14, 213–227.

## Sources

Observatoire International des Prisons–Notice 2008, http://www.oipbelgique.be. Accessed 14 Oct 2014.

http://www.lachambre.be: Loi organique des services de renseignements et de sécurité, bill n. 638/18-21. Accessed 14 Oct 2014.

http://www.lachambre.be: Le Rapport du Comité permanent de Contrôle des services de renseignement et de sécurité. Accessed 14 Oct 2014.

http://www.lachambre.be: Cour Européenne des Droits de l'Homme, Condamnations, Serif c. Grèce n° 38178/97, Hassan et Tchaouch c. Bulgarie No. 30985/96. Accessed 14 Oct 2014.

# Part II
# Religious Diversity on the Way to Recognition in Secular Prison Rehabilitation Programmes

# Chapter 5
# Religion, Reintegration and Rehabilitation in French Prisons: The Impact of Prison Secularism

Corinne Rostaing, Céline Béraud and Claire de Galembert

## 5.1 Introduction

What place can religion have in French prisons, in a country which has defined itself as *laïque* (secular) since the 1905 Law on the Separation of the Churches and the State? In order to answer this question, our analysis has endeavoured to focus on religion in its most ordinary forms (Piette 2003) as it is applied and administered in penitentiary institutions. Inspired by the theory of symbolic interactionism, we conducted an in-depth ethnographic study between January 2011 and October 2012, both "from above" (in administrative centres and at the top of religious institutions) and "from below" (in eight French prisons), just as much from the point of view of prison administrations, chaplains of all denominations and prisoners, by observing, among other things, cultural activities or chaplains' visits to cells, and through face-to-face interviews with prisoners, the Prison Administrations Directorate (members of the directorate, correctional officers, social workers) or other people working in prisons (doctors, trainers, managers, etc.).

The intention of this initial sociological study on the religious phenomenon in French prisons as a whole (Béraud et al. 2013; Rostaing et al. 2014) is to combine approaches both focused on the sociology of prisons and the sociology of religion. It aims to explore, from a comprehensive sociological perspective (Weber 1922), the place and role which prison authorities, chaplains and incarcerated people attribute to religion, in particular in terms of rehabilitation. The point of view that is

C. Rostaing (✉)
Centre Max Weber (CNRS), University of Lyon, Lyon, France
e-mail: corinne.rostaing@univ-lyon2.fr

C. Béraud
CerreV, University of Caen, Caen, France
e-mail: Celine.Beraud@gmail.com

C. de Galembert
Ecole Normale Supérieure de Cachan, Cachan, France
e-mail: galember@isp.ens-cachan.fr

© Springer International Publishing Switzerland 2015
I. Becci, O. Roy (eds.), *Religious Diversity in European Prisons,*
DOI 10.1007/978-3-319-16778-7_5

presented will therefore be centred on what happens during and not after the incarceration, nor on the possible role of associations, often denominational, with people coming out of prison.

Since the very introduction of penal prisons in France, at the time of the French Revolution, the legitimacy of a sentence rests on the principle of a "good sentence" which, in addition to providing for the protection of society, will enable the delinquent or criminal person to be transformed through, among other things, labour, discipline or religion. It is in line with optimistic philanthropic theories, which believe in man's capacity to change, even those who have committed a crime. Opinions in the eighteenth century varied on how this moral healing could be achieved. Some advocated complete isolation, others silence, some labour (forced or not, paid or not), others reflection with a focus on religious guidance, while others again championed education, which then, however, harkens back to the idea of amendment. "Rehabilitation" is the term that is then used to describe efforts aimed at transforming prisoners, in order to "straighten" them or morally "heal" them. Chaplains therefore appear as being able to effectively contribute to the moral reform of prisoners. Already in the 1870s, however, a number of observers seem to concur on emphasising the ineffectiveness of chaplains in the moral reform of prisoners: "Instrumentalised, misled, discredited even, the chaplain emerges from this picture as a weakened figure." (Artières 2005, p. 197). It is precisely at the time when they are going through a crisis of legitimacy that chaplains are confronted with two waves of secularisation in prisons, which occur between 1880 and 1889 and then between 1900 and 1908 (Langlois 1984). Despite this reference to secularisation, from an historical point of view, there is a strong connection between Christianity and prisons, a connection which associates ideas of amendment or of rehabilitation. The idea of moral transformation, however, gradually mutates into a more prescriptive idea, with connotations of rigour and discipline. It becomes a question of cutting the delinquent away from his pathogenic environment in order to curb his amoral instincts, to keep him constantly occupied, to instil good physical hygiene or to apply strict rules to favour good behaviour or respect for a way of life in accordance with religion. With the increase in the number of professionals, "reintegration" is the term most frequently used in the Code of Criminal Procedure (CPP). This refers to the preparation of convicts for release from prison and their ability to adapt to a new life by finding a job and place in society. If the concept of rehabilitation refers back more to the work of chaplains, the notion of reintegration is more linked to social workers who fulfil their mission within the Prison Integration and Probation Service (SPIP). Yet, the reintegration mission is a by-product in relation to the security mission within French prisons, even though the former mission is what is meant to give the system its entire coherence. For example, the institution employs five times more wardens than social workers who also manage the follow-up process in open environments.

In this context, what role does the prison administration attribute to religion in general and to chaplains in particular in reintegration issues? To begin with, we will first present the specific French framework with its peculiarities and the rather marginal position occupied by religion in prisons as well as the meagre means allocated to chaplains. We will then explore the different stances adopted by chaplains, whether they be universalist, secular, denominational and occasionally moralistic, which are not mutually exclusive. Then finally we will analyse by which process religion can constitute a biographical turning point and sometimes help convicts to exit criminality.

## 5.2   The Context of Prison Secularity: Low Ambitions in Matters of Reintegration

It is in accordance with the principle of secularity, deriving from Article 1 of the Constitution, that religion is taken into account by prison administrations. Secularisation, much more than a legal principle, refers to a specific conception of a public regulation of religion, which is the legacy of a turbulent history. Although, historically speaking, the 1905 secularisation law contributed to restricting the rights and means granted to chaplains, today it is used to respect the principle of equality and the rights of religious minorities to practice their faiths.

### 5.2.1   French Singularity

The rather marginal status granted to religion and its representatives in prisons, is reflected in the poor resources allocated to them and by religious actors being represented more as external participants than partners. Nevertheless, the 1905 law has not severed the strong link between prisons and Christianity (Liwerant 2006). The architecture of old establishments and the presence of chapels—even if many of them have been converted into cells—are proof of this Christian past (Rostaing et al. 2014). Another important trace of this Catholic heritage is undeniably to be found even today in the presence of a few nuns working in women's prisons (Rennes and Fleury-Mérogis), paid by the directorate. Inside women's prisons, nuns have also played a moralising and rehabilitative role. The Amor Reform in the 1950s then facilitated the vast entry of diversified personnel (teachers, medical staff, paramedics, social workers) as well as people from civil society (cultural representatives, chaplaincy members, visitors), each of them fulfilling a rather positive function, focused on the rehabilitation of the person, which occasionally fuels an element of competition between them. The role of chaplains has been significantly reduced in this field.

Another French peculiarity manifests itself in the difficulty of finding a place for new faith groups. Six faiths are officially recognised (Catholic, Protestant, Muslim, Jewish, Orthodox and Buddhist) and are permitted to propose religious activities that come in addition to social activities available in prison. Taking into account this new pluralist religious landscape often turns out to be more restrictive in comparison to prevalent trends in European countries or the USA. The manner in which religion is treated in French prisons distinguishes itself by a kind of minimalism, which is often reflected in the random character of worship facilities in prisons, the poor status and low remuneration of chaplains, as well as the limited cooperation between prison administrations and religious figures on reintegration issues. The places allocated to worship have often been forgotten or sacrificed for the sake of rationalising space in prisons which, due to the increase in the number of inmates, is in great demand. The wave of construction initiated by the "15,000" (places) Plan, launched in 1987, did not include provisions for worship spaces. The "13,000" Plan, launched in 2002, takes into account religious elements and provides multi-faith places of worship, although they are very small and require arrangements to be made between different religious groups and thus proved as a better plan. According to our study, religion in prisons is a fairly minority phenomenon, even though we do not have any statistics on religious practice, since statistics of this kind are forbidden in France. In this regard, the absence of religious and ethnic statistics in France is one of the republican traits which contribute to the difficulty of evaluating the needs of faith groups. This also applies to the status of prison chaplains, which is far less favourable than in England and Wales where there are not only many chaplains, but they are civil servants who are well paid (Beckford and Giliat 1998). However, a significant increase is to be noted in the number of prison chaplains, which has doubled over the past 15 years, an increase which by far outstrips the growth in the prison population. This increase is a consequence of religious pluralisation and concerns in particular Muslim chaplains, although also ministers of older faiths have been increasingly appointed. The management of this plurality represents a challenge for prison administration, which in accordance with the 1905 law, must ensure non-discrimination in the free exercise of religion. Does this particular context offer prison administrations an opportunity to increasingly envisage religion as a vector of reintegration?

### 5.2.2   Religion Not Conceived as a Vector of Reintegration

The issues of the connection between religion and reintegration in the prison framework have barely been investigated in France. Moreover, when it comes to the adjustment of sentences, the invocation of one's religion as evidence of moral reform does not have the same positive effects it has on the other side of the Atlantic. There is no mention of the issue of religious practice in the activity reports of the Prison Administrations (PA) Directorate between 1950 and 1998, which nevertheless review aspects of prison life, which are deemed relevant to reintegration, such as educational, sociocultural and sporting activities. It was not until 1998 that half a page was devoted to "religious activities": Ten lines under the heading of "context" recall the great principles of the CPP and deal with chaplains in the "Spiritual Assistance" section of a chapter devoted to "preparatory actions for the reintegration of convicts". Another paragraph limits itself to listing the numbers of chaplains. There is no evidence until then of any kind of policy to take the religious element into account in prisons. From 2007 onwards, however, the annual activity report from the PA Directorate is substantially enriched because an entire page (p. 44) is now devoted to the issue under the heading "Access to Religion". The editor insists on the "triple obligation": neutrality, "the establishment of access to religious practice for the members of the prison population who are unable to exercise their religious freedom" and to resist "all forms of proselytism and sectarianism" (PA Directorate 2007, p. 44). Prison administration distances itself from any involvement in religious life and endeavours to control excess. A brief presentation of the principal religions now forms part of the training of prison wardens, who are thus initiated into respecting religious practices.

The manner in which religious actors intervene in the field of reintegration has also been impacted by prison secularisation. Even though the provisions of the CPP regarding chaplaincies appear in the preparation for the social reintegration of convicts section, suggesting that chaplaincies can facilitate reintegration, there is no mention, however, of any concrete actions which these religious actors might specifically undertake to meet that objective. This void leaves it up to pluralist associations to set up actions for the maintenance of social bonds, vocational training or access to employment or the housing of people coming out of prison. Only a few of these various associations claim any clear denominational identity or close links with Catholic chaplaincies. As a whole, they provide material help to destitute people, endeavour to limit isolation by visiting prisons and exchanging correspondence, and offer teaching in prison or accommodation for those being released from it. Even though each chaplaincy works in liaison with selected partners, there is no global "reintegration" action programme that has been organised or structurally coordinated to prepare and support inmates before their release and return to civilian life and, in the long term, their release from prison.

From that point of view, this concept of the participation of religious actors in reintegration has strictly nothing to do with what may happen in the countries of, among others, North America where *faith-based prison programmes* (activities promoted by religious associations) have developed considerably since the Bush administration (Dammer 1992; Sundt and Cullen 2002; Kerley et al. 2005). Broadly speaking, at the request of the Federal Government, these programmes consist in delegating the prison sentence mission to religious actors. The religious organisations thus become responsible for the prisoners that request it, and follow up on this monitoring even in the postprison phase. Here we find a symptomatic manifestation of the strong link that persists between religion and rehabilitation in American penology (Ignatieff 1978). The term "rehabilitation" with its religious connotations suggests that the prisoners could be changed morally after being subjected to a specific regime.

Numerous studies have been conducted in the USA in an attempt to discuss or measure the effectiveness of these faith-based programmes, in order to ascertain if they reduce recidivism (Johnson et al. 1997), if they facilitate rehabilitation (O'Connor and Perreyclear 2002) or reduce deviant behaviour in prison (Camp et al. 2006). According to the authors, upstream religion would tend to prevent the commitment of a crime, and the faith-based programmes offered to prisoners during the terms of their sentences tend to help to avoid the commitment of offences in prison, reduce recidivism on re-entry and favour social reintegration. The idea, even though it is far from proven, that religion protects against crime and delinquency, and that it favours desistance, i.e. the halting of a delinquent path, is very much alive. This issue is rarely raised in France. Only one book compiled by M. Mohammed (2012) raises the issue of exiting delinquency, without establishing a direct link with religion. Reference to religion is only made in two articles whereas reintegration through employment or life as a couple seems to be the most frequent option.

### 5.2.3 The Personnel: Religion Appeases, but Does It Contribute to Reintegration?

In the field, however, our investigation noted that religion enjoys a certain legitimacy and even receives explicit recognition for some form of social usefulness. Secularism in the prison world is distinguished by a form of appeasement and pragmatism, which distances it from the ideological debates and tensions that can be observed in other types of public institutions, schools in particular. This is evident in particular in the *topos* of "any religion that appeases" which manifests itself in a kind of bureaucratic common sense with regard to it. As far as the prison personnel are concerned, "Anything that can help and calm the prisoners helps us too…".

But in what way can it participate in the rehabilitation of prisoners? Wardens talk more about the logic of maintaining order through religion. The positive influence of religion is hailed for its effects on prison life. Therefore they say things like: "keeps them occupied on Sundays" (worship is often the only activity on weekends), "it calms them", and "religion does them good".

But the statements of many of the personnel during the course of our investigation revealed their doubts on the authenticity of the religious beliefs of prisoners. To them, "if they really believed, they wouldn't be in there…" Religious belief is considered to be a convenient faith, an illusion entertained by the prisoner who thinks it will fix everything, that God will help them keep in check. The personnel's criticism is most often targeted at the Islamic faith, at those who "think they can become virgins again through prayer and can't even manage to complete the Ramadan". In addition to this criticism, they mention the issue—mainly in relation to the Islamic religion—of proselytism and the radicalisation of certain prisoners.

Religion can therefore catalyse tensions between prisoners and the personnel. These tensions often concern "lay" wardens (of the Gallic category, for example fierce supporters of secularity) who feel that "there's too much religion about in the name of freedom of religious practice". These staff members then criticise the space that is allotted to denominational activities, a space that is growing and adding to the workload. The development of other cultural activities seems preferable to them, and vocational training is deemed to be more useful than religious practices in matters of social reintegration.

There is, however, recognition of some social usefulness of religion even though this is more on the grounds of security than from the point of view of reintegration. Some staff members, many of whom are believers or practising wardens, would therefore have a greater tendency to evaluate the influence of religion on prisoners.

With the backing of testimony, they even attribute long lasting changes to religion, transformations that can lead to a new relationship with the prison institution. It can even be a source of personal rehabilitation by virtue of the ethical and moral points of reference that it can give prisoners, thus enabling them to put their lives back into order, to give them a meaning and to even project themselves in the future. Religion is considered to be a moralising tool that should have a beneficial effect on reintegration and the prevention of recidivism.

However, wardens insist on the fact that religion only interests a small portion of the prisoners. A number of them express their doubts on the durability of the religious fervour beyond the prisoners' release, and have little faith in the potential role of religion in matters of reintegration. The fact that religion is not explicitly conceived of as a vector of reintegration by the institution and its personnel does not mean that it is of no value in the dynamics of rehabilitation and reintegration, particularly from the point of view of chaplains.

## 5.3   Chaplain Practices Focused on Personal Rehabilitation

Twenty years ago one could have thought that chaplaincies were in decline, partly condemned by the secularisation process and the professional specialisation of prison staff. Our field study revealed a developing institution and a reactivation of the function of chaplaincies with the entrance of new religions, in particular Islam. There are more than 1200 chaplains operating in French prisons. Even though Christian chaplains are to be found in the country as a whole with an average of three catholic representatives per establishment and at least one protestant per prison, this is not the case for Muslim or Jewish chaplains, who often have to spread themselves between several establishments, or for the newly integrated religions that still have few chaplains. (In 2013, for example, there were four Buddhist chaplains in French prisons as a whole.)

An ethnographic approach enabled us to observe chaplains in their working context and in action (in their places of worship, in cells, corridors, at meetings and in training sessions), and this enabled us to gain a better understanding of how they define their mission.

### 5.3.1   Humanising Agents, but Not in Charge of Reintegration

The chaplain is a person who is not a member of the prison staff; he/she is a civilian and "external" figure to the prison world while moving freely through prisons since he/she has keys to cells in most of the establishments. He/she is often seen as an impartial figure, devout and often benevolent. He/she is a resource as a person who can bring information, goods, spiritual or social assistance, but above all, a presence, as Jean-Bernard puts it:

To be a chaplain is above all to be a presence in the broadest sense of that term. (…) We're there for them, we're there for free. We have to be available to go see them in their cells, listen to them. (priest, jail1)

Chaplains have often valued this free listening, which differs from that of other professionals. As Jean-Paul (Catholic chaplain, jail2) points out, they have the time: Thus they can "spend five minutes or two hours in a cell with a prisoner". Their mission, however, is difficult to determine. It is not clearly defined in the CPP, as Pierre-Paul explains:

I would say that the Code of Criminal Procedure sets a clear framework. It states clearly that the chaplain is neither a psychologist, nor a social worker, nor a warden, nor a judge, nor a friend. He is there to provide spiritual and moral support. How can that be put into practice? I realised that it was very easy to break out of the framework. You can very swiftly feel the urge to be a social worker. Which is what I did when I wanted to find work for a prisoner who was about to be released.... And in doing so, I overstepped my function. (Protestant chaplain, prison1)

Chaplains therefore have a different role to those of social workers and therapists. It is therefore a question of avoiding any competition or indeed conflicts with other agents and professional, to find one's "right place" in the division of labour. Thus, Marthe undeniably feels a certain pride for the appeasement she manages to provide, from the blessings she gives to the prisoners she visits, including those who suffer from psychological or even psychiatric disorders. However, she takes care to ensure she places herself on another level to that of the psychologist. Similarly, Roger, the Catholic chaplain in the *Maison Centrale* prison (MC2) considers "the issue of reintegration is one we deal with without it being ours". According to him, the chaplain does not provide any "concrete help", but through his work he contributes to "the rehabilitation of the person". On talking about her long experience as a prison chaplain, Isabelle Le Bourgeois (2006, p. 133–134) above all sees herself as a humanising factor and refuses to take on the responsibility of reintegration:

First of all, we are not responsible for the reintegration of prisoners when they leave prison. Nor do we have any explicit responsibilities as nurses. That's not exactly our task. We are there in the name of the Gospel: "I was in prison and you visited me", Jesus said (Mt 25, 36). Our intervention is therefore aimed at helping people to rediscover that part of humanity which is temporarily or long-lastingly enclosed behind walls, the part experiencing profound human misery and which reveals the power of evil present in all of us in a more visible way.

Above all, chaplains offer a non-bureaucratic relationship within the prison organisation (Becci 2012). "We see the prisoner as a human being, not just a number in the register or a file", one pastor insists. Therefore, in the eyes of the inmates, they are defined and perceived as re-personalising and humanising figures, by re-including the prisoners in a joint humanity:

The chaplain is a person who is sent into prisons to meet prisoners, to share a piece of humanity with them, rediscover a common dignity as children of God and tell them that salvation is for all of us. (Bernadette, regional Catholic chaplain)

According to this presentation, we get the impression of a meeting without any stakes. Thus, according to the national Catholic chaplain, the approach to spiritual assistance is "a free meeting without any stakes, without any obligations for re-sults". Behind these general terms, there is a great diversity of professional prac-tices among chaplains in terms of their clientele and mission definitions.

## 5.3.2   Occasionally Moralistic Stances

A high number of chaplains endeavour to be impartial in their actions: not to judge and to be prepared to hear everything. They insist on the horizontal nature of the relationships they have with prisoners. And in a significantly different way, others veer towards a more vertical and top-down stance of a normative and moralistic nature, as a continuation of the educational role. They therefore often appear as teacher-chaplains, in reference to the figure of the Imam teacher (Jouanneau 2011) who is in charge of ensuring the prisoners' good knowledge of religion. This is how Karim and Marouan, both of whom were trained in the Great Mosque of Paris, de-scribe their roles, in particular with regard to incarcerated people, who start to prac-tice their religion again after having lapsed for a long period. A very good example of this kind of evolution is to be found in young people of North African origin, who have abandoned the practice of their faith, often during their adolescence, and then return to Islam. Having noted the poor knowledge of the young inmates they meet, the chaplains aim not only to offer them a basic religious socialisation but also, for Marouan, to combat interpretations which they deem to be false and even to teach *laicity*. Both of them devote a part of their services to giving lessons and aim to promote the practice of a moderate form of Islam. In this way they also contribute to controlling certain forms of radicalisation, but more mundanely their mission involves teaching inmates how to read the Koran, pray, do ablutions and to initiate one's self in the duties of a Muslim.

> The regional chaplain told me: "Broadly speaking, our goal is to teach inmates how to pray, do ablutions, simple things. How to pray in groups. In other words, the basics: That's how I function. I already know that if an inmate manages to pray correctly that's already not bad. On top of that they're there to learn, it's not to go into any depth." (Karim, jail1).

This more moralistic stance is also reflected in conversations. This is the case of the Protestant chaplain in prison3, a former teacher, whose leitmotiv to the recidivist inmates he visits is the following: "Shouldn't you just take out a subscription to prison and finally decide to put an end to all this bullshit!" Chaplains therefore ap-pear as being able to effectively contribute to the moral reform of prisoners. Thus, they participate in the mission to reform the prison population. According to Farid, on the basis of the motivations of Muslim spirituality, it is a case of disseminating an ethic that is designed to get the inmate back "on the right path":

> Our mission is religious and educational. Because religion is a way of educating people (…). Yes, it's a way of educating people (…). Because religion prohibits us to steal, hold people up, it forbids us to drink alcohol to avoid all our problems, forbids us to sell drugs, leads us to respect our neighbours, respect the elderly…. Religion—not just Islamic reli-gion but all religions—pushes us to respect others and to respect ourselves. (Farid, Muslim chaplain, prison2)

Chaplains' statements do not always allude to a direct reintegration mission, even though they may contribute to it on the sidelines, and the presence of the religious element in prisons appears as a sign of the failure of the re-socialisation project. Chaplains participate in the personal rehabilitation of inmates, a vital stage in the social rehabilitation process due to desistance. Their solicitous approach places them on a level at which prison professionals have largely failed: to open up to "the possibility of forgiveness (…) the fruit of a possible renewal" (Caillé and Fixot 2012, p. 8). It is a question of giving meaning back to life, even to those who have committed serious crimes in order to enable inmates to establish a link with the period before, during and after their incarceration. Chaplains may sometimes accept to act as witnesses in the trial of an inmate they have followed, in order to talk about the path they have taken and to therefore publicly account for the work the person they have accompanied has done on him/herself. Irrespective of their religions, all the chaplains we met had some nice stories to tell about inmates who, through their contact, managed to reorganise and even transform their lives during the period of their sentences. But often the role of a chaplain is comparable to that of a "nurse, who in a palliative care service, gives out medication that eases the pain without curing the disease." (Le Bourgeois 2006, p. 9)

## 5.4    Religion as Identity Support for the Prisoners

Imprisonment entails an upheaval for the inmate: It is an ordeal, a painful experience, which distances them from normal social life, an experience one does not emerge from unscathed. It marks an interruption in the ordinary course of life and implies diving into a totally alien world. It means a lot more than the simple deprivation of freedom: It results in the deprivation of belongings, heterosexual relations, autonomy and even security (Sykes 1958). Incarceration entails a triple ordeal. On one hand, the inmate is subject to an enveloping institutional take over within a restrictive organisation. This organisation imposes a limiting spatial/temporal framework on the inmate and strict regulations. It maintains people in a position of permanent subordination with a prolonged loss of responsibility, which may result in a certain inability to assume ordinary responsibilities. Being arrested, incarcerated and sentenced can, on the other hand, undermine a person's sense of identity: By being perceived differently by other people, they perceive themselves differently as well (a feeling of degradation). Finally, incarceration and prison conditions constitute an infringement on dignity due to the impossibility of maintaining any intimate spaces (Rostaing 2006, p. 39).

Religion in a prison environment constitutes a personal resource and a shield to protect one's self from others. It also represents a right for prisoners, the right to practice their religion freely, which the prison administration must guarantee. It brings instrumental or useful benefits, such as the search for security, material comfort, access to external people or to social relations (Clear et al. 2000, p. 64–69). It offers a structuring framework, which facilitates life in prison; an opportunity to rehabilitate one's self through forgiveness can even be a vector of change with a view to reintegration (Sarg and Lamine 2011).

### 5.4.1  Religion as a Structuring Framework

Imprisonment therefore constitutes a moment of reflection which, often through the encouragement of close ones, leads to "reforging the path towards God", finding the "right path" again and rejoining a spiritual tradition. Our investigation revealed that this resource is mainly used by those who have had a religious socialisation. A large number of people who have undergone religious socialisation then report an intensification of their religious practice in prison; others renew their faith. The profile type of this category of reconverts is that of a young person educated in a religious denomination or people from a diversity of cultural and/or religious backgrounds who say they have become interested in religion for the first time in their lives. Their delinquent and even criminal paths partly explain this realisation and this resolve to be seen "in a good light" by the family that supported them during their imprisonment, and this serves as a token of their desire to be reintegrated. For a lot of them, religion seems to constitute a "lifeline": Support that enables someone to stay alive, to prevent themselves from sinking into the depths of despair, and to "cling back on to something". It can often intervene in the reordering of one's life in a process in which it is not so much the outcome as the vector and instrument, by enabling the person to, for example, define stages and personal objectives. On this point, Dammer (2002) mentions the hope which religion can give rise to for people who are imprisoned by giving them a sense of direction and goals to be reached. The progress achieved in terms of religious knowledge is highlighted by the followers as a way of emphasising the efforts that have been made and the path that has been followed. Hakan, a 23-year-old man of Turkish origin and a reoffender serving a 3-year sentence for armed robbery, has assiduously started practising his religion again 7 years ago. He likes measuring his progress by learning new and increasingly difficult *surahs* every day.

Religion, with its rites and prescriptions, also organises their relationship with time. From a structuring point of view, it helps to keep one going in prison, to overcome the daily frustrations linked to the pressures of imprisonment and even to find "a certain peace of mind" (Dammer 2002, p. 41). For some, it is a way of learning "more civilized behavior, such as a positive attitude, politeness, humility, calm and self-control" (Dammer 2002, p. 42). The occupational and pacifying virtues of religious practice contribute to the acceptance of the punishment and a reflection on the acts that have been committed.

Meetings with chaplains are sometimes the only social link in prison, particularly for the most isolated inmates. The chaplain, who is a reminder of the common humanity they share, contributes to a personal revaluation and participates in a repersonalisation. The 46-year-old Jules, who was a Protestant since his youth and a devout follower felt he "wasn't worth anything" after he received his 20-year prison sentence for crime. Having served 17 years in a jail, he feels rehabilitated through his relationship with the Catholic chaplain:

> It's Robert, the old Catholic chaplain who suggested I come along. Initially I was very surprised by this openness because I'm not a Catholic. I was very close to him, he saved me in a way. Thanks to him, I was able to pull through difficult periods. We could confide in him, always looking out for others, that hope. When he preached, we felt it really concerned us. He understood the weight of a prison sentence. Afterwards you feel like you're worth something, that you can still get out of this place and lead a normal life with some peace.

Spirituality can, in fact, act as an instrument for the reconstruction of an identity at times when the self is threatened; it can be an element of identity (not the only one) to counterbalance the stigma of prison and being an ex-convict. It can enable people to regain a positive image "for one's self" and for others, which is the first stage that is sometimes necessary for those who have committed "hideous" crimes or who consider themselves as monsters. The belief in a "fundamentally good self" is in fact one of the three essential criteria which encourages desistance according to Maruna (2001).

## 5.4.2   The Rehabilitation of the Self Through Forgiveness: Spirituality and Sin

The invocation of a God who saves also provides a way of finding one's feet again and regaining some form of moral dignity that one thought had been irremediably lost. It can help prisoners escape the stigma of monstrosity, of an amorality or immorality that excluded them from the community of mankind. It enables them to come to terms with their moral failings, as Marie-Thérèse, a 61-year-old Catholic and mother of seven, who has served 4 years, testifies. She says she has "laid down her sins" and feels lighter: "It did something to me, it's as if a weight lifted from me. That night I slept like a baby".

There may be an explanatory key in the fact that the evocation of the Final Judgement is frequently mentioned in discussions with inmates, whether they be Jewish, Christian or Muslim. The fear of hell is, in fact, a recurrent theme, in the discussions of certain inmates.

Gloria, a 22-year-old woman of Brazilian origin, who claims to be a Catholic but was socialised as a Pentecostal, and who very brutally murdered a close one, seems to be more concerned with the issue of salvation than her upcoming trial. In view of the crime she has committed, hell seems inevitable:

> I'm in jail because I didn't want to listen to all those church people, not only my mother.... My mother says: God can forgive everything. But I took someone's life, the life of one of God's children. I don't think he can forgive me. I go to church. I pray. I tell myself I'm going to burn in hell. It's very difficult to live with that. Sometimes I crack. At night we're alone in our cells. You feel like doing yourself in. Even I'm afraid of myself.

The nature of the offence or crime committed undeniably weighs on any potential need to rehabilitate one's self through forgiveness. It is significant that the most ardent followers in the clienteles of chaplains are the authors of sexual attacks, who are considered by their fellow inmates as "sexual criminals" or murderers who have committed "hideous" crimes. The latter became scapegoat figures (Chauvenet et al. 2008), and even though participation in religious practices may not erase the identity of a paedophile, it more or less neutralises the reactions that this identity can give rise to (insults, violence and aggression). Even though this may be some form of "positive illusion", its performative effects are undeniable.

Religion therefore offers a cognitive space, which reshuffles the cards, not only in relation to one's self but also in relation to others. Frequent talks about "restarting from scratch" seem to facilitate the conversion of convicts with heavy criminal records. This repentance dimension is particularly valued by Muslim inmates. In the words of some, settling one's religious duties can be a way of "wiping the slate clean". The force of this use of religion can be gauged from the criticism it gives rise to among the personnel and social workers, who see it as a slightly easy way for some convicts with long sentences to shirk their responsibilities and even cultivate a form of denial.

For others, religion can contribute to tough introspective work. "Before I didn't know what was evil". The 44-year-old Yves in jail who was sentenced to 25 years for rape converted to Islam 5 years ago, a conversion which he experienced as a rebirth process in the eyes of God. He feels he has spent his life in jail ("I was in jail at the age of 18, came out at 35. I came back at 35 and I'll be out at 60".) and describes the path he has followed as "a huge journey" (both religiously and therapeutically) during which he learned to differentiate between good and bad and to think of his victims and no longer just his "own pleasure".

The ordeal of prison can also be reinterpreted as a spiritual penance and no longer as a penalty imposed by man. According to Aurélia, a 45-year old of Italian origin, the fact that she has been put to the test by God by being imprisoned has enabled her to recognise her wrongs. Educated as a Catholic "through family conditioning", to use her own words, she then moved away from religion and committed scams for which she has asked God's forgiveness in order to be at peace with herself.

> So now I can say I no longer look for excuses for my faults. I know where I went wrong and I no longer have any problems asking for God's forgiveness when I make mistakes in my life. God has helped me a lot to find some peace in myself. I thought a lot about the fact that it's too easy to go and pray when we're in need and then, when everything is going well, to forget to thank God for that. I admit it was very tough in the beginning, but I think it was Him who helped to put up with a lot of things. Now I'm no longer anxious, I feel good inside my head. It's positive in any case. And I think without this experience I probably would have continued along the same…path I had taken recently. And that's also when I said that "if I'm here it's because God agreed to it". Maybe…in the end, it's a gift. Prison arrived and I have peace.

In addition to realising one's errors, religion can offer the means to take on another path. Many inmates use metaphors such as "tortuous path" or "wrong track", counterposed against "the right path": As the 28-year-old Younès, of Algerian origin, who received a Muslim education and started practising again in prison, says: Religion can bring one back to the "right path". Having been imprisoned in a jail for the fourth time for theft, he has the feeling that God can enable him "break out of the deadlock".

### 5.4.3   Is Religion a Vector for Changing One's Self?

For some inmates religion has represented the prospect of a self-transformation in the longer term, which initiates a life change associated with a probable exit from delinquency. This deep change occurs through some real work of reflection on one's self and one's path, and it requires the realisation of one's responsibilities and the will to give one's life a meaning, as explained by the 25-year-old Leïla, who is serving a 7-year sentence for violent theft. She talks about how, after a period of isolation which enabled her to realise the gravity of her actions, religion helped her to assume her responsibilities, and gave her the desire to "become a good person". As the offspring of a mixed couple—a Christian mother and Muslim father—she was certainly baptised as a child, but she says she "has always felt drawn to the Muslim religion". The path to her conversion predates her incarceration, but it was in order to "access forgiveness" that she took the step in prison and that she now knows who she is and where she wants to go:

> Religion enabled me to, for example, see the bad that I'd done, the act I'd committed, to gratuitously attack people for money, it wasn't me. And I learned, in fact, to put myself in other people's shoes; to put myself in victims' shoes. To understand, try to understand, not to see myself as a victim, far from it, but try to also understand what I would have felt as a victim. That meant that I felt really bad, I felt really bad in my own skin. In fact, after feeling that, I wanted to try to change, try to become a decent person because all religions advocate good and not evil. In fact, it enabled me to understand where I was and to live it too, with that new little space that had just opened in my brain, to know who I am and where I want to go. It's true that it's more difficult to become a good person than it is to do evil.

"Becoming a good person" after having done bad things requires a profound change which religion can contribute to, through the reading of texts on the meaning of life, prayers or conversations with chaplains. It constitutes a "source of norms and values, it helps the inmate to structure or restructure his or her life" (Sarg and Lamine 2011, p. 101). Denominational commitment constitutes an enriching identification model, which offers a new path for getting out of delinquency, whether it be Christian (Giordano et al. 2008) or Islamic (Calverley and Farrall 2012). It is a question of breaking habits, making friends in other communities, breaking away from "bad company", maintaining or even renewing links with one's family, showing one's change of behaviour to one's close ones and demonstrating one's resolve to get out of it.

These recurring discourses on following the right path, not coming back to prison, doing good, were particularly frequent in the jail, the type of establishment where activities, training and work are rare and where the attendance of religious services is the highest (compared to penitentiaries). They are also the detention centres in France where there are short sentences and where the recidivism rates are the highest. It is a question of "believing" in God's power to control one's bad actions, while at the same time being aware of the limits of this type of invocation. Religion is therefore associated with a hope, that of managing to persist over time, by defining a stricter framework and practices.

Sami, a father of three, who was given a 2-year sentence for a drug case, says he is increasingly interested in religion. This 38-year-old Franco-Tunisian, who is a non-practising Muslim and drove his father to the mosque for 18 years without ever entering the building, promised himself that when he gets out of the jail he will go to the mosque with his father and practice.

Some inmates, who consider the cessation of their religious practices or their distancing from religion to be the original source of "their problems", believe that their coming closer to God will act as a protection for the future, "to get out of the bad life". In the words of Roger, a 38-year old from Martinique, who was sentenced to 18 years for a crime and has served 8 in a jail:

> My aunt wanted to bring me back closer to God because she thinks I ended up in prison because I wasn't praying properly, that I wasn't close enough to God. I call on the Eternal One to ask him to put wisdom in our hearts. My prayers gave me a little strength, a little bit of spiritual strength. I deepen my personal wisdom. And also it can help me to get out of bad living, yes, it helps. In life you never know when you might find traps, obstacles, you call upon the Eternal One so that he'll always protect you.

Some of the inmates we met shortly before their release doubted before even being freed whether they would be able to follow the good path or not. The 63-year-old Armande, who received a 25-year sentence for ordering the murder of her husband and has already served 16 years, prays in the chapel a lot and "devotes every minute of her free time to Him". She, who has always been a practicing Catholic, talks about this fear she has in connection with her release, which she expects to be in 2 years' time: "In leaving I'm afraid I'll forget him, that I'll talk less to God." A 32-year old Christian, who is serving a 3-year sentence for striking and inflicting wounds with weapons, and is a reoffender known for violent behaviour and is psychologically fragile, tells us about his fear of being released, his fear of meeting "the devil", of crossing "the enemy" (the victim in the fight) who might incite him to do the irreparable. According to him, only religion could stop him from "doing bad".

The meetings we had with re-incarcerated inmates showed the fragility of commitments when returning to a normal life and how paths can be reversed. Several of the inmates that we met mentioned their poor practice of religion when they left a previous prison before they were re-incarcerated. As much as they have time in prison to practice, as much life outside seems to reassert itself and offer many temptations.

## 5.5   Conclusion

During our investigation, few inmates presented religion as a means of pulling through, even though it may be mentioned as one of the possible dimensions of desistance. The people we met use religion more as a structuring force in the meaning of Sarg and Lamine (2011) and focused more on the here and now rather than a restructuring perspective geared towards reintegration. Of course, these two perspectives are linked since, by constituting a resource for personal and even social rehabilitation in prison, religion can favour reintegration. It can, however, be noted that this perspective is limited to people who have already received religious socialisation. Our interviewees are more situated in the continuity of their careers, whether they be religious or not, since there are few conversions in prison. Moreover, very few inmates evoked religion as the sole tool of rehabilitation. If it was mentioned by a few, particularly by Muslims with the idea of putting things back into order; for example, it was associated with a slightly vague hope of personal reform without it being expressed in any concrete plan, however. Through the humane skills they exercise, chaplains in any case offer inmates a privileged space in which to reaffirm their dignity and humanity. To inmates they represent a possible resource for withstanding imprisonment or at least to endeavour to neutralise some of its degrading effects and they often contribute to giving a meaning to the sentence. There is no proof, however, that they perform better in terms of rehabilitation than other listening professionals that operate in prisons, but they contribute to it. Contrary to what happens in other European or American countries, where it is strongly linked with reintegration programmes, in France the prison authorities seem to see religion more as an appeasing resource or as a means of "withstanding incarceration", or even as tool for maintaining order, without any real ambition for reintegration. From that point of view, prison is a manifestation of the varied geometry of secularism and an excellent indicator of the ambivalences of French secularism, which sometimes represses religion as an unacceptable element in public life, while at other times, calling on its supposed potential to pacify souls and act as an agent of social control. These forms of religious utilitarianism betray an institutional admission of the vacuous meaning of sentences, as well as the illusory, even mythical, character of the supposed re-socialising virtues of modern sanctions.

# References

Artières, P. (2005). L'aumônier, le médecin et le prisonnier Ã la fin du XIXe siècle. In O. Faure & B. Delpal (Eds.), *Religion et enfermement (XVIIe-XXe siècle)* (pp. 193–202). Rennes: PUR.

Becci, I. (2012). *Imprisoned religion: Transformations of religion during and after imprisonment in Eastern Germany*. Farnham: Ashgate.

Beckford, J. A., & Gilliat, S. (1998). *Religion in prison. Equal rites in a multi-faith society*. Cambridge: Cambridge University Press.

Béraud, C., de Galembert, C., & Rostaing, C. (2013). *Des hommes et des dieux en prison*, Paris: research subsidized by the Prison Administrations Directorate (DAP) and the GIP Law and Justice research mission.

Caille, A., & Fixot, A.-N. (2012). Presentation "leaving prison". *Revue du Mauss, 40,* 5–22.

Calverley, A., & Farrall, S. (2012). Individual, family and community: Ethnocultural ways out of delinquency? In M. Mohamed (Eds.), *Les sorties de délinquance. Théories, méthodes, enquêtes* (pp. 131–156), Paris: La Découverte.

Camp, S., Klein-Safran J., Kwon O. K., Daggett D. M., & Joseph, V. (2006). An exploration into participation in a faith-based prison programs. *Criminology and Public Policy, 5*(3), 529–550.

Chauvenet, A., Rostaing, C., & Orlic, F. (2008). *La violence carcérale en question*. Paris: PUF.

Clear, T., Harydman, P. L., Stout, B., Luken, K., & Dammer, H. (2000). The value of religion in prison. An inmate perspective. *Journal of Contemporary Criminal Justice, 16,* 53–74.

Dammer, H. R. (2002). The reasons for religious involvement in the correctional environment. In T. O'Connor & N. Pallone (Eds.), *Religion, the community and the rehabilitation of criminal offenders* (pp. 25–58). Binghamton: Haworth.

Dammer, H. R. (1992). *Piety in prison: An ethnography of religion in the correctional environment*. New-Jersey, UMI.

Direction de l'administration pénitentiaire, Ministère de la Justice. (2009). Rapport d'activité 2007. http://www.justice.gouv.fr/art_pix/Rapport_activite2_DAP_2007.pdf.

Giordano, P., Longmore, M., Schroeder, R., & Sefferin, P. (2008). A life course perspective on spirituality and desistance from crime. *Criminology, 46*(1), 99–132.

Ignatieff, M. (1978). *A just measure pain: The penitentiary in the Industrial Revolution 1750–1850*. London: Penguin Books.

Johnson, B. R., Larson, D. B., & Pitts, T. C. (1997). Religious programs, institutional adjustment, and recidivism among former inmates in prison fellowship programs. *Justice Quarterly, 14,* 145–166.

Jouanneau, S. (2011). "Ne pas perdre la foi dans l'imamat". Comment se maintiennent les "vocations" d'imams bénévoles en France. *Sociétés Contemporaines, 84,* 103–125.

Kerley, K. R., Matthews, T. L., & Blanchard, T. C. (2005). Religiosity, religious participation, and negative prison behaviors. *Journal for the Scientific Study of Religion, 44*(4), 443–457.

Langlois, C. (1984). L'introduction des congrégations féminines dans le système pénitentiaire français (1839–1880). In J.-G. Petit (Ed.), *La prison, le bagne et l'histoire* (pp. 129–140). Genève: Ed. Médecine et Hygiène.

Le Bourgeois, I. (2006). *Espérer encore* Paris: Desclée de Brouwer.

Liwerant, S. (2006). Evasion spirituelle en détention autorisée: en détention, prière de réinsérer. *Droit et Cultures*, n° 51.

Maruna, S. (2001). *Making good: How ex-convicts reform and rebuild their lives*. Washington: American psychological association Books.

Mohammed, M. (2012). *Les sorties de la délinquance, théories, méthodes et enquêtes*. Paris: La Découverte.

O'Connor, T. P., & Perreyclear, M. (2002). Prison religion in action and its influence on offender rehabilitation. In T. P. O'Connor & N. J. Pallone (Eds.), *Religion, the Community, and the Rehabilitation of Criminal Offenders* (pp. 11–33). New York: Haworth Press.

Piette, A. (2003). *Le fait religieux. Une théorie de la religion ordinaire*. Paris: Economica.

Rostaing, C. (2006). La compréhension sociologique de l'expérience carcérale, Revue européenne de sciences sociales, septembre 2006, Tome XLIV, n° 135, 29–43.

Rostaing, C., de Galembert, C., & Béraud, C. (2014). Des Dieux, des hommes et des objets en prison. Apports heuristiques d'une analyse de la religion par les objets, Champ Pénal, vol. XI.

Sarg, R., & Lamine, A.-S. (2011). La religion en prison. Norme structurante, réhabilitation de soi, stratégie de résistance. *Archives de Sciences Sociales des Religions, 153,* 85–104.

Sundt, J. L., & Cullen, F. T. (2002). The correctional ideology of prison chaplains: A national survey. *Journal of Criminal Justice, 30*(5), 369–385.

Sykes, G. (1958). *The society of captives. A study of a maximum security prison*. New York: Princeton University Press.

Weber, M. (1995 [1922]). *Economie et société* (vol. 2) Paris: Presses Pocket.

# Chapter 6
# Institutional Logic and Legal Practice: Modes of Regulation of Religious Organizations in German Prisons

Sarah J. Jahn

## 6.1 Introduction

What happens if a Muslim inmate wants to attend Friday prayer in a German prison? What happens if Jehovah's Witnesses or another religious organization wants to celebrate religious meetings in this prison? Each prison has to find its own ways of negotiating these and other questions concerning 'religion'. The proposed solutions must correspond to German law and the institutional specificities of the prison. My own study of 'the legal practice of positive religious freedom in German prisons' has clearly shown that 'religion' is considered as a private good.[1] But whether individual and corporate religious freedom can be used as a tool for negotiation depends not only on the legal framework, but also on the interpretation of the law, institutional logic of the prison, and the individual's understanding of 'religion'.

---

[1] The article refers to some results of my research project about the legal practice of positive religious freedom in German prisons. In my project, I explore the negotiation and organization of religious diversity in German prisons. I focus on prisons for male offenders with a long-term sentence of at least 3 years. The goal of the research was to analyse how the right to religious freedom is negotiated in the German penal system. Based on the approaches of the sociology of law and the study of religion, I conducted field studies in German prisons and semi-structured guideline interviews with both prison staff and prison inmates in several German prisons. The selection of the prison-sample was related to regional differences (e.g. urban, rural, or religious landscape) in order to get a broad base of empirical data. For the studies on site, I took 1 week to explore the particular circumstances of each institution. In sum, I collected 80 interviews, numerous documents, and conducted six field studies by way of participant observation. The data was analysed anonymously and by means of the method of qualitative content analysis (Mayring 2010). The results of the project will be published in 2015.

---

S. J. Jahn (✉)
Center for Religious Studies—CERES, Ruhr-University Bochum, Universitätsstraße 90 A,
44789 Bochum, Germany
e-mail: Sarah.j.jahn@rub.de

© Springer International Publishing Switzerland 2015          81
I. Becci, O. Roy (eds.), *Religious Diversity in European Prisons,*
DOI 10.1007/978-3-319-16778-7_6

Taking a neo-institutional approach, religion and law are understood as institutions that form not only a regulative, but also a normative mechanism of social action (Scott 1999, pp. 57, 59). Furthermore, the interpretation of the law is based on the understanding of the 'good' organization of everyday life in prison and the 'good fulfilment' of prison goals (rehabilitation and security). Allowing religion into prison depends fundamentally on the institutional logic of the prison and its legal structure/framework. But what is 'religion'? In this chapter, the focus is on organized 'religion', such as religious organizations. Yet within this formalised view, 'religion' is also understood as a generic term (Beckford 2003, pp. 11–29), because there are questions as to what is a 'religious' organization and what is not organization. The understanding and the definition or non-definition of religion is more than a legal or scholarly question; it is also a question of negotiating and organizing religious diversity in public institutions such as prisons, hospitals, or schools. Following Winnifred F. Sullivan, I assume that:

> [i]n each of these cases [where religious freedom is requested] a court or a legislature or an administrative official must make a determination as to whether the religious practice in question is legally religious. In other words, in order to enforce laws guaranteeing religious freedom you must first have religion. (Sullivan 2005, p. 1)

Based on these preliminary ideas, this chapter explores the modes of regulation affecting religious organizations in German prisons. It does so by looking at regulatory factors such as structural and legal conditions, and by studying individual modes of negotiating religious organizations. These individual modes of dealing with religious diversity in German prisons that take place under well-circumscribed conditions: On the one hand, they are defined by the specific relationship of state and religion in Germany. The so-called 'cooperative partnership' between state and religion permeates all legal and institutional levels, including the Basic Law for the Federal Republic of Germany (Basic Law), the prison house rules, and the Act concerning measures of rehabilitation and prevention involving deprivation of liberty and the execution of prison sentences (Prison Act). On the other hand, they are defined by the legal practice towards religion, and by the prisons' logic and the practical interpretation of it.

To understand the logic of the prison and its legal practice towards religious organizations, I will first present which religious organizations are present in German prisons, and how the choice of religious organization is tied to the logic of the prison. Using the example of an Evangelical organization and Jehovah's Witnesses, I will illustrate that the institutional logic is interpreted differently depending on which religious organization is concerned, and to the extent to which this is related to the external perception of religious organizations. Comparing these two examples shows that religious organizations are included in the prison structure when they are perceived as actors of rehabilitation, independently of their status in public law. If, on the other hand, a religious organization is perceived as a security risk, it is excluded regardless of its status in public law. This means that in practice, it is more important that the perception of the religious organization fits with the purposes of the institutional logic, and less important that it be given legitimacy by the law.

## 6.2   Presence of Religious Organizations in German Prisons

The various ways in which religious organizations are present in public institutions depends on inter-religious, intra-religious, and denominational processes, as well as processes between religious organizations and specific societal institutions, such as law, economy, etc. Categorizations of religious organizations in German prisons are affected by different types of organizations and communitarizations, as well as differing internal and external perceptions. In addition, as the model of the 'religious market' will illustrate, the relations among religious organizations and within the prison are dynamic and depend on various factors.

### 6.2.1   Variety of Religious Organizations in German Prisons

The figure below shows the religious organizations as they were observed during field research.

As presented in Fig. 6.1, it is evident that most religious organizations in prison have a Christian background. Organizations associated with 'Islam' are an exception. The strong representation of Christian organizations in prison is due to the history of European religion, and the history of European prison, which are both tightly entwined with Christian groups (Becci 2012, pp. 33–38, Jahn 2011).

In German prisons, prison chaplaincy, Christian welfare organizations, as well as nongovernmental and non-church-related associations for inmates and ex-offenders, are organizations with a Christian self-understanding. While from a historical perspective, they have a common origin, they are now completely different

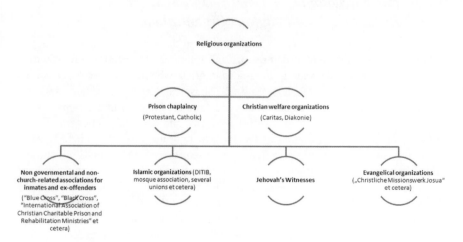

**Fig. 6.1** Religious organizations in German prisons

types of organizations. As such, they are good examples of intra-denominational to inter-denominational processes of differentiation. As religion scholar Günther Kehrer writes, the church as a religious organization is so highly differentiated that it has constructed its own structures and initiated exchange processes with the environment in which it is situated, in such a way that the current network of organizations is determined by specific goals and not by a theology (Kehrer 1982, pp. 124–125). Though Christian nongovernmental and non-church-related associations for inmates and ex-offenders share a common origin, they have moved away from the church and have formed independent organizational structures. Examples of such organizations are the 'free churches' like the Baptists, Mennonites, Salvation Army, and several Evangelical and Pentecostal groups. Other examples include the 'umbrella unions' where different organizations are members because they share a common theme, for example, welfare. Islamic unions in Germany such as the Turkish-Islamic Union for Religious Affairs (DİTİB) and Millî Görüş (IGMG) are prominent examples of 'umbrella unions'. Islamic organizations have various political, ethnic, and religious backgrounds and have various types of organizations, such as unions and associations (Amir-Moazami 2005, pp. 267–286). In contrast to 'umbrella unions' certain religious organizations have no specific targets beside religion. These include Jehovah's Witnesses and the Evangelical organization *Christliches Missionswerk Josua*, which will be described further in Sect. 4.

The following analysis of religious organizations demonstrates different types of communitarization in prison. On the one hand, there are religious organizations that uphold a clear religious self-understanding. On the other hand, there are religious organizations that see themselves more as interest groups pursuing specific purposes. Those religious organizations that understand themselves as religious rather than purpose oriented are led to use an 'organized rationality' (Kehrer 1982, p. 12).

## 6.2.2 Categorization: Old, New, Established, and Institutionalised Religious Organizations

In addition to the different structures of each religious organization, one can also distinguish them based on the following categories: whether they are old, new, institutionalised, and/or established religious. These categories are related to the internal understanding of the religious organization and the offer that they present in prisons, the perceptions of officials of the prisons, and the legal framework. While *old* and *new* as temporal dimensions show how long the particular religious organization has been in the prison system, the dimensions of *institutionalised* and *established* indicate the quality of integration. Established religious organizations are those that have gained social recognition. Institutionalised religious organizations are those legitimated by the law and which are part of the prison structures. The following table shows how a number of religious organizations fit in these categories. Two more categories are presented in the table, to indicate which organizations are externally perceived as *social* or *religious* (Table 6.1).

**Table 6.1** Categorization of religious organizations in German prisons

| Religious organization | Institutionalised | Established | Old | New | Religious | Social |
|---|---|---|---|---|---|---|
| Prison chaplaincy | X | (X) | X | | X | X |
| Christian welfare organizations | X | X | X | | | X |
| Nongovernmental and non-church-related associations for inmates and ex-offenders | (X)[a] | X | X | | (X) | X |
| Jehovah's Witnesses | | | | X | X | |
| Islamic organizations | (X) | | | X | X | |
| Evangelical organizations | (X) | X | | X | X | |

[a] Bracketing means that in some cases the organization is 'institutionalised', 'established', 'religious', but not in any case.

The categorization of corporate religions in prisons shows that an *old religious organization*, such as the prison chaplaincy, may admittedly be institutionalised, while it does not need to be equally established. *New religious organizations*, such as Islamic organizations and the Evangelical organizations, may be established and show first signs of institutionalisation. It is also clear that not all religious organizations are perceived as exclusively religious. The prison chaplaincy and the nongovernmental and non-church-related associations for inmates and ex-offenders are recognized as both religious and social organizations. The Christian welfare organizations are recognized as socially oriented only. As I will describe in the section below, the perception of these organizations as religious or social does not necessarily depend on the external perception of these, but also on differentiation processes within religious traditions and the resulting forms of community that are thus created.

The categories described above can also be analysed as a 'religious market' (Stark and Finke 2000). The model of the religious market is presented here from the perspective of the provider. While the theoretical approach of the religious market can be criticised because of its assumption of rational action (Sen 1982), as the metaphor rather systematically represents the dynamics of religious organizations in prison, it is still useful within our analysis.

Offers on the religious market are generally divided into institutionalised and noninstitutionalised providers. These offer religious or social services that can be more or less well established. Prison chaplaincy and Christian welfare organizations like *Diakonie* and *Caritas* are institutionalised providers that still have a strong presence on this market. But the influence of other organizations steadily grows, especially nongovernmental and non-church-related associations for inmates and ex-offenders, for example, Evangelical organizations like the *Christliches Missionswerk Josua*, and Islamic organizations. On this market, we also find groups like

Jehovah's Witnesses that are neither established nor institutionalised. Overall, we notice two related tendencies: the dissolution of the monopoly of traditional Protestant and Catholic prison chaplaincy, and the establishment of new providers.

*The dissolution of the monopoly* The religious market, on the providing side, tends to be in constant motion; not only because of the various treatment religious organizations receive in prisons, but mainly because of the establishment of new religious providers within an institution. Institutionalisation does not necessarily mean that the provider is established simply because consumers accept the offer. Several of my field studies make clear that chaplaincy is not established in all prisons—even if it is institutionalised by state–church contracts in public law. One reason is that chaplains sometimes do not have a full position in a prison. They may be working fulltime, halftime, or voluntarily in the prison. My data shows that the more the chaplain is present on site, the more his chaplaincy is established. In regions which are largely secularized, the chaplain oversees several prisons while at the same time he still leads a parish. As a result, the chaplain is rarely on-site, to the extent that the staff and inmates may wonder 'what the clergyman does at all in prison'.[2]

It is different when the chaplain in prison is on site more consistently. In such cases, chaplains assume many tasks that are normally associated with social and psychological services. And as the chaplains have a budget (church funding) and dispose of their time independently, they can better perform certain tasks compared to other prison staff members, including prison officers, psychologists, and social workers. These are often tasks in rehabilitation, for example, family reunification, transition management, organizing outgoings and events, and so on. In these cases, the religious self-understanding blurs with the social offer. If there are only a few inmates who take part in Sunday service and individual care, the prison chaplain often acts as a kind of social worker.[3]

*New providers getting established* Today, many inmates who had previously accepted the offer of the prison chaplaincy now attend nongovernmental and non-church-related associations for inmates and ex-offenders[4], or Evangelical organizations which engage in prison work as one of their activities. The Blue Cross is the largest and most established organization that was represented in each of the prisons in which I conducted research. While the Blue Cross provides individual groups or individual care for addicted inmates in every visited prison, in one prison, a separate station for alcohol-addicted inmates was provided in addition. The *Christliches Missionswerk Josua*, an Evangelical organization, is also a very well-established religious organization, which operates only regionally, and organizes prison work as one of its minor activities.

---

[2] This was a primary result of field-studies in prisons in northern and eastern Germany.

[3] This was primarily a result of field studies in West Germany and northern Bavaria prisons.

[4] These are religious organizations who understand themselves in opposition to the so called 'mainstream churches' (Protestant Church of Germany and Roman Catholic Church of Germany) as so-called 'free-churches' or smaller groups.

As new providers, Islamic organizations are of particular interest. 'Islam', as a collective term for different Islamic traditions in Germany, is now the third largest religious community in Germany and grows continuously (Haug et al. 2009, p. 11). This trend is also noticeable in prisons: for example, one prison offers halal food and adopts religious rules for Ramadan. While in many institutions, individual religious practice does not seem to be a problem, some federal states are currently discussing the possibility of institutionalising Muslim chaplaincy as a continuous offer (Jahn 2014). In the context of my own research, the diversity of offers and the different ways to regulate them shows that prisons are able to adapt to specific modes. But these individual modes are also only interim solutions while there is still no general modus vivendi based on the law and administration principles. In three of the six prisons I examined, a religious representative of *DİTİB* comes into the prison at irregular intervals to offer Qur'an readings for Turkish inmates. In one prison, a volunteer Muslim and a social worker organize something like an Islamic social service, which provides social care and support for imprisoned Muslims regardless of their national origin. In two prisons, there is no special offer for Muslim inmates. In the cases studied in my own fieldwork, there was no institutionalised Islamic chaplaincy. However, the first comprehensive approaches to develop pastoral concepts for Muslim inmates have started: In 2008, Wiesbaden initiated the project MUSE in order to ensure an institutionalised Muslim chaplaincy on a local level (MUSE Wiesbaden 2014). In 2009, the state of Lower Saxony established a working group with the intention to establish pastoral care in state institutions, such as prisons and hospitals, together with Muslim organizations. In 2012, the Lower Saxony Ministry of Justice and some Islamic unions signed an agreement which included the concern of Muslim chaplaincy in prisons (Justizministerium Niedersachsen 2012). In 2013, similar contracts were signed in the federal states of Bremen and Hamburg (Stadtstaat Hamburg 2014). The examples cited, as well as other unknown local initiatives, are still in process. In some places, the cooperation between religious organizations and prisons works very well, as the case of the imam Husamuddin Meyer working in a prison in Wiesbaden shows (Schnell 2014). Other prisons face large difficulties to establish cooperation. Berlin, at the end of 2013, is one such example. The German Press Agency reported:

A dispute over Muslim prison chaplaincy arose between the federal state of Berlin and the Islamic unions. The Muslim representatives cancelled their participation in the Islamforum for Thursday. (German Press Agency 2014)

The dispute had begun because the Office for the Protection of the Constitution had expressed concerns about security problems regarding people in the working group.

## 6.3 The Institutional Logic of the Prison Institution

Considering those organizations which are new providers that are becoming established, within the context of the institutional logic of German prisons, it becomes clear that the possibilities of rehabilitation help to get a religious organization included into the prison, and that, conversely, issues of order and security will keep a religious organization excluded from the prison. That is, if religious organizations are perceived as rehabilitation actors, they are integrated into the everyday life of imprisonment and the formal structures of the prison. When the presence of a religious organization is perceived as a potential risk towards order or safety, it is not considered as part of the prison, and accordingly, it is not integrated into the prison. To clarify this trend, the following section will describe the institutional logic of prisons in general, and will illustrate some of the practical understandings of religion.

The institutional logic is determined dogmatically by the Prison Act; more specifically, by the prison acts of each federal state, as Germany is a federal republic.[5] These acts consist of specific administrative regulations for penal institutions and German Basic Law, the overall legal text. The logic is defined in the first title of the act, named 'principles'. Section 2 defines the 'objectives of the execution':

> By serving his prison sentence the prisoner shall be enabled in future to lead a life in *social responsibility* without committing criminal offences (objective of treatment). The execution of the prison sentence shall also serve to *protect* the general public from further criminal offences.[6]

Based on this key understanding of imprisonment, rehabilitation, and security, Section 3 of the Prison Act describes the practical implementation of these:

> (1) Life in penal institutions should be approximated as far as possible to *general living conditions*.
> (2) Any detrimental effects of imprisonment shall be *counteracted*.
> (3) Imprisonment shall be so designed as to help the prisoner to reintegrate himself into civil life at *liberty*.

While the first and third point comprise the tension between liberty and imprisonment, normal life and imprisoned life, the second point refers to consequences of imprisonment which have to be counteracted. While Secion 3 is relevant for criminology, my focus is more on Section 4 of the Prison Act:

> The prisoner shall be subject to such restrictions of his *liberty* as are laid down in this Act. Unless the Act provides for a *special regulation*, only such *restrictions* may be imposed on him as are indispensable to maintain *security* or to avert a serious disturbance of *order* in the penal institution.[7]

The italicised words are key terms of the institutional logic, especially with regards to a specific understanding of processes of regulation and practical implementation. But the Prison Act and its actual implementation in prisons does not fully match up. As the head of one correction house described, not all 'general living conditions' are possible:

---

[5] As the laws of the federal states vary on this point only in order, but not in content, the national law is quoted throughout. The used translation is provided by the Language Service of the Federal Ministry of Justice and Consumer Protection. The translation includes the amendment(s) to the Act by Article 4 of the Act of 5.12.2012. Italics added by the author.

[6] Italics added by the author. The first sentence is a common understanding of 'rehabilitation' and 'security' like Cornel 2009 describes.

[7] Italics added by the author.

In normal life, outside the prison, it is quite difficult anyway, but in here it is also restricted by the house rules. I cannot allow all different religions at different times of their calls to prayer from the cell […]. I cannot. I will not be able to set up here that we have a Hindu temple next to a mosque next to a synagogue, and so on…. But in private area, if there is still a private area, the inmates must be allowed to live their religion, to the extent that the house rules allow.

The head of the prison uses an emphatic explanation to describe the (im)possibility of negotiating religious diversity in prison in an equal way, while also referring to the problems of managing them outside, in society. In fact, many conflicts about 'religion' are present in the German public sphere. The public debates on mosques are one prominent example (Schmitt 2012). Another example is the dispute regarding the status of Jehovah's Witnesses as a corporation under public law, which shows that the state has to clarify the question of what constitutes a religious community (Besier and Besier 2001). Currently, there is a debate on 'Islam' within the German public sphere (Torpey and Joppke 2013, pp. 48–84). In prison, these questions arise as well, but there they have to be considered alongside the institutional logic presented above, and the specific conditions in prisons. These prison conditions lead to the deprivation of liberty, the deprivation of goods and services, the deprivation of heterosexual relationships, the deprivation of autonomy, and the deprivation of security, as Gresham M. Sykes writes in 'The Society of the Captives' (Sykes 2003, pp. 63–83). Moreover, the prison as a 'total institution' has different possibilities and limitations to deal with (religious) diversity, because the institution is inhabited by people who act according to general rules, but also according to understandings shaped by individuals or groups. According to Erving Goffman's definition of 'total institutions':

> Their encompassing or total character is symbolized by the barrier to social intercourse with the outside and to departure that is often built right into the physical plant, such as locked doors, high walls, barbed wire, cliffs, water, forests, or moors. These establishments I am calling *total institutions* […].[8] (Goffman 1961, p. 4)

The described institutional logic has to be understood in its dogmatic and practical form. Different tensions emerge among the described key terms because they all stand in relation to each other, as the figure below shows (Fig. 6.2):

For the study of the legal practices that shape prisons, it is interesting to observe how rehabilitation and security are understood separately and in relation to each other, and how they are implemented in everyday life in prison. I will illustrate this with two examples.

### 6.3.1   Established Due to its Potential Ability to Help with Rehabilitation: Christliches Missionswerk Josua (CMJ)

CMJ is a new and established religious organization in one of the prisons I conducted research on, and serves as an example for the establishment of Evangelical

---

[8] Italics by Goffman.

**Fig. 6.2** Institutional logics

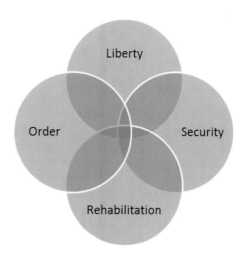

organizations in German prisons. The attribution *new* should be understood in two ways: First, the CMJ is active in prison only since 2010. Second, the organization was founded in 1990 (Christliches Missionswerk Josua 2014).

CMJ offers individual counselling, transition management, and an Alpha Course. The Alpha Course covers Christian and social values and offers an introduction to Christian faith. The organization itself has a definite Christian self-understanding. Besides a general theology with Jesus at its centre, the concept of 'mission' is an important concern. One citation from the homepage of CMJ states the following:

> We want to pass by word and action the gospel at home and abroad that Jesus Christ is the hope of every person.

This citation is not just about proselytising, but also about mission, which is understood to be an active aid in certain social sectors, including prisons. The work in prisons is regarded as working on relationships, as the pastor of the organization summarises:

> I think, first, that God is not Protestant or Catholic. God is God. The crucial question is how we live in relationships. This comes back in the Alpha Course: How do I live in relationship with myself? How do I live in relationship with my neighbour? How do I live in relationship with God? [...].

While the CMJ has a unique Christian understanding in its organization, theology, and offer, the prison administration understands the organization and its offer in terms of rehabilitation. As the head of the prison says:

> But these providers offer their religious views not in the foreground [...]. They are very worldly oriented, geared to the needs of these inmates. Inmates learn to reflect on meaning and to consider their personal development critically; or to realize through many conversations whether they can perhaps change their own sense of life or not. And that is the main intention.

As the above quote makes clear, the offer is adapted from its religious background into the institutional framework of the prison. So, when deciding whether or not to allow the offer, it is neither the legal status of the religious organization (or private association), nor the right to religious freedom based on the German Basic Law, that is relevant. Rather, it is rehabilitation, which is a function of imprisonment, that is taken into account. The religious offer is understood as therapy rather than religious service. The head of a prison sums it up in this way:

> Our task is to provide offers for the inmates which enable them to change their personality. From this perspective, the Alpha Course is a possibility next to other offers.

### 6.3.2   'Mission' as a Security Risk: Jehovah's Witnesses

While CMJ is, from an institutional perspective, perceived as an organization oriented towards social work, and its offer is understood in the context of the rehabilitation of inmates, Jehovah's Witnesses are perceived as an organization oriented towards religious work. In contrast to the CMJ, Jehovah's Witnesses are not considered as established, although they were recognized as a corporation under public law in Germany in 2006, which means that religion benefits from a special cooperation with the state in several public spaces (Robbers 2001).

That Jehovah's Witnesses should be treated differently despite having the same public status as the Protestant and Catholic churches is justified by prison administration on two levels. The first level refers to tradition and identity: the Protestant and Catholic churches in Germany have a 'special status' in history and culture. The second level refers to the institutional logic: Jehovah's Witnesses are considered a security risk. As the head of the prison explains:

> So I would not allow, for example, that they [Jehovah's Witnesses] can go from prison cell to prison cell as it happens outside when they go from door to door. [...] In prison, this quickly takes on the character that inmates should not be exposed to, things that they do not have to accept outside either.

Security, here, is not understood in the sense of protecting the public from criminal activity. Rather, it is a threat specific to the inmates, who sometimes need to be protected from those who come from outside the prison. Because the prison has the function to protect inmates too, the missionary activity of Jehovah's Witnesses is regarded as a security risk for the prison because, by the deprivation of their liberty, the inmate have no chance 'to go out of the way' of the missionaries.

### 6.3.3   Legal Practice and Practical Understanding of Institutional Logics

Two aspects become particularly evident in both examples. First, the public status of a religious organization does not seem to testify for 'security'. Second, 'mission' is used as an argument to justify the classification of certain (but not all) religious organizations as security risks. This first aspect is striking because the legal status of a religious organization as a corporation under public law is awarded the status of partner of the state. Religious organizations with the status of a corporation under public law have to fulfil certain conditions, as article 137, paragraph 5 in the Weimar Constitution states:

> Religious societies shall remain corporations under public law insofar as they have enjoyed that status in the past. Other religious societies shall be granted the same rights upon application, if their constitution and the number of their members give assurance of their permanency. If two or more religious societies established under public law unite into a single BE, it too shall be a corporation under public law. (Federal Law Gazette 2010)

Those organizations also have certain privileges—as article 137, paragraph 6 in the Weimar Constitution states:

> Religious societies that are corporations under public law shall be entitled to levy taxes on the basis of the civil taxation lists in accordance with Land law. (Ibid)

Beside taxes, there is a comprehensive contract system. The contracts regulate, for example, religious education in state schools, theologies in state universities, the funding of religious buildings, or even the pastoral care in state institutions such as prisons. But even though Jehovah's Witnesses have a corporate status, no state contract has been concluded with them. Contracts for pastoral care in prison are signed with the Catholic and Protestant churches, in some federal states with the Central Council of Jews in Germany, and with Islamic organizations (Jahn 2013).

The second aspect is that 'mission' is used as an argument to justify the classification of Jehovah's Witnesses' work as a security risk. With regard to other religious organizations, however, mission is not considered a security risk, even when it is a central part of many of the religious traditions (Kollman 2011) which are present in prisons. Remembering Fig. 6.1, there is a majority of organizations with Christian traditions in prison, all of which have an explicit understanding and positive meaning of 'mission'. Evangelical organizations like CMJ also have a specific focus on mission, as I wrote above. It is not mission in itself, but rather the specific type of mission, which constitutes the security risk. Jehovah's Witnesses have a literal understanding of the Bible. When they talk about 'mission', they have two sections of Matthew in mind:

> Matthew 28:19, p. 20: 'Jesus told his followers to make disciples of people of all the nations.'
> Matthew 10:7, pp. 11–13: 'When he sent out his early disciples, Jesus directed them to go to the homes of the people.'

These two sections are the basis of the 'door-to-door' understanding of mission of Jehovah's Witnesses.

## 6.4   Discussion: Inclusion and Exclusion of 'Religious' Organizations

These explanations make clear the various ways in which prisons perceive religious organizations and their offers, and the role of institutional logic in relation to the regulation of religious organizations in prisons. However, the results presented here

**Table 6.2** Religious organizations as rehabilitation actors

| Rehabilitation program | Religious organizations |
|---|---|
| Therapies for sexual and violent offenders (e.g.) | / |
| Social training | Christliches Missionwerk Josua |
| Therapies for addicts (e.g. drugs, alcohol) | Christian welfare organizations, Christliche Straffälligen- und Gefährdetenhilfen |
| Employment and education agency | Prison chaplaincy |
| Maintain social ties (e.g. visits in prison, marriage and family seminars, prison breaks) | Prison chaplaincy, Christliche Straffälligen- und Gefährdetenhilfen, Christian welfare organizations |

should also be considered in a more general context. I will discuss these empirical findings with regard to two analytical questions: Rehabilitation by religion? Security versus (religious) freedom?

### 6.4.1  Rehabilitation by Religion?

The first general context deals with the question of 'rehabilitation by religion'. This does not refer to a rehabilitating effect of religion, but to how religion as a normative and regulating variable is involved in the task of rehabilitation. More specifically, one could ask to what extent religious organizations are included in the rehabilitation task, which is understood as a secular task in public law.

Within my wider research, I have come to the conclusion that religion is an important rehabilitation factor in the German (secular) prison sphere.[9] Individual volunteers with an explicit religious self-understanding and religious organizations assume important tasks in this area, as shown in Table 6.2, below.

We may consider whether both the religious organizations and the prison give up a part of their internal understanding and function in order to realize this development. As religious organizations take over tasks of the secular rehabilitation program, they are no longer perceived as religious organizations. For example, while CMJ still has a religious self-understanding, the development of Christian welfare organizations shows that, in the long term, the religious self-understanding transforms itself in favour of the secular tasks carried out in prison. The religious self-perception and external perception are transformed through the participation of the religious organization in the prison. Using the example of *Caritas*, I will briefly describe this development.

*The 'Self-secularization' of Caritas*  In the internal understanding of Christian welfare, the grace of charity is central. This is based on Matthew 5:43:

---

[9] 'Prison sphere' is a wider understanding of 'prison institution' while the first one includes not only the house where the prison sentence is carried out. The 'prison sphere' also means transition management after the detention or alternative penalties.

You have heard that it was said, 'you shall love your neighbour and hate your enemy'.

There are differences between individual acts of charity and organized charitable activities. While individual charity is incumbent on each individual Christian, organized charitable activities have traditionally been fulfilled by the deacon. Even if charity is a core concept to Christian action in church history, institutions like *Caritas* have developed out of the church and have professionalized these tasks. *Caritas* is one of the largest welfare organizations and one of the largest social employers in Germany (Caritas 2014). The preamble of the organization states that *Caritas*:

'[…] is recognized by the German Bishops' Conference as institutionalised assembly and representation of the Catholic Caritas in Germany.' (Ibid)

*Caritas* is present in prison through several offers. In the prison facilities I studied, the following activities were offered: addiction counselling (alcohol, drugs, gambling), social training, debt counselling, and transition management. The offer is volunteer-based or on the basis of paid fee, with a contract that is signed between *Caritas* and the prison facility or the federal state Ministry of Justice. It is clear that the offer is primarily social rather than religious. The following part of an interview transcription with a prison-psychologist summarises the way *Caritas* is perceived by others:

The [Caritas staff] are here more on the social worker level. We have concluded contracts here with Caritas referring to addiction counselling. We buy the addiction counselling at Caritas. But we do not buy a missionary order or something. […] We chose the Caritas offer because it is a large agency around here.

This brief excerpt shows that *Caritas* is no longer perceived as a religious organization, but as a social organization, by acting as a provider of diversified social services. According to a research project at the Ruhr-University Bochum, this transformation started in the 1960s. At the time, changes in social legislation led to the primacy of welfare organizations. At the same time, the denominationally shaped institutions experienced a loss of tradition (Jähnichen 2010, pp. 11–14). This ambivalence between external stabilization by legislation and modified self-perception led to what former President of the Council of the Protestant Church in Germany, Wolfgang Huber, called 'self-secularization' (Huber 1999, p. 10).

*Is it a Secular or Religious Understanding of 'Rehabilitation'?* The example of *Caritas* shows that, as less human and financial resources are available to fulfil the rehabilitation mandate of prisons, it becomes increasingly necessary for civil society actors to participate. But the path of privatizing and delegating important areas of rehabilitation to the civil sector is also dangerous. The first danger is in the economization and rationalization of the prison system, and the associated abandonment of the ethical ideal of rehabilitation. The second danger lies in delegating originally governmental functions to the private sector. This could lead to the abandonment of the principle of the welfare state, in favour of economically organized areas that have a decidedly religious understanding, as is the case of *Caritas* and other religious organizations (those mentioned in Table 6.2). This shift means that the understanding of the social and the secular state would be abandoned. Questions regarding religious freedom partake in the blurring of the boundaries between the religious self-understanding of an organization, and the adoption of governmental functions. Considering the emergence of the contemporary law concerning the relations between religion and the state in Germany, the separation between religion and state is not only a freedom *of* religion, but also *for* religion. The individual is not only free to choose one or no religious affiliation; religious organizations are also exempt from state claims. The state, in turn, is (theoretically) ready to fully accept religious pluralism because *one specific* religious self-understanding is no longer a genuine property of the state. In the dogmatic understanding of law, the German state holds *no* religious self-understanding. This arrangement, which set out to guarantee religious freedom, is abandoned by religious organizations in favour of participation, and by the state for the benefit of cost and personal savings.

Winnifred F. Sullivan has studied the consequences of this development for the USA (Sullivan 2009). In the US context, these organizations are known as Faith-Based and Community Organizations (FBCO). Former President George W. Bush founded the 'White House Office of Faith-based and Community Initiatives' on 29 January 2001 to support the situation of social services:

> The underlying premise of the President's Initiative is that a more open and competitive Federal grantmaking process will increase the delivery of effective social services to those whose needs are greatest. Thus, Federal agencies have successfully undertaken a variety of measures to do this, including: Making information more accessible; Providing training and technical assistance; Broadening program eligibility; Changing regulations; Streamlining grant applications; Focusing on the unique needs of grassroots organizations; and Eliminating preferential treatment for existing and former grantees. (White House Office and Faith-Based and Community Organizations 2014)

Most important is that, through this program, original state functions are delegated to religious and secular organizations, as is the case in Germany with regards to prisons.

### 6.4.2  Security Versus (Religious) Freedom?

In a nutshell, the question of 'security versus (religious) freedom' leads to the insight that security, as a part of institutional logic, has an exclusionary influence on religion. That, however, does not constitute a direct attack on religious freedom. Rather, it is an indirect result of decision-making processes that relate to the interpretation of institutional logic, as the example of Jehovah's Witnesses has shown. It is also clear that the understandings internal and external to religious organizations are different. The prison's perception of religious organization is the decisive factor in whether inclusion or exclusion of religion takes place.

To understand the prison's perception of 'religious organizations' and the understanding of the institutional logic in general, we must look at the inherent tensions between liberty and security. This is the reason for bracketing (religious) in the chapter title above. The political scientist Gert-Joachim Glaeßner has worked on the category of 'security' as a central concept in social sciences (Glaeßner 2006; 2003; 2002; 2001). According to him, the term 'security' is a key term in the context of the History of Ideas. In addition, 'security' is not only a central concept and key term in the social sciences, but also serves as a classical public good in a normative understanding (Glaeßner 2001, p. 337). Glaeßner postulates that:

> [T]he development of modern occidental societies [...] can easily be written as a history of the formation of structures and institutions to ensure security. (Ibid)

In this understanding, 'security' certainly is an integral part of state theories since the treatise of Thomas Hobbes. Hobbes understands the primary role of the state to be in the protection of citizens (Hobbes 2010 [1651]. Another classical treatise, written by Charles-Louis Montesquieu, emphasises the freedom of the citizen from the state. That is, the state does not only have the function to protect the citizen, but the citizen must also be protected from the state (Montesquieu 2006 [1748]). The inherent tension between security and liberty is to be understood in this context.

Both texts are classical positions on the concept of a liberal state, and a specific understanding of the individualisation of rights in the ninetieth century (Glaeßner 2002, pp. 4–5). The invention of basic and human rights in the twentieth century represents the culmination of this development. Taking this line of thinking a step further, we may consider that this public good has to be protected by the state and by the citizen. In this understanding, 'security' does not only have a technical meaning (protecting people in any kind of conflicts); it also has a normative and social dimension: it is a value and an emotion. The right to religious freedom has to be seen as a part of this development. In a long-term perspective, the individualisation of rights leads to multi-polar worldviews. This raises the problem that public goods, like individual freedom and security, theoretically have to be protected equally. In practice, however, the state cannot guarantee different worldviews in their full extent (Glaeßner 2002, p. 12). According to Glaeßner, this leads to the expansion of security institutions of the state (Ibid).

With regard to the question of modes of regulation of religious organizations in German prisons, this insight is important insofar as the prison, as a concept, is only possible in connection with the idea of *security*, and the guiding principle of imprisonment the deprivation of someone's *freedom*.

The prison system, as an institution of the security of the state, is therefore also a part of the history of ideas and current social trends described above. The 'protection of society' and the 'security needs of the public' play a crucial role in Germany. The Criminologists Michael Alex and Thomas Feltes have brought out these tendencies and have connected them with general developments in relation to aspects of social security (Alex and Feltes 2009). They describe the 'step-mother' role of prisons in two ways: how prisons are widely disregarded in German politics, and prison's relationship to the perception of social changes:

> The significant changes [...made to the prison system] have no empirical or rational background, but exclusively express punitive settings in politics and media. (Alex and Feltes 2009, p. 92)

They conclude that even in prison, the new security thinking is already firmly anchored (Alex and Feltes 2009, p. 98). In my research, the security mentality was also very influential. However, it was handled differently in every single prison.

## 6.5  Final Statement

As we have seen, there are different modes of regulation of religious organizations in German prisons. The modes of regulation mainly depend on the external perception of the religious organizations and their offers, but also on perceptions and developments inside of religious organizations.

Overall, it can be stated that research on religion in prison, and on the relation of religion and law, should take place on various levels and from different perspectives because there are several understandings of what is meant by 'religion', and several legal practices. Both these *understandings* relate to each other. In addition, the empirical findings have to be set in an inner-institutional and societal context to explain causality. On the question of the 'impossibility of religious freedom', according to Sullivan, we must ask what is meant by religious freedom, and by religion in literal, practical, and theoretical dimensions.

## References

### Monographs and Article

Alex, M., & Feltes, Th. (2009). Von der Pathogenie des Strafvollzugs. In H.-J. Lange et al. (Ed.), *Auf der Suche nach neuer Sicherheit. Fakten, Theorien und Folgen* (pp. 89–102). Wiesbaden: VS Verlag für Sozialwissenschaften.

Amir-Moazami, S. (2005). Muslim challenges to the secular consensus: A german case study. *Journal of Contemporary European Studies, 13*(3), 267–286.

Becci, I. (2012). *Imprisoned religion. Transformations of religion during and after imprisonment in Eastern Germany. Farnham, Surrey.* England: Ashgate.

Beckford, J. A. (2003). *Social theory and religion.* Cambridge: Cambridge University Press..

Besier, G., & Besier, R.-M. (2001). Jehovah's Witnesses request for recognition as a corporation under public law in Germany: background, current status, and empirical aspects. *Journal of Church and State, 43*(1), 35–48.

Cornel, H. (2009). *Resozialisierung. Handbuch.* Baden-Baden: Nomos.

Glaeßner, G.-J. (2001). Sicherheit und Ordnung. Politisch-soziologische Reflexionen zu einem (wieder) aktuellen Thema. *Berliner Journal für Soziologie, 11*(3), 337–358.

Glaeßner, G.-J. (2002). Sicherheit und Freiheit. *Aus Politik und Zeitgeschichte, 10*(11), 3–13.

Glaeßner, G.-J. (2003). *Sicherheit in Freiheit. Die Schutzfunktion des demokratischen Staates und die Freiheit der Bürger.* Opladen: Leske + Budrich.

Glaeßner, G.-J. (2006). Security. In A. Harrington et al. (Ed.), *Encyclopedia of social theory New York* (pp. 538–540). London: Routledge.

Goffman, E. (1961). *Asylums. Essays on the social situation of mental patients and other inmates.* Garden City: Anchor Books.

Haug, S., et al. (2009). *Muslimisches Leben in Deutschland. Eine Studie im Auftrag der Deutschen Islamkonferenz.* Nürnberg: Bundesamt für Migration und Flüchtlinge.

Hobbes, Th. (2010 [1651]). *Leviathan or the matter, forme, & power of a commonwealth ecclesiasticall and civill.* New Haven: Yale University Press (reprint).

Huber, W. (1999). *Kirche in der Zeitenwende. Gesellschaftlicher Wandel und Erneuerung der Kirche.* Gütersloh: Gütersloher Verlagshaus.

Jahn, S. (2011). Gefängnisseelsorge in der Bundesrepublik Deutschland. In M. Klöcker et al. (Ed.), *Handbuch der Religionen* (pp. 1–31.). Landsberg/Lech: Olzog.

Jahn, S. J. (2013). Religiöses Feld im rechtlichen Raum: Religion im Strafvollzug. In P. Antes et al. (Ed.), *Konflikt - Integration - Religion. Religionswissenschaftliche Perspektiven* (pp. 121–137.). Göttingen: V&R unipress.

Jahn, S. J. (2014). Zur (Un-)Möglichkeit „islamischer Seelsorge" im deutschen Justizvollzug. *Cibedo-Beiträge,* (1), 20–25.

Jähnichen, T. (2010). Caritas und Diakonie im „goldenen Zeitalter" des Sozialstaates. Auf- und Umbrüche in den konfessionellen Wohlfahrtsverbänden in den 1960er Jahren. In T. Jähnichen (Ed.), *Caritas und Diakonie im „goldenen Zeitalter" des bundesdeutschen Sozialstaats. Transformationen der konfessionellen Wohlfahrtsverbände in den 1960er Jahren* (pp. 11–14). Stuttgart: Kohlhammer.

Kehrer, G. (1982). *Organisierte religion.* Stuttgart: W. Kohlhammer.

Kollman, P. (2011). At the origins of mission and missiology: A study in the dynamics of religious language. *Journal of the American Academy of Religion, 79*(2), 425–458.

Mayring, Ph (2010). *Qualitative Inhaltsanalyse. Grundlagen und Techniken.* Weinheim: Beltz.

Montesquieu, Ch.-L. (2006 [1748]). *The spirit of laws.* Cambridge et al., University Press (reprint).

Robbers, G. (2001). Religious freedom in Germany. *Brigham Young University Review,* (2), 643–668.

Schmitt, Th. (2012). Mosque debates as space-related, intercultural, and religious conflicts. In B. Becker-Cantarino (Ed.), *Migration, religion, and Germany* (pp. 207–217). Amsterdam: Rodopi.

Scott, W. R. (1999). *Institutions and organizations.* Thousand Oaks: Sage.

Sen, A. (1982). *Choice, welfare, and measurement.* Cambridge, Mass.: MIT Press.

Stark, R., & Finke, R. (2000). *Acts of faith. Explaining the human side of religion.* Berkeley: University of California Press.

Sullivan, W. F. (2005). *The impossibility of religious freedom.* Princeton, NJ: Princeton University Press.

Sullivan, W. F. (2009). *Prison religion. Faith-based reform and the constitution.* Princeton: Princeton University Press.

Sykes, G. M. (2003). *The society of captives. A study of a maximum security prison.* New York: Princeton Paperbacks.

Torpey, J., & Joppke, C. (2013). *Legal integration of Islam: A transatlantic comparison.* Berlin: De Gruyter.

# Internet Resources

Caritas Germany. (2014). Caritas as employer. http://www.caritas.de/fuerprofis/arbeitenbeidercaritas/arbeitgebercaritas/caritasalsarbeitgeber.aspx. Accessed 22 Feb 2014.

Christliches Missionswerk Josua. (2014). About us. http://www.missionswerkjosua.de/ueber-uns. Accessed 29 Sep 2014.

German press agency. (2014). Quarrel in Islam forum. http://www.berlin.de/aktuelles/berlin/3251308-958092-krach-um-muslimische-seelsorge-islamforu.html. Accessed 13 Aug 2014.

Justizministerium Niedersachsen. (2012): Justice Minister Busemann signed agreement between the Muslim associations and the Ministry of Justice. http://www.mj.niedersachsen.de/portal/live.php?navigation_id=3745&article_id=111512&_psmand=1. Accessed 13 Aug 2014.

MUSE Wiesbaden. (2014). About us. http://muse-wiesbaden.de/. Accessed 13 Aug 2014.

Schnell, L. (2014). From prison to jihad: Islamists seek supporters among German inmates. http://www.spiegel.de/international/germany/islamists-seek-support-in-german-prisons-a-978720.html. Accessed 13 Aug 2014.

Stadtstaat Hamburg. (2014): Contract Hamburg. http://www.hamburg.de/contentblob/3551370/data/download-muslim-verbaende.pdf. Accessed 13 Aug 2014.

White House Office and Faith-Based and Community Organizations. (2014) The initiative from the president, available via http://www.whitehouse.gov/government/fbci/president-initiative.html. Accessed 3 Mar 2014.

## Legal Texts

Basic Law for the Federal Republic of Germany in the revised version published in the Federal Law Gazette Part III, classification number 100–1, as last amended by the Act of 21 July 2010 (Federal Law Gazette I p. 944).

Act concerning the execution of prison sentences and measures of rehabilitation and prevention involving deprivation of liberty (Federal Law Gazette I p. 2425; the translation includes the amendment(s) to the Act by Article 4 of the Act of 5.12.2012).

## Translation

Original German quotes and transcriptions are the author's literal translations.

# Chapter 7
# Addressing Religious Differences in Italian Prisons: A Postsecular Perspective

Valeria Fabretti

## 7.1 Introduction

The central topic of this book, that is, the challenges that new religious diversity is addressing to prison employees, inmates, and the institution itself all over Europe, is increasingly an issue in Italy. Although the responsiveness to such challenges is still insufficient, the changes in the ethnic, cultural, and religious composition of the inmate population, with almost 35 % of foreign people, as well as the pressure from the European Union for a general enhancement of the recognition of religious rights and pluralism within the member states, represent relevant factors requiring major attention from our country towards the topic. At least partially, a new collective awareness of the need for institutional cultures and practices more sensitive to the issues linked with different religious belongings is arising, and it regards the case of prisons as well as other relevant public spaces (such as schools and hospitals).

Although it is beginning to be a field of study for social sciences, the topic is still poorly explored. The contributions on the case of prison, in particular, are still few in numbers[1]. In contrast, a quite consistent tradition of study is taking root, with regard to the examination of the different systems implemented in other European countries and their recent inner changes, mostly on the steps of the well-known first works of Beckford and colleagues (Beckford and Gilliat-Ray 1998; Beckford

---

[1] Irene Becci's reflection on the transformations of rehabilitation with respect to religion and of the inmates' spiritual life considers Italy in comparison with East Germany and Switzerland (Becci 2011, 2012). Mohammed Khalid Rhazzali explores the presence of Islam in prisons, with a more exclusive focus on the subjective dimension of the prisoners and their beliefs and practices (Rhazzali 2010).

---

V. Fabretti (✉)
Department 'Scienze e Tecnologie della Formazione' (STF) and 'Centre for the Study and Documentation of Religions and Political Institutions in Postsecular Society' (CSPS), University of Rome Tor Vergata, Rome, Italy
e-mail: valeria.fabretti@uniroma2.it

© Springer International Publishing Switzerland 2015                                           101
I. Becci, O. Roy (eds.), *Religious Diversity in European Prisons,*
DOI 10.1007/978-3-319-16778-7_7

et al. 2005). As this volume attests, such studies suggest that despite the differences between cases, a common attempt is taking place to widen the boundaries between states and religions, to allow the inclusion of both traditional and "new" denominations, and to make this inclusion compatible with the rooted secularization models of each society and the pursuit of the prisons' own institutional goals.

In other words, the various scenarios drafted by the national reconstructions attested in the past, and still attested in more recent years, that prisons must be considered as exemplary social spaces able to reflect the features of the broader (old and new) relations between the secular and the religious in given societies, on the one hand, and to generate new models through the dynamism of the local level, on the other hand. We approach the Italian case from this starting point and provide knowledge that will further advance the topic.

In this chapter,[2] I briefly clarify, at first, the theoretical frame and design of the research. Second, and in a more extensive way, I highlight the main findings, with particular attention to some of the crucial areas of prison life supposed to be engaged with religious issues. To conclude, I attempt to clarify how our findings can provide a general understanding of the current situation in Italy.[3]

## 7.2  Prisons as Postsecular Spaces? How We Looked at the Italian Case

Three broad sociological premises guided our study. First, religion remains a central factor in today's collective life, despite what is learned from simplistic secularization theories. Second, it is increasingly clear that its importance goes beyond the private and the individual: Religion concerns collective identities and groups within the public, social, and political spheres (Casanova 1994; Davie 2007). The third sociological condition is the increase in religious pluralism in Western, European societies (to keep to our ground), which contributes to the overcoming of monopolistic situations by the part of one or more religions in particular. Such a "picture" has much to do with the idea of a *postsecular society*, which is the notion we used

---

[2] I dedicate this essay to the memory of Massimo Rosati (1969–2014). Massimo was a friend, most of all, and the colleague I had the pleasure of collaborate with at the centre he established at the University of Rome Tor Vergata, the *Centre for the Study and Documentation of Religions and Political Institutions in Post-Secular Society* (CSPS). Massimo has unexpectedly and suddenly passed away in January 2014, leaving us too soon. His energy, creative ideas, and scientific work have been very inspiring for me and all of us who took part in the CSPS initiatives. The research project on religious assistance in prisons I am presenting in this chapter developed within the CSPS environment and under Massimo's direction. Although obviously under my full responsibility, these pages are the fruit of a reflection largely shared with him. To Massimo goes my deepest and endless gratitude.

[3] For a comprehensive analysis of the research findings, see Fabretti 2014. I have also tried to deepen, in particular, the mutual representations and relationships between secular and religious actors in: Fabretti 2015.

as a frame for our research. Taking into account the skepticisms about the suitability of using a postsecular framing to study religion in prison (Beckford 2010, 2012), the study wanted to test the usefulness of the notion in social sciences on both the theoretical and the methodological ground, moving beyond the attempt to clarify its main features. In our understanding of the postsecular,[4] it first refers to the three basic conditions mentioned above. In general terms, a postsecular society is characterized by a new awareness of the persistent and renewed public presence of religion, and the actual coexistence within the public sphere of secular and (*pluri*) religious worldviews and practices.[5] Generally speaking, the notion highlights a fourth crucial point: a "response" on behalf of Western modernity, *a change in mindset*, potentially resulting from those conditions. The postsecular refers not to desecularized contexts, but to contexts in which an increased consciousness about the dialectic, and not merely oppositional, relationship between the "religious" and the "secular" (Knott 2005) takes place. Dialectical relationships and "interpenetrations," (Göle 2005) in principle, raise the possibility of new configurations of both secular and religious viewpoints and practices (Rosati and Stoekl 2012). In this sense, the capacity of secular and religious actors to be reflexive and to bring their own logics in dialogue is assumed, and mutual transformation or—in the well-known expression of Habermas (2006a)—*complementary learning* is expected to potentially be triggered.[6]

According to these premises, the study is primarily concerned with the responses of penal institutions, rather than the inmates' personal religious and spiritual experience.[7] We considered prisons as social spaces in which one can recognize the reflexes of broader social features. Here, our focus goes on two main points: consolidated models of secularization and views of the secular and the religious on the one hand and impacts of religious collective dimension and of religious pluralism on the institution on the other hand. Moreover, we consider prisons as a potential

---

[4] The understanding of the notion of the postsecular that we developed is obviously derived from a deep scrutiny of the existing literature, but it does not overlap completely with any other concept. Among the main references: Casanova 1994; Knott 2005; Habermas 2006a, 2006b; Molendijk et al. 2010. The following brief clarification is in substantial agreement with the meaning of postsecular proposed, in particular, by Massimo Rosati. Consider mainly: Rosati and Stoeckl 2012; Rosati 2015.

[5] The postsecular also refers to the presence of a marked difference between secular and religious traditions with regard to the dimension of *the sacred*, that has an immanent and civil form in the first case, and a heteronomous transcendental form in the second (Rosati and Stoeckl 2012).

[6] Using this formula Habermas (2006a, p. 258 ->A or B) defines the postsecular as a process engaging religious and secular social actors in a dialogue through which "both sides can, for cognitive reasons, (…) seriously take into account each other's contributions regarding controversial themes in the public sphere." Complementary learning is required for secular and religious actors to practice the virtue of epistemic humility; secular groups do it in the name of public reason, while religiously oriented groups do it in the name of a "principled tolerance" (see on this point: Seligman 2004).

[7] Contributions focused on the latter issue, concerning different cases, including Italy: again, Becci (2011, 2012) and Rhazzali (2010). See also the research project by Céline Béraud, Claire de Galembert and Corinne Rostaing, *La religion en prison au prisme d'une sociologie de l'action*.

reflex signaling an increase in awareness and in the capacity of institutional actors to address religious issues in a secular environment.

## 7.2.1 Indications on the Methodology Adopted and Research Questions

The one year research project[8] has provided multiple case studies, examining 10 of the 14 institutes existing in the Italian region of Lazio, a territory in which the percentage of foreign inmates is very close to the national average. Within the ten cases,[9] a consistent document analysis, and more than 100 focused interviews with secular and religious actors (directors, educators, guards, psychologists, cultural mediators, volunteers, and obviously chaplains and representatives of the different traditions engaged in religious assistance) have been carried out. A first general aim was to look at how the actors understand the role and space of religion in prison, followed by an attempt to systematically reconstruct the practices of religious assistance and to focus on how they take shape accordingly to actors' representations. Moreover, according to the postsecular perspective, a particular point was relevant. Is the changing social scenario—the increasing religious pluralism and visibility of the different religious groups and demands in the Italian public sphere and institutional spaces—somehow soliciting prisons to better address the new challenges? Do shared practices, mutual exchanges, reflexivity, and complementary learning somehow occur in a space in which secular-institutional and pluri-religious identities are increasingly cohabiting? And finally, which conditions are necessary in order to trigger this kind of dialectic process? As it will become clear with regard to some of the crucial areas of religious assistance we focused on, this positive development has yet to be measured. At least in the cases under investigation, this positive development is hindered by certain limitations and delays: in particular, a still weak pluralistic culture and a tendency to treat religion as a purely private matter.

---

[8] The project has received the financial support by the part of the Lazio regional administration and the Lazio Guarantor for detainees' rights.

[9] The correction facilities taken into consideration are quite different in terms of territory (centre/periphery), dimensions, and number of detainees (big/medium/small size prisons). With regards the typology, the majority of the prisons refers to the category of "*Casa circondariale*," mostly hosting inmates still waiting for the assignment of punishment and/or having received a short term sentence. Only one female prison is included, and in the other cases, the presence of female detainees was strongly limited. For more detailed indications concerning the features of the cases investigated, see the methodological notes in Fabretti 2014.

## 7.3    Religion in the Communication Between Institutions and Inmates

First, we considered the space of religion as a category within the information and communication processes involving prisons and inmates. We observed which procedures prisons follow in the very first phase of the inmates' entrance in the institution—those crucial rituals of imprisonment notoriously described by Goffman (1961)—and the meanings the employees give to such practices. Both "sides of the coin" need to be identified. On one side, it is relevant to find out whether the staff collects data on inmates' religious belonging at the moment they enter the prison, or if they collect this data during the rehabilitation process later on. On the other side, we also need to observe whether religion comes into consideration when inmates are told of their rights and of the possibilities that are available to them during imprisonment. With regard to both points, religion reveals to be *not* a relevant variable in the way institutions relate to detainees. Inmates' religious belonging is usually not recorded, neither at their entrance into prison, nor later on during the rehabilitation programs given by educators, psychologists, and social workers. Intentional and ordinary communications to inmates about their rights concerning religion is substantially lacking, too. Prison personnel assume that this type of information circulates informally among the inmates: They can find it autonomously in the internal regulations, or they can ask prison guards on a personal basis. On the whole, we did not find significant differences among the ten cases we studied.

These two insufficiencies regarding religion in the communication process reflect something more than contingent oversights. As the analysis of the interview transcripts brought to the fore, they are signals of a largely widespread idea that religion is a "very personal and intimate dimension" (an educator), "something that one feels inside" (a social worker). We did not record significant divergences between the employees' points of view regarding this concern. Religion is basically represented as "a private affair" which finds its place in the individual request more than in the official vocabulary of the institutions. In many cases, educators, security agents, and social workers admit that they consider it to be inopportune to ask questions about religion in their conversations with inmates. Such a tendency is often legitimized by the prison personnel by referring to a professional ethic inspired by strict "neutrality" and "respectfulness" toward the inmates' personal differences.

> For me the inmates are all equal regardless of their religious belonging. I do not distinguish on the basis of religion, unless it's brought to my attention…otherwise I prefer not to inquire about what kind of religion they practice. (An educator)

They argued that they needed to limit their own intervention on the theme, as they considered it to be sufficient to simply respond to prisoners when they eventually demanded for religious services and possibilities.

> We don't go and tell them "you can require for [religion assistance]", we never intervene in these matters, it doesn't seem right for me to do it. I mean, we absolutely do not intend to apply pressure, neither positive nor negative. If there's something they need they will ask for it but I don't solicit a request from them, it is a matter of respect for those who

don't practice religion. (...) I fear they may feel attending worships is somehow a duty, for example. (...) I think one should have a secular orientation towards religion, so to speak. It means not to interfere and therefore to only eventually respond to their requests, and this certainly applies for all. (A prison director)

This is a first crucial result. The influence of such a representation on practices of communication with inmates tends to hinder a systematic implementation of religious assistance, prior to possible requests by single inmates. In fact, if knowledge about the plural religious affiliations is precluded (indeed prison directors and staff often do not seem to "have their pulse on the situation" about it), it can be assumed that the consequent planning of services for religious care is precluded too. And if the communication to inmates of their religious right is limited, the availability of information enabling inmates to access the existing religious services may be limited, too. Under these conditions, the visibility of the different religious groups mostly depends on the evidence of their demands and, in turn, the rising of requests derives in a large part on the clearness of the offer (e.g., highlighting information about the presence of a certain religious minister in many cases determines an increase of inmates requiring his assistance). In other terms, the blurring of the category of religion in the communication process between prison and inmates is likely to induce a narrowing of the overall process of religious care. In very recent years, something might be partially in progress about this point. The Italian Minister of Justice has adopted a "Charter of Rights'" which, in principle, is aimed at a more explicit and effective communication to inmates. Significantly, however, the document still reserves only minimal consideration to religious rights and services. It limits the argument to the sole "right to benefit from the Catholic Chaplain' spiritual care and to take part in the religious rites in the catholic chapels or in spaces arranged for worships of other denominations."[10] Whatever the specific forms of communication that prisons adopt, the point relative to a conscious and systematic communication appears crucial, both as a test of cultural maturation of the institution, and for its potential impact in making the demand of religious assistance emerge.

### 7.3.1 The Chaplaincy

The history of the chaplaincy in Italy is strongly linked to the religious history of the country and to its largely Catholic composition. Although profound changes are affecting the Italian religious landscape, with a gradual pluralization of affiliations, and although Italian jurisdiction on religious freedom and assistance in prison has significantly changed from the thirties to the present,[11] the position of monopoly traditionally held by Catholicism in penitentiaries remains substantially unchanged. It is true that the process of secularization, touching prisons like other

---

[10] The document is published on the Italian minister of justice official web site: http://www.giustizia.it.

[11] A crucial step was signed in 1975 by the Law 354/1975, which for the first time recognized the detainees' rights to faith and worship.

social institutions, has resulted in the removal of functions traditionally granted to the chaplain, referring among other things to rehabilitation and custody. However, it is also true that, as can be observed in some other European cases, chaplaincy still plays (a more or less explicit) role in the organization of prison life and in the sphere of "control."

According to prison regulations (DPR n. 230/2000), Catholic worship, education, and spiritual care are secured by one or more chaplains entrusted by prison administration. In every correction facility, a Catholic chaplain paid by the state works for about 18 h a week, equipped with an office and a chapel.

In the cases we have studied, religious practices associated with Catholicism depended mostly on factors such as the individual personality of the chaplain, his habits and routines, and the resources—temporal and spatial, but also human, economic, etc.—available to him. These aspects vary significantly from prison to prison and contribute to delineating a variety of chaplaincy "styles." In most cases, the chaplains guarantee regular visits, but concentrate on one or another of their duties, according to their personal understanding of chaplaincy: These range from economic and material to human and relational support, in addition to specifically spiritual and religious forms of support. In the prisons in Rome especially, the chaplain runs a well-structured support group of volunteers coming from the Catholic community (priests, nuns, lay volunteers, etc.). Overall, the chaplaincy possesses a certain autonomy. A reliance on the chaplain's space for action—more than that enjoyed by other religious figures—is part of the particularly close relation between him and the direction or, in general, the prison staff. As for penal institutions, they seem to delegate to (or "capitalize on") the chaplaincy to make up for the structural lack of resources when responding to the various needs of inmates.

Catholic chaplains only partially participate to, and facilitate, the management of religious and spiritual care for other religions. On the whole, the chaplains we met tended to consider the implementation of spiritual care of different religions mainly on the basis of the relations historically established between the Church and these other religious traditions. From what we observed, these included a positive orientation towards Orthodox religious ministers, a minor involvement in the services of protestant ministers, a certain tension with Jehovah's Witnesses, and a lack of links with Muslim communities. Such inequalities in Chaplains' facilitations of other denominations is likely to be detrimental to their potential contribution to a more balanced estimation of the different needs associated with religious care.

In Italy as in various European countries, a gradual rethinking of prison chaplaincy, in the extent to which its composition is representative to the inmates' religious belongings, is at stake. It is particularly interesting to have a look at the cases of the UK and France, which started with a similar situation of monopoly by one or more religious groups, and gradually grew into an openness and inclusiveness of Chaplaincy towards other traditions. These processes have of course been the object of controversies and conflicts. They nevertheless bear witness to the fact that institutions can have relevant capability in interpreting and governing social changes.

## 7.3.2    Ministers and Services of "Other Religions"

According to the Italian legal frame, ministers of other religions can give assistance in response to specific requests from one or more inmates. Chaplains gain their access on three formal levels. First, specific agreements (*Intese*) between religious communities and the state allow representatives of some religions to enter the prison without any control. This was the case of Jewish and Protestant communities during the period of our field work. A second possibility is to have a state permission for specific requests, which is subject to strict control by prison central authorities, as is the case of Imams or Jehovah's Witnesses. Finally, religious groups can rely on a specific article of the Penitentiary Regulation,[12] which allows contributions by external actors in rehabilitation approved by each prison autonomously. This was the way in which, for example, Buddhists could offer their services in the prisons we studied. At the time of our research, inequalities and unbalanced distribution of power and autonomy between religious actors largely affected this system. The recent extension of the agreements with the Orthodox, Buddhist, and Hindu communities[13] is likely to partially change the situation soon.

The study of different religious actors' perspectives and practices in prison has taken a large place in the fieldwork research, in which many pieces of evidence useful in understanding the overall features of the Italian case have been collected.

In the ten prisons, the ordinary visits by non-Catholic ministers were quite limited. The majority of the ministers we met were Jehovah's Witnesses (33), Protestants (6), and Orthodox Christians (4). Remarkably, especially considering the significant number of Muslim inmates, no Imams were seen to provide regular religious care for extended periods, although they were present during Ramadan in some cases. The shortage of official Imams actually encourages "secondary paths," often informal and out of the prison's control, of spiritual care for the many Muslim inmates (e.g., inmate leaders or cultural mediators who act as Imams or providers for strictly religious needs). It also proves unhelpful in dealing with issues of security and risks of proselytism and fundamentalism, which represent priorities in the eyes of the Italian penal administration. Furthermore, there is a clear difference in Lazio between the "center" and the "periphery." Prisons in Rome, like "Rebibbia" and "Regina Coeli," are part of an urban reality which offers a diversified and vital framework of religious and secular organizations, they present a more consistent set of initiatives compared with prisons located in provincial areas.

On the whole, as for the case of Chaplains, ministers of other religions interpret religious assistance differently and largely accordingly to their own tradition. We can distinguish between: a *relational care*, based on the priority of human contact; *spiritual care*, i.e., guidance in a personal itinerary aiming at interior growth; *pas-*

---

[12] Law 354/75, Article 17.

[13] Agreements are currently in place with the Valdensian Church, the Assemblies of God in Italy, the union of Seventh-day Adventist church, the union of Jewish Communities, the Christian Evangelical Baptist union and the Lutheran Evangelical Church, the Orthodox Archdiocese, the LDS (Mormon) Church, the Apostolic Church, the Buddhist Italian Union, and the Hindu one.

*toral/catechetic care*, teaching inmates about the founding principles of a religious system; and a *legal/religious care*, concerning required behavior in conditions of reclusion with respect to religious rules. In adherence to the consideration of the collective dimension of religions, we assumed that practices linked to the latter and more "visible" area of assistance would have a particularly strong impact on the institutional dimension of the prison. The celebration of rituals, the respect of liturgical calendars, and of the different rules in everyday life, makes manifest the presence of the different religious identities, while on the other hand, the personal, human, even spiritual affair between the inmates and the single ministers may instead stay hidden. It is evident that, when approached with requests by ministers and/or inmates linked to the respect of the legal dimension of religion, prison actors show major difficulties. It is in these cases that they are mostly forced on finding a balance between religious assistance and the rules and routines within the prison.

Evidence about the latter aspect can be found when considering the forms that relationships between different religious and secular actors take. According to the analysis of the narratives that emerged in the interviews, four ideal-typical forms of relationships can be drafted.

The first is *misrecognition*. Even when their entrance and service is facilitated by the agreement with the state, as in the case of Protestants, religious ministers often disclosed that they are made to feel "transparent" in the eyes of the institutions, which as a result creates a feeling of isolation and loneliness. They receive no guidelines or instructions from the administration, no—at least no systematic— information about the inmates, and no proposals of involvement in meetings or decision-making bodies. Moreover, prison directors are sometimes not even aware of the exact number of religious ministers present in their institutions, neither the religious denomination they belong to, nor the activities they are engaged in. This is what we mean by "misrecognition"; not some form of harsh and explicit refusal, but rather a soft and silent marginalization. Moreover, as noticed above, a sort of mutual misrecognition—or more simply, a "disconnection"—is apparent between the prisons, especially those in the periphery, and the local Islamic communities.

A second form is *accommodation*. In this broad category, we find, on the one hand, forms of instrumentalization, by prisons, of religious groups and services; and, on the other, attempts of adaptation—mixed to underground practices of "resistance"—by religious representatives. This point needs to be briefly clarified. Religion is most commonly categorized as part of the rehabilitation process by prisons staff. Considering the Quran or Buddhist meditation to be something that can relax and relieve possible forms of conflict is a representation quite widely believed. Therefore, staff responds positively to requests from religious groups, in part due to calculations of the utility of religion in terms of control. For their part, numerous members of religious groups seem to accept this attitude for instrumental reasons. Buddhists, for example, tend not to be recognized as religious groups but rather as cultural or recreational ones. Nevertheless, they do provide religious services. More generally, religious actors are aware of the need to compromise and to accommodate their service to the institution's requirements. They are adapting to the ways that their own religion is viewed in a basically Catholic context, while in actuality they are maintaining their identity (Fabretti 2015).

A third form of relationship is *conflict*. A certain intra-Christian antagonism, in relation to religious assistance in prisons, mostly involves Chaplains and Jehovah's Witnesses (but also Protestants in some cases). Other strands of relational friction can be identified, for example, the case of Islam (e.g., controversies between a director and a cultural mediator—informally acting as Imam—on the use of a space for Friday prayer). However, in these and similar circumstances, no explicit forms of real conflict have resulted, and this is another relevant element. The absence of conflicts seems to largely stem from the general efforts of prison administration and staff to establish a climate of moderation and "benevolence." This attitude reflects a common feature in Italian institutional behavior, which has roots not only in a Catholic legacy but also in a wider culture, characterized by what Max Weber has called an "ethic of brotherliness" (1920). This ethos, despite its virtuous effect in reaching compromises on a daily basis, actually prevents opportunities for direct and genuine confrontations *on* and *between* diversities. By calming latent conflicts, the ethic of brotherliness deprives prisons of the enhanced reflexivity and awareness that could potentially be gained through the "disruptive" visibility of religious groups in public spaces (Göle 2011).

Following a postsecular perspective, we also focused on the potential relational form of *cooperation*. The month of Ramadan, which is generally respected in the prisons we observed, can be taken as a good point in case. Its organization often involves Islamic communities, prison staff, and Catholic chaplains and volunteers, and is stimulated by administrative policies. Other situations suggest that spontaneous and "bottom-up" forms of cooperation can also take place. The celebration of the baptism of an inmate converted to Protestantism, for example, was an opportunity for the religious actors and the prison staff (especially guards) to interact, to know each other better, and join their services in prison. However, the examples of cooperation stand out from an overall picture in which, as highlighted above, a sort of minimal harmony prevails. While conflicts tend to be avoided, real experiences of working together, side by side, are also uncommon. Relationships between religious actors and prison staff (including Catholic chaplains) were mostly marked by politeness and respect, but strictly speaking, that cannot be understood as cooperation.

As the following paragraphs shall elaborate, taken together, these features indicate that a distance still exists between the current situation in Italian prisons and proper dialectical relationships and interpenetrations between the "religious" and the "secular" potentially arising in a postsecular space.

### 7.3.3  Spaces for Worship and Prayer

A third area of findings regards the presence and the use of spaces for worship and prayer. The topic is particularly relevant according to the research framework. The spatial dimension is becoming increasingly important after the so-called "spatial turn" (Lefebvre 1991), and studies within the field of the science of religion have shown how "spatialization" is a central category to understanding religious phenomena and the interaction between the secular and the religious (Knott 2005).[14] Furthermore, overcoming a purely Christian-centered understanding of religion in a pluralistic context implies that space, as well as the body (see further on), must be duly taken into consideration. Moreover, the sacred spaces have their own "grammar" (Rosati 2012). They answer to specific rules and characteristics, which are different for each tradition.

In other words, there are different options for the use of spaces, which indicate different levels of recognition of the right to worship by the institution. In principle, it makes a difference if the prison provides inmates with dedicated spaces for their religious practice, if it organizes multi-faith spaces, if it offers gym areas or theater spaces to perform sacred liturgies, or, if the prison foresees the exclusive use of catholic chapels to accommodate the needs of inmates from other religious backgrounds, if the space of the cell represents the only space devoted to prayer, and so on. All these possibilities represent solutions that indicate a different awareness by the institution, and a different capability of implementing religious assistance in prison.

In the ten prisons we studied, Catholic chapels are largely available. In several cases, the detainees themselves have contributed to the renovation and decoration of these spaces; in other cases, the setting of the chapels has been enriched thanks to contributions from external organizations. Moreover, in some cases, meaningful locations in the architecture of the prison are reserved to chapels, as in the historical facility in Rome, *Regina Coeli*. Here, the chapel represents the central space and, so to speak, the "heart" of the overall panoptical structure.[15] It is evidently an environment characterized by Catholic symbolism, which fully appropriates its sacred dimension at the time of Sunday Mass and other Catholic celebrations.

On the contrary, the spaces for non-Catholic worships appear to be few and not properly suitable. We found, in one case, a pleasant area available to Buddhists for their meditation. This space was in fact organized into two rooms, one in the men's section and one in the female section. The preparation of the space was carried out with care, according to the indications of the religious community, including the presence of the appropriate sacred objects necessary for religious worship.

In two other prisons, small rooms (even cells) have been made available for Friday prayers, or explicitly set up as mosques. The rooms have been arranged, in these cases, by Muslims inmates, who have set them up, albeit minimally, with prayer mats, copies of the Quran, and writings on the walls. Within the other prisons, non-Catholic worship usually takes place in the chapels and prayer within the cells, or in improvised spaces ordinarily used for social and rehabilitative activities.

---

[14] The centrality given to the "localization" of religion (multi-faith prayer spaces in institutional environments of various kinds), which reflects the application of the "spatial turn" area of sociology of religion, is evident, for example, in the fieldwork of Gilliat-Ray (2005a, 2005b).

[15] As is well known, the significance of the Panopticon, designed by Jeremy Bentham in 1791, as an architecture consonant to the idea of control over individuals and bodies was fully caught by Foucault (1975). Moreover, the Panopticon attests to the centrality of religion—Catholicism—in determining the structure of old penitentiaries.

Significantly, it is largely with regard to the use of spaces that we could measure the religious actors' relational approaches that I described in the previous paragraph. The ministers' attitude to adaptation was present when, for example, Orthodox ministers ordinarily used Catholic chapels for their rites, as we observed in many prisons. Practices of "resistance" and silent protest were also present: One of those ministers was used to bringing his icons with him and arranging them around the space of the Chapel, trying to approximate what a sacred space should look like in his own tradition. Even conflicts were observed: For example, a cultural mediator and some Muslim inmates' of a peripheral prison were expressing their request for a mosque by persistently celebrating the Friday prayer in outdoor spaces, even under the rain.

As is well known, in Italy, prison administration is facing severe problems, such as the degradation of many penitentiaries and dramatic overcrowding. And, according to the prisons staff, the inmates are often aware of the severe structural deficiencies of buildings, so that, in many cases, their potential demand for the use of spaces remains unexpressed. At the same time, those who most frequently cross the corridors of the sections, especially prison officers or volunteers, attest that prisons are places in which people often pray. Alternatively to the institutional provision of formal spaces, cells or areas for rehabilitation become sacred spaces where collective prayers fit in both ordinary life and in specific times of the liturgical calendars.

However, at least in principle, in light of the structural limitations of Italian prisons, it is relevant to consider the criteria taken into consideration in the assignment of the few spaces available for the various activities; such criteria reflect the importance accorded to the different needs and rights of the inmates. As we know, significant examples of a deeper recognition of religious pluralism through the managing of space in prison—as in other public spaces—can be found in Europe (Gilliat-Ray 2005a, 2005b).

## 7.4 Diets and the Body

Respect for precepts concerning food is, in certain traditions especially, an essential aspect of religious observance. In the research project, the issue has been considered in its capacity of making religious differences explicit and in questioning prison's ordinary life.

Special diets according to religions are, at least in principle, an element of religious assistance that has been recognized and implemented promptly in Italian prisons. The penitentiary administration itself has, in recent decades, supported the creation of a system we can now define as "standard." In all the prisons studied, in fact, the service is available to those inmates requesting it. On the whole, the request for specific menus mostly comes from Muslim inmates; as it can be expected, the demand increases during the period of Ramadan. If we consider social representations spread among prison staff and, in particular, within the guards of the prison service, the religious observance of Muslim prisoners, which is expressed in differentiated demand for food, is often categorized as "fundamentalism." This categorization bears witness to a substantial misunderstanding of the very nature of Islam. At the same time, the efforts put in place, by the employees of the kitchen, for the organization of this service reveal some care and diligence.

However, the findings also indicate certain critical points concerning the ways in which prisons are implementing dietary respect. First of all, procedures followed to collect the inmates' requests for this service are quite "informal." Directors are seldom aware of the dimensions and the type of demand that exists in their prison. In many institutions, the issue is dealt with at an operational and "pragmatic" level, in the kitchens. Second, a cuisine that adheres properly to religious traditions tends to be totally absent, like *halal* for Islam or *kosher* for the Jewish tradition. Such proper interpretations of religious diets would require specific procedures for the butchering of the animals and would imply strict controls for correct preparation of the food by religious authorities. In this sense, they would lead prisons to have a more systematic interaction with external religious communities. On the ground we notice the contrary, as the provision of alternative menu is carried out following ministerial tables which indicate the types of food to be considered admissible for different religious traditions, or, vice versa, to be avoided. Therefore, the prevalent mechanism is the substitution of foods (e.g., cheese instead of pork meat).

In brief, the solution used in the visited prisons for the respect of religious dietary rules does not seem to represent an answer that fully recognizes the strict connection between religion and food. Although the service promptly responds to the inmates' requests, it assumes the shape of a minimal symbolic acceptance of the issue.

It leads, in closing, to another point, which has been taken into consideration in the reconstruction of prisons' practices of religious care. A similar underestimation by the part of institutions regards the link—also crucial—between religion and the body. In this regard, as it is well known, there are a number of factors which religious traditions tend to regulate strictly: e.g., hygiene, illness, sexuality, death. However, during the investigation, such a link emerged to a very limited extent. Overall, members of the prisons' staff did not perceive it as an issue on the basis of their own experience, but there were a number of exceptions. Traces of frictions between religious care of the body and prison regulations concerned for example: availability of showers, often not responding to Muslims' hygienic norms; ignorance, on the part of direction and medical staff, about religious precepts in relation to medical treatment and cases of controversies and difficult "mediations" with inmates; difficulties in responding to "individualized" treatments, also on a religious basis, because of a lack of medical staff, etc. Despite such examples, findings clearly indicate that the religious significance of the body's care remains a "grey area." It can probably be explained only recalling that, as stressed above, religion tends to be considered as mainly an interior and spiritual issue. By cutting off bodies and practices (the spatial and public dimension as well), religion is reduced to an intimate dialogue between the believer and his own God.

## 7.5   Conclusive Remarks

Religion in prison appears as a topic not only relevant per se but also as an "exemplar" topic that helps us understand current dynamics between religions and society as a whole. Generally speaking, this analysis has illustrated some ways in which religious pluralism impacts prison's institutional life. If we look at the topic through a lens focusing on the collective and public dimensions of religion, numerous challenges emerge. It is also clear that the solicited changes must come to terms with national jurisdictions as much as with established broad social representations and with local, institutional cultures. From this point of view, it seems appropriate to question the way in which the postsecular frame can help in a critical reading of the case.

We conceived the postsecular as a sociological category with heuristic value, which cannot be addressed in abstract terms. Features and conditions of an ideal-typical postsecular society are empirical features of several Western societies, but their combination and ability to trigger out processes of complementary learning—or instead, their absence and/or ineffectiveness—must be analyzed in relation to specific contexts. In other words, the concept allows not so much to give a diagnostic of the state of accomplished realities but rather allows us to identify the local makings of those processes which, according to the sociological conditions mentioned above (the persistent centrality of religion in contemporary societies, the relevance of its collective dimension, the increase of religious pluralism determining situations of coexistences in the public sphere), can trigger new and multiple interpretations of modernity (Eisenstadt 2003; Rosati and Stoekle 2012): These include practices, negotiations and agreements, forms of relationships, representations of public and private life, and so on. Looking at the European context, we can certainly find examples of systematic facilitations of pluri-religious assistance that allows forms of real cooperation between secular and religious actors.

According to the results of the cases under examination, in Italy, a considerable gap still seems to exist between the sociological dimension of the postsecular and the potentially virtuous move towards mutual understanding, awareness, reflexivity, and change. According to our findings, the gap can be read in light of at least three crucial factors. The first concerns the legal frame and the unequal status of the various religions providing assistance. In this sense, for example, the extension of chaplaincy to non-Catholic denominations constitutes a necessary future step. However, a more egalitarian accommodation of religions in relation to Italian state institutions probably requires, in turn, a growth of religious pluralism in the overall society, which is to be taken as a crucial sociological prerequisite to the progress of its juridical recognition. The second and the third reasons have to do with cultural processes affecting prison actors' approaches towards religious assistance. A widespread vision of religion as an individual issue, limited to the inmates' private sphere, implies an underestimation of the public and collective aspects of religions taken as a whole. Such a vision explains the lack of attention given to organizing and assuring religious facilities *prior to the emergence of a demand*. Here, we come to the third element. It cannot be said that the prison system, in its current conditions, is insensitive or incapable of positive reactions in the face of issues posed by religious assistance. However, prison policies seem to derive more from the intent to satisfy, case by case, the requests coming from inmates, rather than from deliberate, planned strategies of institutional implementation of the right to worship in a pluralist setting. Prison staff's approaches to religious assistance are inspired more by a type of paternalistic humanitarianism and by the "ethos of brotherhood" than by any conscious or intentional response to a mature culture of "the right to rite."

While guidelines for gradual change can be drawn by taking into consideration each of the areas of religious assistance involved,[16] we must be aware that "good practices" and specific innovations are also present in the Italian scenario, although they are not properly monitored yet.[17] Their presence shows how, looking at the case of prisons as an "exemplar," possibilities in "the making of a postsecular society"[18] are open in our country. They are not only dependent on juridical changes but also largely in the hands of secular and religious "creative" interactions at the local level.

# References

Becci, I. (2011). Religion's multiple locations in prison. *Archives de Sciences Sociales des Religions, 153*, 65–84.

Becci, I. (2012). *Imprisoned religion. Transformations of religion during and after Imprisonment in Eastern Germany*. Farnham: Ashgate.

Beckford, J. (2010). The uses of religion in public institutions: The case of prisons. In A. Molendijk, J. Beaumont, & C. Jedan (Eds.), *Exploring the postsecular: The religious, the political and the urban* (pp. 381–401). Leiden: Brill.

Beckford, J. (2012). Public religions and the postsecular: Critical reflections. *Journal for the Scientific Study of Religion, 51*(1), 1–19.

Beckford, J. A., & Gilliat-Ray, S. (1998). *Religion in prison*. Cambridge: Cambridge University Press.

Beckford, J. A., Joly, D., & Khosrokhavar, F. (2005). *Muslims in prison: Challenge and change in Britain and France*. Basingstoke: Macmillan Palgrave.

Casanova, J. (1994). *Public religions in the modern world*. Chicago: University of Chicago Press.

Davie, G. (2007). *The sociology of religion*. London: Sage.

Eisenstadt, S. N. (2003). *Comparative civilizations and multiple modernities* (Vol. 2). Leiden: Brill.

Fabretti, V. (2014). *Le differenze religiose in carcere. Culture e pratiche negli istituti di pena alla prova del pluralismo*. Rome: Universitalia.

---

[16] See "Conclusions" within Fabretti 2014a.

[17] Various agreements between prison authorities and Muslim communities at a local level have been put in place for the organization of Ramadan, including the cases we studied. Attempts for a more pluralistic configuration of the spaces of worship and prayer are arising, in "our" and other institutions. Moreover, one of the most notable cases of innovation, with virtuous impacts also on religious issues, is certainly the experimental penal and rehabilitative project implemented in the prison of Bollate, Milan.

[18] See Massimo Rosati's posthumous book, 2015.

Fabretti, V. (2015). Dealing with religious differences in Italian prisons: Relationships between institutions and communities from misrecognition to mutual transformation. *International Journal of Politics, Culture, and Society, 28*(1), 21–35.

Foucault, M. (1975). *Surveiller et punir: Naissance de la prison*. Paris: Gallimard.

Gilliat-Ray, S. (2005a). 'Sacralizing' sacred space in public institutions: A case study of the prayer space at the millennium dome. *Journal of Contemporary Religion, 20*(3), 357–72.

Gilliat-Ray, S. (2005b). From 'chapel' To 'prayer Room': The production, use, and politics of sacred space in public institutions. *Culture and Religion: An Interdisciplinary Journal, 6*(2), 287–308.

Goffman, E. (1961). *Asylums: Essays on the social situation of mental patients and other inmates*. New York: Anchor Books.

Göle, N. (2005). *Interpénétrations. L'Islam et l'Europe*. Paris: Galaade Éditions.

Göle, N. (2011). *The Disruptive Visibility of Islam in the European Public Space: Political Issues, Theoretical Questions*. Paper discussed at CSPS, University of Rome Tor Vergata, 28 April 2011.

Habermas, J. (2006a). On the relations between the secular liberal state and religion. In H. de Vries & L. E. Sullivan (Eds.), *Political theologies. Public religions in a post-secular world* (pp. 251–260). New York: Fordham University Press.

Habermas, J. (2006b). Religion in the public sphere. *European Journal of Philosophy, 14*(1), 1–25.

Knott, K. (2005). *The location of religion. A spatial analysis*. London: Equinox Publishing Ltd.

Lefebvre, E. (1991). *The production of space*. Oxford: Blackwell.

Molendijk, A., Beaumont, J., & Jedan, C. (Eds.). (2010). *Exploring the postsecular: The religious, the political and the urban*. Leiden: Brill.

Rhazzali, M. K. (2010). *L'Islam in carcere. L'esperienza religiosa dei giovani musulmani nelle prigioni italiane*. Milan: Franco Angeli.

Rosati, M. (2012). Postsecular sanctuaries. Towards a neo-Durkheimian grammar of sacred places. *Etnografia e ricerca qualitativa, 3*, 365–392.

Rosati, M. (2015). *The making of post-secular society. The Turkish laboratory*. Farnham: Ashgate.

Rosati, M., & Stoeckl, K. (2012). *Multiple modernities and postsecular societies*. Farnham: Ashgate.

Seligman, A. B. (2004). *Modest claims. Dialogues and essays on tolerance and tradition*. Notre Dame: University of Notre Dame Press.

Weber, M. (1988 [1920]). Zwischenbetrachtung. Theorie der Stufen und Richtungen religiöser Weltablehnung. In M. Weber (Ed.), *Gesammelte Aufsätze zur Religionssoziologie* (Vol. I, pp. 536–73). Tübingen: J.C.B. Mohr.

# Chapter 8
# Religious Care in the Reinvented European *Imamate* Muslims and Their Guides in Italian Prisons

Khalid M. Rhazzali

## 8.1 Introduction

My purpose, in this chapter, is to analyse the role of the Imam, whose figure is in a constant state of change, in the context of the religious care[1] provided to Muslims in Italian prisons[2]. In the prison environment, the figure of the Imam highlights

---

[1] The use of the term 'religious' care, instead of 'spiritual' care, is an intentional methodological choice. Both in the legislation on the topic and in other writings and conversations with the interlocutors consulted during this research study, all assume the two terms as synonymous. But I wish to keep the two terms as distinct, since we believe that the care that is provided by Muslim care providers is religious in that it refers to a precise and codified tradition (Sunnah), although within this there is a plurality, and it belongs to a group that is, at least symbolically, homogeneous (the Umma, or Islamic Community). Whereas the category of 'spiritual' (in the case of Islam, one would consider the Sufi tradition, and we found no instances of Sufi care providers in prison) refers to a relationship with the sacred that goes beyond identity and belonging, privileging instead the personal experience, over and above dogma and truth. On the ambiguity of these terms, refer to the interesting recent debates in the field of sociology of religion on 'spirituality'. Cf.: Heelas and Woodhead (2004); Giordan (2006); Flanagan and Jupp (2007).

[2] Religious care provided specifically in prisons is the main focus of a multiyear research on Italian jails carried out by the author of this chapter, starting in 2004 and still ongoing. Furthermore, the care provided by Imams in various social settings was also the topic I addressed in three different research projects: the first (2011–2013) was a Programme of National Interest promoted by the Italian Ministry of Education and Universities (PRIN-MIUR—Programma di Interesse Nazionale del Ministero dell'Istruzione, dell'Università della Ricerca Scientifica), conducted jointly by five Italian universities (Padua, Bologna, Rome, Turin and Palermo), which produced a national survey called: 'Il pluralismo religioso in Italia: Per una Mappatura e un'interpretazione delle diverse presenze socio-religiose nella società italiana' (Religious Pluralism in Italy: a mapping and interpretation of the different socioreligious presences in Italian society), directed by Enzo Pace, and in which the author coordinated the research group on the Muslim presence; the second (2011–2013) was a research study financed by the University of Padua called: 'La leadership socio-religiosa

---

K. M. Rhazzali (✉)
Department of Philosophy, Sociology, Pedagogy and Applied Psychology-FISPPA, University of Padua, Veneto, Italy
e-mail: khalid.rhazzali@unipd.it

© Springer International Publishing Switzerland 2015                                    117
I. Becci, O. Roy (eds.), *Religious Diversity in European Prisons,*
DOI 10.1007/978-3-319-16778-7_8

some of the characteristic features that are gradually shaping a new Imamate, with its largely unique and original format, closely linked to the evolution of the Islamic presence in Europe. Taking a reconstruction of the characteristics of Muslim presence in the Italian prison system as my starting point, it is my intention to show how the issue of religious care provided to Muslims—and in particular the situations that come into being as a result of the intervention by an Islamic religious care provider—highlights the link and the reciprocal influence of a whole web of circumstances. These circumstances concern both the specific legal context (which are the result of the political decisions and also of nondecisions by the Italian State) and the specific composition of Muslim immigration to Italy, with its characteristics that are to a large extent exasperated in the prison population; they also concern the sociocultural transformation that the European Islamic communities are undergoing, where the evolution of their religious and theological culture is engaging in a problematical exchange with the transformations of a community that is becoming increasingly rooted in the European context. In particular, I wanted to study what forms the figure of the religious care provider takes on, in relation to these needs and these limitations, and how religious communication and intercultural mediation are interlinked and overlap in his activity, to extents and in ways that are rapidly changing.

As a result, the figure of religious care provider (Imam) is emerging as one of those aspects of the Imamate, as it is progressively reinvented by the European Islamic experience, that is especially important in the transformation of the authority figures in the Islamic diaspora (Saint-Blancat 1995). As such the Imam represents a strong link between the prison and the outside world, by virtue of the very nature of the communication it provides. And the experience gained in prison acquires considerable importance for the debate within Islamic organizations, where the training of Imams is becoming increasingly topical, in the perspective of opening up to sociocultural and political issues, and to a generation of religious care providers trained in Italy, among whom women play a role that is now not at all secondary.

The very nature of the subject that I was investigating and outlining informed my main methodological choices: in the context of symbolic interactionism, I chose the *Grounded Theory* constructivist perspective[3]. Equally consistent with the configuration of the subject, was its placement within the field of intercultural research, a

---

dell'imam in Italia in prospettiva europea' (The socioreligious leadership of Imams in Italy, seen in a European perspective); the third was a joint research and action project on religious care provided to Muslims detained in Italian prisons (2012–2013), carried out by Youssef Sbai as his project work during his Master's on the Study of Islam in Europe, under my supervision. This last study involved mapping the Islamic religious care in all prisons: it included 15 semi-structured interviews and the preparation for a daylong training workshop at the University of Padua for about a dozen Imams from the Union of Islamic Communities and Organizations in Italy (UCOII), who were active care providers in the prisons of Northern Italy.

[3] As is well known, the *Grounded Theory* proposes an innovative relationship between data collection and theoretical organizing, and also between quantitative and qualitative methodologies: on this subject cf. Glaser and Strauss (1967); Strauss and Corbin (1990, 1997); Paillé (1994); Glaser (2003); Tarozzi (2008).

perspective that is very closely related to the interactionist and constructivist theories, which I consider particularly useful for the analysis of issues concerning Islam, a subject that—even in the work of social researchers—is all too often fixed in the rigid configuration given to it by theological, historical and political definitions. Looked at from an intercultural viewpoint, the reality of Islam is thus conceived of as a dynamic and shared entity, negotiated and challenged by the members of the community of believers and also in its 'contact zones' (Hermans and Kempen 1998), rather than as a pre-existing fixed 'body', to which individuals need to be constantly brought back to. Thus, cultural and religious differences do not disappear in the fixed and rigid identity that conceals any evidence of transformative processes, and annuls the decisive importance of interaction between different individuals; rather, such differences are seen as being internal to the dynamics of meeting and exchange. For nothing, today, in the evolution of the reality of European Islam appears to be interpretable without taking into consideration the constant interaction of its various components, in relation to all the most important issues, with their European context. This context involves European Islamic communities in a variable but continuous process of osmosis, which highlights how unrealistic is the interpretative key that characterizes essentialistic or generically multiculturalist approaches[4]. The methodological choice described above appears to us to be the only way of preventing Muslims in general, and Imams specifically, as individuals and as members of a group, and all the other players who are in contact with them over the different stages of their lives, from being separated from the interactive flow in which they are in effect immersed, and thus morphing into useless—or worse, harmful—stereotypes.

## 8.2 Muslims in Italian Prisons

The radical change that has occurred over the past two decades in the make-up of the population in Italian prisons, due to not only the effects of migration but also the political and legal management of migration as a phenomenon, has forced the prison system, with its guiding principles and regulations, to address issues and questions of such magnitude that the system's very foundations have been shaken. Religious care, traditionally identified in Italian jails with the Roman Catholic chaplain, has now become a service that would need to be provided for a considerable number of faiths. This gives rise to a number of problems that range from practical ones (magnified by the material, logistic and organizational conditions in prisons that are often already verging on collapse) to those connected to the interpretation that should be given to principles such as freedom of opinion and worship, and to the by no means unanimous acceptance in our society of religious pluralism (Giordan and Pace 2014).

---

[4] For a detailed differentiation between the multiculturalist and the interculturalist approach, cf. Blau (1995), Baumann (1999), Benhabib (2002), Mantovani (2008), Rhazzali (2014).

It is often stressed that Muslims constitute the most numerous non-Catholic religious group within the Italian prison population[5]. As we are speaking of Muslims in Italian prisons, it is legitimate to wonder who these individuals, whom we are thus defining, really are. Hence a broader question arises, assuming specific connotations in the prison environment, and full of methodological implications: who are those individuals really, whom we, by convention, define as Muslims?

The answer tends to be provided through a statistical approach. Usually, the following are considered Muslim: those detainees who are nationals of a country where Islam is the state religion, or at any rate where the majority of the population is Muslim. When the host country is, like Italy, a non-Muslim country, all citizens from a Muslim country are considered Muslims, simply because they come from such a country, and this includes even the second and third generations of those (originally) migrant populations: Islam as an inherited trait, as it were. And then there are also autochthonous citizens who have converted to Islam.

The religious element ends by being a national ethnic feature, reducing religion essentially to something akin to a characteristic trait that is assigned automatically. This classification tends to reduce the highly complex reality of Islamic religiosity to an apocryphal *homo islamicus* (Babès 1997). With it comes the neglect for the different ways in which the relationship with Islam is expressed and experienced by individuals and groups, and for the vast range of different lifestyles and behaviours that those whom we call Muslims engage in, beyond their relationship with religious experience[6].

All this means that, based on the importance that in any case must be given to the quantitative aspect, one cannot provide an answer to the question above unless qualitative investigations are carried out[7] in order to address the subjective experiences of Muslims, and to understand the times and ways of their evolution, including the meaning that religion has begun to take on for them, as an identity factor, in relation to the other dimensions that define the uniqueness of their experience.

Bearing in mind these premises, let us examine the statistics. The 22nd report of Caritas-Migrantes (2012) estimates that there are 1,645,902 Muslims in Italy. As far as the Muslim population in Italian prisons is concerned, there is no official estimate. One can elaborate some of the figures using the conventional criterion of deriving the detainee's religion from his/her geographical origin; although, this will yield a figure with the same degree of approximation as the figure relating to the number of Muslims in Italy in general. The Ministry of Justice provides statistics on the population in Italian prisons, as is shown in the table below, from which

---

[5] In recent years, the media have often stressed a correlation between the presence of undocumented (or irregular) migrants and the high number of immigrants in prisons, highlighting the considerable size of the Muslim presence.

[6] It is worth remembering the classic notion of the pluridimensionality of religion as proposed by Glock (1964): apart from the dimension of belonging, he also indicated as equally important the dimensions of experience, of belief, of knowledge and practice.

[7] On the prevalent tendency today, in the methodological debate on the sociology of religions, to combine quantitative and qualitative methods, cf. Berzano and Riis (2012).

we see that foreign prisoners account for slightly more than one third of the total (Table 8.1).

The number of detainees who are not Italian citizens amounts to 20,521, about 34.38 % of the entire number of prisoners. Based on the criteria used by the Pew Research Center (2009), adding the figures for the nationals of those countries where Islam is either the state religion, or is the religion of the majority of the population, we estimate—as you can see from Table 8.2 below—that the number of Muslims in Italian jails amounts to 10,684, i.e. more than half the foreign population (Table 8.2).

More significant and reliable data could be made available to researchers and scholars if the Department of Penitentiary Administration (DAP) were to release the information from the individual detainees' declarations on their religious beliefs, which each inmate is required to give when she/he is first inducted into the prison.

**Table 8.1** Prison population as of 30-04-2014. (Source: Table based on statistics provided by the Ministry of Justice. Cf.: http://www.giustizia.it/giustizia/it/mg_1_14_1.wp?previsiousPage=mg_1 _14&contentId=SST950279)

| Region | Number of prisons | Detainees present | | Of whom foreigners |
|---|---|---|---|---|
| | | Total | Women | |
| National total | 206 | 59,683 | 2521 | 20,521 |

**Table 8.2** Estimated number of Muslim detainees, based on country of origin (30/04/2014). (Source: Table based on statistics provided by the Ministry of Justice. Cf. http://www.giustizia.it/ giustizia/it/mg_1_14_1.wp?previsiousPage=mg_1_14&contentId=SST950282)

| Country[a] | Women | Men | Total |
|---|---|---|---|
| Albania | 27 | 2182 | 2209 |
| Algeria | 1 | 511 | 512 |
| Bangladesh | 1 | 59 | 50 |
| Bosnia and Herzegovina | 20 | 50 | 70 |
| Egypt | 2 | 436 | 438 |
| Iraq | 0 | 51 | 51 |
| Morocco | 44 | 3,670 | 3,714 |
| Pakistan | 0 | 127 | 127 |
| Palestinian autonomous territories | 0 | 56 | 56 |
| Somalia | 0 | 88 | 88 |
| Tunisia | 14 | 2,361 | 2,375 |
| Turkey | 1 | 70 | 71 |
| Other countries | 8 | 536 | 544 |
| TOTAL | *123* | *10,561* | *10,684* |

[a] I use the percentages of Muslims given by the Pew Research Center in all cases, except for those countries (Nigeria, China, India, etc.) in which the migrants to Italy come from regions with nearly no Muslim presence. I also applied a figure of 100 % where the percentage given was greater than 95 %

**Table 8.3** Foreign detainees according to their religious affiliation. (Source: Data provided by the Department of Penitentiary Administration (situation at 31/01/2009))

| Total foreign detainees | Muslims | Other religion | Religion not known |
|---|---|---|---|
| 21,891 | 9006 | 8382 | 4507 |

This information, however, is collected from the prisoners for purely organizational purposes, and contains highly sensitive and personal data: for this reason it cannot be readily released[8]. A statistical elaboration of the information on religious affiliation (Table 8.3) was—exceptionally—made available to a group of researchers, including myself, only once in 2010 (Rhazzali 2010).

A further element that makes this information so important is the fact that at least 80% of prisoners accepted to declare voluntarily their religious affiliation. Whatever the reasons that may have induced the prisoners to declare themselves as Muslims, including mere tactical considerations, here we have a first declaration actually provided by the inmates themselves: it is, of course, influenced by a variety of circumstances, but it is an occasion on which the inmates are speaking their mind, it is something closer to a self-definition than the usual conventional classification.

As compared to other prison contexts in Europe[9], Islam in Italian jails has a specificity that needs to be interpreted in relation to the overall characteristics of the Islamic presence in Italy. It is a migrant Islam, that has grown to reach a considerable size over a relatively short period of time, basically just the past twenty years, and which includes people from a wide range of provenances (Allievi 2009; Rhazzali and Equizi 2013). Unlike other European countries, immigrants to Italy do not come from one or a few predominant country(ies) of origin, as a result of official policies; although it must be added that Italy has, in recent years, entered into specific agreements with some foreign countries (starting with Albania, Morocco and Tunisia), based on two laws on immigration (Law no. 40, dated 6 March 1998, known as the Turco-Napolitano Law and Law no. 189, dated 30 July 2002, known as the Bossi-Fini Law), aimed in part at establishing an annual planning of the flow of migrants, but—more importantly—at securing the collaboration of these States in the repression of so-called 'clandestine' immigration, i.e. the flow of clandestine migrants (by guaranteeing that these countries would take in the migrants that were sent back, and provide cooperation in border surveillance).

Today the presence of irregular, or undocumented, migrants is lower than it was in the early 1990s (the years when Italy was definitely undergoing its transformation from a country of emigration to one of immigration). Yet, in prisons, the majority of foreigners are those called 'irregular' or 'clandestine', for two main reasons: either

---

[8] As far as the prison administration's questionnaires on religious affiliation is concerned, Rosati and Fabretti's report addresses the question from the viewpoint of the prison staff and comes up with a very credible explanation (Rosati and Fabretti 2012, p. 36).

[9] For a detailed reconstruction of the state of the art of Islam and religious care in the prisons of Europe, cf. our contribution (Rhazzali 2010), and the following works: Schneuwly Purdie and Vuille (2010), Schneuwly Purdie (2011) and Beckford et al. (2005).

because, in the majority of cases, a regular migrant loses her/his status as legally registered if she/he commits a crime (except for those cases where the migrant is related to an Italian citizen), or because the very condition of being undocumented was—for a certain period—a crime punished with incarceration.

Therefore, the Islam in Italian prisons, as well as being a 'migrant' Islam, is also a 'clandestine' Islam. Yet this condition is, on the contrary, representative of only a small proportion of Muslims in Italy generally, who are fairly well established in the country. Despite many difficulties, they are quite well integrated although there is always a risk of falling back into a precarious condition, and even into a status of irregularity (government policies on the acquisition of Italian citizenship have ended up creating a sort of 'waiting room', where immigrants, and especially their children and grandchildren, born and raised in Italy, are forced to live in a status of permanent migrants, with reduced rights, and no entitlement to act and exercise their rights in the public space)[10].

Another specificity is the absolute predominance of men over women (Table 8.3). Islam in prisons would appear to be linked to the world of those men who migrate alone, without having a real plan for their new life, and who are exposed to the risk of organized exploitation of undocumented migrants, teetering on the brink of falling into the circuits of organized criminal entrepreneurship. For these men, a period in prison is—paradoxically—more like attending a training course, an induction into crime, rather than a deterrent; or perhaps it is merely that one mistake leads the person to live in a condition where that mistaken lifestyle become the norm (Sbraccia 2007). It is not within the scope of this chapter to provide a complete analysis of the events that lead to such a large proportion of inmates being Muslims, nor is it my task to understand why there is such a huge difference between the numbers of males and females. But it will be useful to gather from these objective characteristics, relating to Islam in prisons, some relevant information for our subject, religious care provided in prisons, and the social actors involved.

## 8.3   Religious Care and Authority: A Testing Ground for Imams in Europe

In most cases, upon entering the jail, these prisoners are not practising Muslims and have very little knowledge of the theological foundations of their religion as has been shown by the rare research projects carried out in Europe on Islam in jails[11]. Nevertheless, either spontaneously or through the pressure of circumstances that fail to honour their cultural diversity, very few would renounce to resorting to the symbolic resource that Islam can offer, whilst attempting an interpretation of their own existence or seeking a form of guidance for their conduct. So it is not entirely

---

[10] On the conditions of the so-called second generations in Italy, cf. the following: Ambrosini and Molina (2004); Rhazzali (2008); Bertani and Di Nicola (2009); Colombo et al. (2009).

[11] Cf footnote 5.

surprising to learn that many become practicing Muslims once again, or undergo a reconversion during their detention (Khosrokhavar 2004; Spalek and El-Hassan 2007; Rhazzali 2010), and that sometimes the reconversion only lasts for the period of their incarceration. Another element is the propensity of Muslim inmates to group together based on their faith, so as to try and organize a lifestyle in prison that is consistent with their religious commitment, and recreate—to the extent that prison regulations allow—the proper settings and rhythms of worship. This matter cannot help but raise issues relating to freedom of worship as a subjective right of human beings, a right connected in its implementation to the relationship between Church and State, both as a result of the mediation with organized confessions, and as the consequence of the secular principle of freedom of thought (Ferrari 2006). In different ways and to varying extents, the constitutional set-up of all European countries acknowledges religious pluralism. This means that in some countries, especially those where the plurality of religions is a historical characteristic of its local population, laws and prison regulations have favoured the adoption of legal and organizational solutions providing religious care for Muslims (Beckford 2011a, b).

It is worth pointing out that, for Islam, the provision of religious care in prisons is a novelty, occurring only in a Western context, and in what in this chapter we have called the European Imamate[12]. There is no similar tradition in the prison systems of Muslim countries, or rather, there is no form of religious care provided, except very recently, as a consequence of a more general introduction of prison systems based on European or American models, resulting from the development of a greater awareness and acceptance of the rights of individual freedoms in the societies and political institutions, thanks to the ratification and adoption of the international declarations of human rights[13].

Over the course of the twentieth century, the space for religious care in prisons underwent an evolution, which was not at all free of problems. The Roman Catholic or Protestant chaplains, or those of other religions in those States where the socio-religious context allowed their presence, witnessed a reduction of their roles as guardians of the prisoner's humanity. And, further, they were gradually also losing their function as providers of the inmates' moral and cultural discipline, which they had acquired during the course of the modern age; this occurred as a more comprehensive set of sociopsychological skills were required, aimed at the management of and care for the detainees, leading towards their recovery and social rehabilitation (in the group of professionals that today addresses the needs of inmates, the

---

[12] The Imamate is a highly important institution for Shi'a Islam, which does not have a direct equivalent in the notion of Imamate pertaining to the Sunni Islamic tradition that the majority of European Islam recognizes itself as belonging to. On this topic there have been several scholarly works in recent years: Shadid and van Koningsveld (2002); Lewis (2004); Frégosi (2004); Cesari (2004); Cohen et al. (2004); Ciaurriz (2004); Saint-Blancat and Perocco (2005); Dassetto (2011); Caeiro (2010); Jouanneau (2013).

[13] Groups of Islamist detainees in the prisons of Arab-Muslim countries, such as Morocco and Tunisia (in the past), have referred to the rights envisaged in the international declarations in submitting their demands for facilities in which to hold prayer sessions and the request to be granted Imams as prayer-leaders.

chaplains share their role with psychologists, educators, social workers). On the other hand, it is at least since the 1960s, although at different times and in different ways in the various countries of Europe, that migrations and their consequences on the prison population have highlighted the importance of the religious phenomenon. In particular, the presence of several faiths that do not originate from Christianity has given rise to the need to organize religious worship in jails in an entirely new way. The chaplains resume their important role, either because they, as Christian religious care providers, take it upon themselves to acknowledge the right to worship of other confessions; or because a religious care provider from other confessions is organized as a mirror image of how they are organized, with these new figures acting in a sense under the auspices—or in the shadow of—the Christian chaplain. Even in those cases where there has been an acknowledgement, in principle, of the right of Muslims to enjoy the benefits of religious care, the life of the person who has been called upon to provide such care in the prisons was certainly not easy.

Islam is probably the most striking example of a religion appearing to resist formatting (Roy 2008), in other words resisting against its neutralization through standardization into a common, shared and sedated religious dimension, a process borrowed from the customary adaptation of Christian churches to the needs of their interaction with statehood; and, more recently, from the religious and cultural homogenization promoted by the processes of globalization. And, actually, it is precisely in the context of religious care provision in prisons that we can get a fuller understanding of the still unresolved tension between the formatting of Islam and the spontaneous and noncompliant reaction of the European Muslim world to the pressure of the 'formatting forces' pressure. When the admission of an Imam to a prison setting is considered plausible, through a forced analogy with the figure of the Christian chaplain, as we shall see below, undoubtedly what we are witnessing is an episode of the pressure exercised by European institutions on Islam, to shape its forms so as to match those of the Christian churches. At the same time, in the figure of the Imam, the function of the religious care provider acting within the penitentiary system's organization appears to merge with the function of the representative of the Islamic community outside the jail. And this double function is one of the most distinctive features of the new and radical reinvention of his role, which results in the creation of a new Imamate, which can be considered a novel development within European Islam. The fruits of that belaboured process through which European Islam has tried to react creatively, feeling the need to refuse to be merely the passive object of transformations resulting from its involvement in processes that change its habitat, and affect its sociocultural condition and development.

In traditionally Muslim countries the Imam, as he who leads the community in prayer, or as the khatib[14], the preacher, or the person who gives the Friday sermon, has a clear place within a fairly complex and diversified system of figures representing religious or legal authority (even in the absence—at least in the Sunni context—of a clergy that is comparable to the Christian model). In the European context,

---

[14] Important, for the topic of Imams, are the studies that Reeber (2004) devoted to the Khutbah (Sermon) in France.

however, this organized system of authority figures is totally lacking. The functions that were shared among them, as well as other functions that have emerged as needs in the experience of the newer communities of believers in their interactions with their social and institutional surroundings, are all condensed in the evolving but ever-present figure of the Imam. The Imam, thus, ends up becoming an agglomeration of formal and, more often, informal roles. Apart from ensuring the essential services related to worship, the Imam's community of faithful—and more frequently the Islamic organizations that are responsible for the place of worship in which he preaches—demands that he addresses a wide range of issues. In different situations, individuals with the most diverse life-stories, in their role as Imams, create for themselves a personal mosaic of activities that may range from leading the faithful in prayer, to providing care for the sick and for prisoners, to celebrating weddings, to teaching Arabic or religion to the youth. In European countries, the latter activities are moving towards a form of institutionalization that is clearly modeled on the role of the Christian priest (Allievi 2009), although in some communities a clearer division of roles and professions is beginning to take root (the Imam-chaplain, the administrator of mosques, the teacher of religion in public schools, etc.). And the Imam can even become the community's administrator, keep the books of their associations, manage their public relations; if he is well-versed in the dominant rhetoric circulating in the public arena, he may even take on the political representation of his community, maybe even in order to gain access to benefits or advantages that religious organizations are entitled to, through European welfare systems (Dassetto 2003). In such cases the outcome is that of an Imam who is the leader of his community, a figure who can cross paths—but this is a topic that is beyond the scope of this chapter—with religious leaders, lecturers and speakers, preachers, and sociocultural mediators, who are becoming increasingly important in European (Frégosi 2004) and transnational (Caeiro 2010) Islam.

However, his raison d'être lies in being able to perform activities that will enable the Islamic heritage to remain alive in the present, and from this he obtains legitimation for his service as 'Islamic action' (Dassetto stresses this, in a Weberian analysis of categories, 2011). Although it may at times appear to be less evident in the tangled web of negotiations practised by the Imam, this element remains decisive and represents a non-negotiable symbolic nucleus, from which the renewal of the energy produced by the interactions of Islamic communities through religion depends.

This last aspect is essential, if we are to understand how the religious care provider—precisely in order to be able to perform all those complicated and wide-ranging 'secular' functions that pertain to him—must in any case, even in these innovative forms, embody a clear continuity of religious inspiration.

## 8.4 The Imam-Religious Care Provider: Profiles

In Italy religion is commonly equated to Catholicism and also in the provision of religious care for the inmates of the prison system this notion is expressed in full force. To actually give real space to other faiths is something that is accepted in principle, but has a difficult time in being implemented in practice, since it needs to overcome anything from inertia to outright suspicion (Ferrari 2013). The idea of Muslims, as held by the Ministry's penitentiary administration bureaucrats, appears still to be primarily preoccupied with the potential links between Islam and terrorism, and the officials still consider that spaces for Muslim worship, granted for use inside prisons, need to be kept under constant vigilance, and the religious care providers as well, so as to ensure that the activities carried out do not become those extremist political gatherings that the administration fears[15]. The prisons we have visited over recent years (Rhazzali 2010, 2014) act according to decisions taken to some extent at their own discretion, which means that some periods are more favourable than others towards collaboration with Muslim detainees and with the Islamic organizations and associations outside the prisons.

In the prisons, on the other hand, there is a pragmatic approach, in which the main restrictions to worship are those imposed by the organizational constraints of the jail, whereas the presence of religious leaders and groups of inmates getting together based on their common faith, so that they can worship together, is often seen as an indirect contribution towards making the prison more governable, since the more devout inmates, apart from being forceful in demanding their rights to freedom of worship, are quite unlikely to create disturbances or serious conflicts in the prison. The general climate in prisons, however, is still suffering from the consequences of 9/11, affecting the relations between prison administrators and Islamic organizations. Combined with the fact that there is still no formal agreement between the State and the Islamic communities and no financial backing that would allow for an agreement to be implemented, this means that the effectiveness of the existing provisions is truly limited, with no chance of actually finding a positive solution for many of the issues. The President of the Republic's Decree no. 230, dated 30 June 2000, addresses in Article 35 the question of the guarantees to be provided to foreign detainees in relation to cultural-linguistic differences and promotes the role and action of Intercultural Mediators. Article 58 then explicitly states that prisoners have the right to participate in the religious celebrations of their own faith, as long as they are not in any way in conflict with 'the order and security of the institute'. The display of religious symbols in cells is allowed and individual worship is permitted, if it occurs in the inmate's free time, and is therefore not in competition with any activity planned by the institution's regulation. The same Decree establishes the right of detainees of a faith different from Roman Catholicism to enjoy the guidance of a minister of their own faith, chosen by the prison governor from the list of those granted accreditation by the Ministry of the Interior.

The degree to which the rights guaranteed by law are actually implemented in practice depends on a variety of circumstances. First of all, it will depend on the level of willingness and initiative of the prison administrators; second, on the

---

[15] Cf. the references to Imams and prayer facilities in the report on religious care provided to Muslims in prison by the Ministry of Justice, in section III (Analysis and monitoring) where the results of the monitoring are described as useful contributions to the work of the Inter-Ministerial Committee on Terrorism. Cf.: http://www.giustizia.it/giustizia/it/contentview.wp?previsiousPage=mg_14_7&contentId=ART149091.

organizational skills and the actual number of inmates interested in making use of the right to worship under the guidance of the religious care provider; then, on the existence in the geographical area where the prison is located of religious organizations that are open and responsive to the needs of prisoners and willing to mobilize in their favour; on the ability of the individual Imam or community leaders to propose themselves as organizers of the service; on the activism of the secular social workers and volunteers, and also on the solidarity of the Roman Catholic chaplain (Rhazzali 2010; Sbai 2013). In other words, also in this case the quality of regional policies regarding intercultural practices and social intermediation, and the local cultural traditions relating to the provision of welfare services can play an important role, together with the readiness to stimulate synergies and raise awareness among the prison administration.

How many people are there today that, in various different roles, are involved in the provision of religious care in Italian prisons? There is no way of getting hold of exact figures, and there are no official data. We have to rely on estimates drawn up by some Islamic organizations that are active in this field. The estimate of religious care providers, active in 206 Italian prisons, suggests a figure of not more than 50, including those that are only active occasionally. In our opinion this is a fairly reliable estimate, since it takes into consideration the number of Muslim clerics authorized by the Ministry of the Interior, which is only 29 (Rosati and Fabretti 2012, p. 47), and the fact that not all these clerics are actually active, since they provide their services on an entirely voluntary basis, and are therefore restricted by their other work commitments.

Bearing in mind all these considerations, our research study has produced the following identification of the different sociocultural types of Islamic religious care providers in Italian prisons:

### 8.4.1 The Imam from the Mosque

This figure is currently the emerging figure of an authority in the Islamic world in Italy and Europe. The Imam may be the president of a local religious association that is in charge of managing a small Islamic centre, where he embodies almost all the official roles (Saint-Blancat 2008), including the role of providing care to those detained in nearby prisons. The more specifically religious functions (worship and prayer), including caring for detainees, may be performed by an Imam paid by the organization that manages the mosque or the Islamic centre; this Imam may perform these functions over and above a paid job. In Italy, though, the Imam performs his functions prevalently as an unpaid volunteer. These voluntary Imams come from a wide range of different life experiences. In order to establish an effective and successful relationship with the prison world, however, it is essential for the Imam to have considerable experience in dealing with Italian institutions and nongovernmental organizations, and he must therefore also be very proficient in the local language. Due to this last aspect, in the prisons in Italy there is very little space for Imams who were trained outside Italy and who, sometimes, are acting on behalf of the governments of their country of origin, or on behalf of organizations who appreciate them especially for their theological scholarship, acquired in their own country; these organizations frequently prefer this kind of Imam, with high level theological qualifications, to the ones who have developed their skills within the local community in Italy, who are on the other hand well acquainted with the Italian situation and have many good relational ties to the local institutions, but whose theological scholarship is rather the result of a well-meaning religious do-it-yourself education (Leclerc 2002; Lenoir 2003; Trombetta 2004).

### 8.4.2 The Detainee Imam

This figure is usually a detainee capable of meeting a widespread need expressed by the inmates: he will take on the task of organizing the worship and prayer functions for inmates of his same religion, and is also willing to represent them and their needs in dealing with the prison's administration. Although these men have not had any theological training, they know how to make the most of their personal charm, charisma and credibility; they often have an external support, or benefit from the help and suggestions of other detainee Imams from other prisons, with whom they correspond by letter, sharing information, experiences or simply the text of sermons. The importance of their action is especially evident in those cases where the prison population is such that the administration has decided to organize entire sections of the jail for Muslim inmates only, separating them from the others; in these cases, the detainee Imam plays a decisive role in organizing the prayer sessions and also acts as an interface with the top administrators of the prison. This form of Imam is the most widespread, precisely because he performs so many roles and functions, which usually eliminates any fear that his activity may develop into a form of fundamentalist proselytising or some kind of political preaching. On the other hand, those individuals considered, whether rightly or wrongly, as complicit with illegal organizations, or even worse with jihadi organizations, are subjected to a special regimen in Italian prisons. Usually this sort of do-it-yourself Imam is an emblematic representation of the attempt to transform incarceration into the rediscovery of a new life path, aimed at regaining personal dignity, in which a new self-narrative may become a positive self-affirmation, taking the first steps in prison of a path towards a change in the conditions of one's existence.

### 8.4.3 The 'Accredited' Imam

In recent years there has been a tendency in Italy to attribute a specialized profile and configuration to the Muslim religious care provider in several sectors of welfare and social affairs. Over the past few years the Ministry of the Interior has drawn up a list of 'accredited' Imams, which envisages a list of requirements that must be satisfied in order to be included. Furthermore, some Islamic states, through their diplomatic circuits, provide financial support to their own nationals in Italian jails in the organization of specific projects, on the occasion of the major Muslim festivities, especially Ramadan. Consequently, what has gradually developed is a space where religious care in prisons takes on the semblance of an activity which is religious, but is also sociocultural and quite distinct from the activities outside the prison system. Those who perform these functions and roles can to a certain extent compare themselves to the Roman Catholic chaplain, and this is in fact one of the demands put forward by the Islamic organizations and the practicing Muslim inmates. On the other hand, the relatively small number of 'accredited' Imams, who perform their functions as volunteers and who have a certain kind of recognition of their function, but very partial, are still a long way from being considered equal to the Christian chaplains: they do not even share the title of *cappellano*. Unlike the situation in other European countries, where the figures of the *aumônier* or the *chaplain* in the prison system have existed for some time, even in the case of an 'accredited' Imam in Italy, he is still merely an Imam. And his specificity ends up by becoming yet another element in that ongoing process where the forms of what we have called the 'European Imamate' are further elaborated, defined, but also frequently further confused.

### 8.4.4   The 'Intercultural Mediator' Imam

The prevalently religious dimension characterizing the functions of the Imam in Italian prisons is complemented by the role of the Intercultural Mediator. This figure occupies almost always an experimental and temporary position, with its roles and functions constantly redefined (Luatti 2006). Although language mediation represents the original justification for the creation of this profile in the social services, in recent years it has evolved into a figure who is capable of understanding and meeting the needs of religious and cultural minorities in the prison, and conveying those needs to the administration. With his presence, the Intercultural Mediator bears witness to the need the prison system has of finding a way to understand the psychological and sociocultural complexities of the humanity that is entrusted to its custody. In theory, its role is based on a purportedly secular vision of cultural diversity. At the same time, however, the Intercultural Mediator is also the figure that stresses the concreteness of the life of the inmates, breaking from the reassuring stereotypes to highlight the importance of the symbolic dimension, when this becomes the most important cultural and existential resource for the prisoners. From his position, which is in itself entirely separate from any kind of religious role, the Mediator is often the person who confirms that a specifically religious care for the inmates is not just useful, but can actually be indispensable. This occurs when distress pushes a Muslim inmate into behaviour patterns that are especially difficult to manage, such as severe depression, incidents of self harm, or suicide attempts, and serious psychic disturbances; in such instances, when a 'secular' diagnosis or treatment is incapable of solving the problem, at times a partial solution can be provided by reactivating a micro context of social–religious experience, stimulated and borne out of the presence of a figure such as an Imam, embodying religious authority and providing a familiar context, even for a small group, that recreates the rhythms and meanings of *Salat* (prayer).

The Mediator can thus become the go-between between the prison and the Islamic centre outside, facilitating the access of an Imam into the prison, but also occasionally replacing him when he is absent, holding conversations on religious topics, performing a sort of bland form of religious instruction, in both cases even having to negotiate the boundaries of the topics addressed with the prison administration (which, in turn, may choose to assign to him a role in training projects on Islamic culture addressed to the guards and other prison staff), or even simply providing copies of the Quran or publications on Islamic topics in the inmates' languages. It is in situations like those described here that this figure of the Imam-Intercultural Mediator has developed. He can be a combination and meeting point of several different life experiences and roles: there is the case of an Imam who practices in a mosque or an Islamic centre, or exercises his functions in an itinerant fashion, in many different places, and then has a position as Intercultural Mediator, which is a proper form of employment that provides him with earnings; he is legitimated by his position as Intercultural Mediator to gain access to the prison, or to other institutions, but once in prison as an Intercultural Mediator, is also able to meet the religious needs of detainees, as an Imam. Then there is the Intercultural Mediator who is a Muslim and who, in many cases, feels that he can improvise as a religious care provider, relying on whatever knowledge he may have of theological doctrine, and offering his services to those who, based on his experience as a Mediator, he believes are in need of religious care. In this case, the lack of clear rules has actually favoured a sort of approximation to a specific professional role. It is worth stressing that the roles described above give rise to a very close interrelation between religious functions and intercultural practices; this means that the requirements perceived as needed for the figure of the Imam are increasingly characterized as being a combination of theological knowledge, and of a great sensitivity and awareness of the sociocultural circumstances of the members of the community of believers. The prevalence of women among the trained Mediators further leads to this idea: in the function of cultural mediation and in establishing an active intellectual relationship with their faith, women find an opportunity for personal development and a potential for gaining increased social standing, in a context in which all those representing authority in European Islam are undergoing a considerable transformation.

In any case, all these types of Imam-Chaplain in Italian prisons highlight all the different facets of a need that exists, and that is unlikely to find a solution with a resource outside the sphere of what can be provided by religion. This is not a need felt unanimously by Muslim detainees, but certainly it is a widespread need, very much part of the inmates' experience. In the vacuum left by the very generic secular culture that characterizes public policies, including the prison sector, the resources of the symbolic world offered by Islam become the support system that provides a Muslim prisoner with the means of examining his status, enabling him to break out of a condition of passivity and confusion. On the one hand, this may seem like—and, at times, may indeed be—a way of seeking refuge in one's Islamic self, identifying with the supposed moral and political self-sufficiency of an idealized and imaginary Umma (Rhazzali 2010). But, on the other hand, those detainees who return to an earlier religious practice from which they had lapsed, and benefit from the religious care provided, may actually begin a new life experience, starting on a new path that enables them to relate more personally to the context in which they are living. From this point of view, the religious care provider is also faced with the necessity to relate the symbols of his faith to the needs of interpreting daily life experiences: thus, the re-proposed theological message will tend to give rise to a further operation of cultural mediation, even if this is sometimes done unwittingly.

Even in the case of religious care in prison, the European Imam finds himself having to coordinate his communication, and also his relationship with the theological tradition, with the fact that he is constantly in a contact zone, an in-between zone, not only between Muslims and non-Muslims but also in the very heart of the faithful of his community who are Muslims in Europe. The fact that he acts in a space that appears prevalently to be the space defined by the interactions between public welfare and an attempt at Islamic welfare—partly in competition, partly in subsidiarity—reflects a more general condition of Muslims in Europe. Comparison with the institutional relationship with the State enjoyed by Christianity, on the one hand, and with the relationship with political representation and leadership on the other, becomes the benchmark for the new Imamate, where the Muslims put their participation in the European context to the test, in their attempt at developing an original cultural invention that is capable of going beyond a mere statement of identity.

## 8.5   Religious Care in Prisons and the Initiative of Islamic Organizations in Italy

What is emerging is the need for Muslims to break free of the sterile alternative between reaffirming the standard abstract statement of their identity or being subjected to a form of ready assimilation that comes in a variety of ways from the contexts where they live, and of which the formatting of the Imam as a cleric to be modelled exactly on the Christian priest or pastor, but always lower in status, is an example. In this scenario, the role of Islamic organizations, especially national ones, appears in all its importance. These are federations of several associations whose purpose and mission is to provide a cultural and political representation of Italian Islam: coming from different backgrounds and looking at the questions from different perspectives, they aim at creating the conditions for a more effective elaboration by the Islamic community of its role and place in Italian society. This is an objective towards which several different projects and players have worked over the past few years, with results that have not always been useful (Allievi 2010). Today we see that two organizations in particular have come to the fore: although they differ in how they make up their membership and in their strategies, they both coordinate a considerable number of mosques and Islamic centers throughout the country.

The Islamic Confederation of Italy (Confederazione Islamica Italiana, CII) is an organization that was established following a fairly complex federative process between 2009 and 2012; it is connected to the government of Morocco and to several institutions in that country; it has federated 209 mosques and prayer centres (Rhazzali and Equizi 2013), but has not yet elaborated a programme of religious care to be provided to Muslims in prison[16]. On the other hand, the Union of Islamic Communities and Organizations in Italy (Unione delle Comunità e delle Organizzazione Islamiche in Italia, UCOII), whose history dates back much further (active since 1990) and which can boast of a widely disseminated presence throughout the country (250 mosques and prayer centres), in recent years has made an effort at trying to coordinate the presence of religious care providers in prisons.

For this purpose UCOII acts through a network which reportedly consists of about 30 individuals (not a small number, if we consider the overall number of religious care providers authorized by the Ministry of the Interior)[17], who provide religious care in the broadest sense, carrying out activities which can range from offering real religious guidance like the Imam from the mosque to the role of a community leader who acts as continuing link, forging a network between the inmates and the outside community, its institutions and associations to the Intercultural Mediator. This latter figure appears to perform a sort of balancing act between the proposals put forward on the Islamic side and the innovations that the State institutions are willing to accept. In other terms, as we wait for the memorandum of understanding between the State and Islamic organizations to finally be agreed upon, or for the system of approval and 'accreditation'—which already exists—to be properly and systematically implemented, so that a cleric that is not a Catholic can finally be recognized, it is actually on the role of the Intercultural Mediator that the Muslims rely, in order to approximate the de facto implementation of the figure of religious care provider for Muslims.

Around this core group, other components have gathered, developing a serious professional profile, with a body of knowledge ranging beyond Islamic theology, to include human, legal and social sciences, existing alongside each other, even interacting in a completely new interdisciplinary manner, on some occasions collaborating with Italian universities such as Padua, La Sapienza in Rome, the Salesian Pontifical University.

Based on the research we have conducted over the past few years, we have clearly noticed a growing awareness—in the reflections shared by the members of the Islamic organizations—of the importance that experiences in the Italian prisons can have for a more general perspective, stimulating an explicit discussion on the

---

[16] It is worth mentioning the initiative, that began a couple of years ago, of Hilal, a Moroccan association that benefited from funding from the Moroccan government and organized activities targeting Moroccan detainees especially during Ramadan. Cf. http://it-it.facebook.com/pages/Il-Carcere-una-Terra-comuneسجن-أن-ضي-ة-مشترك ة/173298056197427?sk=info

[17] Cf. Rosati, Fabretti, op. cit., p. 47.

renewal of theological communication strategies and also of the role of religious guides or leaders in European Islamic communities. In Italy, in particular, as can also be seen by observing the UCOII experience, religious care providers are for the most part also active as Intercultural Mediators. This just goes to confirm the fact that the role of religious care provider is totally precarious and unrecognized, since most of those who perform it can only afford to do so by combining it with the (only marginally) more officially recognized function of Intercultural Mediator, which at least guarantees some form of remuneration. The training of Intercultural Mediator, who is also the religious care provider, is for the most part the result of activities offered by secular public and private entities, and which therefore concentrate on providing him with the skills of mediator. This raises the issue of the theological education of these men: in the context described above, the religious function is likely to be the most important function the person needs to perform, while it is undoubtedly the one for which he has the least training. In another dimension, there is a need to reflect more on a new and organic project of cultural and religious education for those who provide religious care in various social settings, also in view of how their training and their activities exert an influence on, and in turn are influenced by, the overall evolution of the religious expression of the Muslims of Italy and Europe.

UCOII is an organization that is increasingly coming to recognize its mission as the establishment of a form of Islam that is more rooted in the European experience, and which must therefore accept the challenges of innovation. The debate within UCOII, for example, has taken into account the absolute novelty of the fact that there is a prevalence of women among Intercultural Mediators; it has therefore began an in-depth internal debate on the role of women in the organized system of religious leaders and authorities.

This laboratory of the new European Imamate, seen from a viewpoint that catches the intercultural aspects running through it, is thus reaffirmed, as we were saying above, as a space where many different instances of negotiations develop; a space in which the various contact zones push, on the one hand, for practical adjustments in areas where for a long time matters were left up to religious do-it-yourself and improvisation, and on the other, attempt to promote courageous innovations of conceptual paradigms. These innovative paradigms may become important indicators of trends for the future of European Islam and for its ever more rapid and more intense reciprocal relations with the cultural evolution of Islamic countries. It is well worth remembering here—and this is an element that is truly relevant to a discussion of the European Imamate—the redefinition in Moroccan institutions of the figure of the Morchida, who is not properly a female Imam, but a female Morchid, i.e. a recognized religious guide or leader: she is trained as a religious guide (degree in Shari'a and Islamic thought) and holds the title of a new, formally designated religious authority, envisaged as a social role to be performed in the community (religious education, literacy courses for women, helping people in their dealings with the institutions and so on). In this case, too, there is a sort of overlap between cultural and religious communication, in which the impetus of socioeconomic processes, with all the innovations they introduce into the material conditions of the daily life of Muslims, play an important role (as in the case of the very high numbers of requests for religious care providers in European prisons). And the cultural and religious communication increasingly contributes to the organization, in Luhmann's (1995) sense, sharing a mutual relationship between the system and its environment, becoming for each other a context that raises problems and produces cultural elaboration that engages it, stimulating the emergence of constantly new resources.

## 8.6   Conclusions

An analysis of the forms characterizing Islamic religious care in Italian prisons needs to take stock, first and foremost, of a decisive element: The strong attraction exerted in prison on Muslim detainees of the notion of returning to an actively practiced worship. This element can be interpreted as an attempt by the inmates to find in the language of Islam the words through which they can weave a new fabric, give a meaning to their personal life stories and perhaps also to the life and existence of the community as a whole. Islamic religious care has only recently begun to exercise its functions in Italian prisons; amidst considerable difficulties, it is growing, trying to meet this need. The forms it takes on, and which this chapter has attempted to analyse, display a wide variety, in some cases based on conflicting notions; but what does appear to prevail is not an unchangeable, unequivocal definition of Islamic identity, but rather a dialogue with the concrete situations that bear witness to the difficult task of reconciling to traditional criteria the living conditions of Muslims who are permanently immersed in the spaces, rhythms and flows of communication of a world which is not informed by the guidelines of the historical manifestations of Islam. The various figures that have come to the fore in this field, each one with specific traits that often tend to overlap with those of the others, bear witness to the fact that the sociocultural reality of Italian Islam is highly dynamic, and to the fact that manifold complications make it difficult to provide an effective and original self-definition. A significant fact is that, in many cases, the religious care provider has developed out of the world of Intercultural Mediation.

This is where the question of Islam in the prison system intersects the issues related to a new configuration of the Imam, in a context of rapid transformation of the functions of authority and leadership in European Islam. As this chapter has attempted to show, the prison context exasperates issues which are actually central to the overall experience of Muslims who have lived through the experience of migration first and then of integration, with all their related difficulties: many aspects of their integration have been successful, although they themselves—and the autochthonous communities as well—tend to interpret their integration as incomplete. The space in which the Imam merges his various roles, selecting the ones for each situation, is the space where negotiations with the local contexts and with the many institutional interlocutors intersect the elaborations ongoing within the conscience of Muslim individuals and communities, where the religious change takes place. This gives rise to a pre-eminently intercultural dimension where although it is possible to distinguish the more specifically religious aspects from the sociocultural ones, it is impossible to analyse each one separately, ignoring the extent to which they influence and condition each other.

It is this very engagement, with the cultural fabric permeating the contexts in which Muslims are involved in a dense network of exchanges, that urges religious communication to adopt a highly original stance in its relationship with the reality of a world in rapid evolution, which the Muslims now share on a stable basis with 'others'.

# References

Allievi, S. (Ed.). (2009). *I musulmani e la societÃ italiana. Percezioni reciproche, conflitti culturali e trasformazioni sociali*. Milano: FrancoAngeli.

Allievi S. (2010.) *La guerra delle moschee*. Venezia: Marsilio.

Ambrosini, M., & Molina, S. (Eds.). (2004). *Seconde generazioni. Un'introduzione al futuro dell'immigrazione in Italia*. Torino: Edizioni Fondazione Agnelli.

Babès, L. (1997). *L'islam positif. La religion des jeunes musulmans de France*. Paris: L'Atelier..

Baumann, G. (1999). *The multicultural riddle. Rethinking national, ethnic, and religious identities*. London: Routledge.

Beckford, J. A. (2011a). Prisons et religions en Europe. Les aumôneries de prison: une introduction au dossier. *Archives de Sciences Sociales des Religions, 153*, 11–21.

Beckford, J. A. (2011b). Religion in prisons and in partnership with the state. In J. Barbalet, A. Possamai, & B. S. Turner (Eds.), *Religion and the state. A comparative sociology* (pp. 43–64). London: Anthem Press.

Beckford, J. A., Joly, D., & Khosrokhavar, F. (2005). *Muslims in prison: Challenge and change in Britain and France*. Basingstoke: Macmillan Palgrave.

Benhabib, S. (2002). *The claims of culture. Equality and diversity in the global era*. Princeton: Princeton University Press.

Bertani, M., & Di Nicola, P. (Eds.). (2009). *Sfide trans-culturali e seconde generazioni*. Milano: FrancoAngeli.

Berzano, L., & Riis, O. P. (2012). *New methods in the sociology of religion. Annual review of sociology of religion* (Vol. 3). Leiden-Boston: Brill.

Blau, P. M. (1995). Il paradosso del multiculturalismo. *Rassegna italiana di Sociologia, 1*, 53–63.

Caeiro, A. (2010). Transnational Ulama, European Fatwas, and Islamic Authority: A case study of the European Council for Fatwa and Research. In M. van Bruinessen & S. Allievi (Eds.), *Producing Islamic knowledge: Transmission and dissemination in Western Europe* (pp. 121–141). London: Routledge.

Caritas-Migrantes. (2012). *Dossier Statistico Immigrazione. XXII rapporto*. Roma: Idos.

Cesari, J. (2004). *L'islam Ã l'épreuve de l'Occident*. Paris: La Decouverte.

Ciaurriz, M. J. (2004). La asistencia religiosa islámica en los centros públicos. In A. Motilla (Ed.), *Los musulmanes en España. Libertad religiosa e identidad cultural* (pp. 137–165). Madrid: Trotta.

Cohen, M., Joncheray, J., & Luizard, P.-J. (2004). *Les transformations de l'autorité religieuse*. Paris: L'Harmattan.

Colombo, E., Domaneschi, L., & Marchetti, C. (Eds.), (2009). *Una nuova generazione di italiani. L'idea di cittadinanza tra i giovani figli di immigrati*. Milano: FrancoAngeli.

Dassetto, F. (2003). *L'islam in Europa*. Torino: Fondazione Giovanni Agnelli.

Dassetto, F. (2011). *L'Iris et le Croissant. Bruxelles et l'islam au défi de la co-inclusion*. Louvain-la-Neuve: Presses Universitaires de Louvain.

Ferrari, S. (Ed.). (2006). *Islam ed Europa. I simboli religiosi nei diritti del Vecchio continente*. Roma: Carocci.

Ferrari, A. (2013). *La libertÀ religiosa in Italia. Un percorso incompiuto*. Roma: Carocci.

Flanagan, K., & Jupp, P. C. (2007). *A sociology of spirituality*. Hampshire: Ashgate.

Frégosi, F. (2004). L'imam, le conférencier et le jurisconsulte: Retour sur trois figures contemporaines du champ religieux islamique en France. *Archives de Sciences Sociales des Religions, 125,* 131–146.

Giordan, G. (Ed.). (2006). *Tra religione e spiritualità. Il rapporto con il sacro nell'epoca del pluralismo*. Milano: FrancoAngeli.

Giordan, G., & Pace, E. (Eds.). (2014). *Religious pluralism: Framing religious diversity in the contemporary world*. New York: Springer.

Glaser, B. G. (2003). *The grounded theory perspective II: Description's remodeling of grounded theory methodology*. Mill Valley: Sociology Press.

Glaser, B. G., & Strauss, A. L. (1967). *The discovery of grounded theory: Strategies for qualitative research*. Chicago: Aldin.

Glock, C. Y. (1964). *Toward a typology of religious orientations*. New York: Columbia University Press.

Heelas, P., & Woodhead, L. (2004). *The spiritual revolution: Why religion is giving way to spirituality*. Oxford: Blackwell.

Hermans, H. J. M., & Kempen, H. J. G. (1998). Moving cultures. The perilous problems of cultural dichotomies in a globalizing society. *American Psychologist, 53,* 1111–1120.

Jouanneau, S. (2013). *Les imams de France. Une autorité religieuse sous contrôle*. Paris: Agone.

Khosrokhavar, F. (2004). *L'islam dans les prisons*. Paris: Balland.

Leclerc, G. (2002). *Le bricolage religieux*. Monaco: Éditions du Rocher.

Lenoir, F. (2003). *Les métamorphoses de Dieu. Des intégrismes aux nouvelles spiritualités*. Paris: Plon.

Lewis, P. (2004). New social roles and changing patterns of authority amongst British "ulama". *Archives de Sciences Sociales des Religions, 125,* 169–188.

Luatti, L. (2006). *Atlante della mediazione linguistico culturale*. Milano: FrancoAngeli.

Luhmann, N. (1995). *Social systems*. Stanford: Stanford University Press.

Mantovani, G. (2008). *Intercultura e mediazione. Modelli ed esperienze per la ricerca, la formazione e la pratica*. Roma: Carocci.

Paillé, P. (1994). L'analyse par théorisation ancrée. *Cahiers de recherche sociologique, 23,* 147–181.

Pew Research Center. 2009. Mapping the global Muslim population: A report on the size and distribution of the World's Muslim population. http://www.pewforum.org/2009/10/07/mapping-the-global-muslim-population/#map2. Accessed 21 Sept 2013.

Reeber, M. (2004). La prédication (khutba) dans les mosquées en France et en Europe: enquête d'une nouvelle légitimité? In M. Cohen, J. Joncheray, & P-J Luizard (Eds.), *Les transformations de l'autorité religieuse* (pp. 187–198). Paris: L'Harmattan.

Rhazzali, K. (2008). Le seconde generazioni sulla soglia. Trickster, 6. http://masterintercultura. dissgea.unipd.it/trickster/doku.php?id=seconde_generazioni:khalid_soglia.

Rhazzali, K. (2010). *L'islam in carcere. L'esperienza dei giovani musulmani nelle prigioni italiane*. Milano: FrancoAngeli.

Rhazzali, K. (2014). The end of life from an intercultural perspective. Mediators and religious assistants in the health service. *Italian Journal of Sociology of Education, 6*(2), 224–255.

Rhazzali, K., & Equizi, M. (2013). I musulmani e i loro luoghi di culto. In E. Pace (Ed.), *Le religioni nell'Italia che cambia Mappe e bussole* (pp. 47–63). Roma: Carocci.

Rosati, M., & Fabretti, V. (2012). *L'assistenza religiosa in carcere. Diritti e diritto al culto negli istituti di pena del Lazio. Rapporto di Ricerca*. Roma: CSPS University of Rome Tor Vergata.

Roy, O. (2008). *La sainte ignorance. Le temps de la religion sans culture*. Paris: Seuil.

Saint-Blancat, C. (1995). *L'islam della diaspora*. Roma: Edizioni Lavoro.

Saint-Blancat, C., & Perocco, F. (2005). New modes of social interaction in Italy: Muslim leaders and local society in Tuscany and Venetia. In J. Cesari & S. McLoughlin (Eds.), *European Muslims and the secular state* (pp. 99–112). Aldershot: Ashgate.

Saint-Blancat C. (2008). Imām e responsabili musulmani in relazione con la società locale. In A. Pacini. *Chiesa e Islam in Italia: esperienze e prospettive di dialogo* (pp. 57–82). Milano: Edizioni Paoline.

Sbai, Y. (2013). L'assistenza religiosa ai musulmani detenuti nelle prigioni d'Italia. Unpublished Master's Thesis (project work), University of Padova.

Sbraccia, A. (2007). *Migranti tra mobilitÃ sociale e carcere. Storie di vita e processi di criminalizzazione*. Milano: FrancoAngeli.

Schneuwly Purdie, M. (2011). "Silence… Nous sommes en direct avec Allah". Réflexions sur l'émergence d'intervenants musulmans en contexte carcéral. *Archives de sciences sociales des religions,* 153(1), 105–121.

Schneuwly Purdie, M., & Vuille, J. (2010). Égalitaires ou discriminatoires? Regards croisés sur l'exercice de la liberté religieuse dans les prisons suisses. *Revue internationale de criminologie et police scientifique et technique, 63,* 469–490.

Shadid, W. A. R., & Koningsveld, P. S. van (Eds.). (2002). *Intercultural Relations and Religious Authorities: Muslims in the European Union*. Leuven: Peeters.

Spalek, B., & El-Hassan, S. (2007). Muslim converts in prison. *The Howard Journal of Criminal Justice, 46*(2), 99–114.

Strauss, A. L., & Corbin, J. M. (1990). *Basics of qualitative research: Grounded theory procedures and techniques*. California: Sage.

Strauss, A. L., & Corbin, J. M. (1997). *Grounded theory in practice*. London: Sage.

Tarozzi, M. (2008). *Che cos'è la Grounded theory*. Roma: Carocci.

Trombetta, L. P. (2004). *Il bricolage religioso. Sincretismo e nuova religiosità*. Bari: Dedalo.

# Part III
# New Approaches to the Junction of Rehabilitation and Religion in the Prison Realm

# Chapter 9
# Doing Yoga Behind Bars: A Sociological Study of the Growth of Holistic Spirituality in Penitentiary Institutions

Mar Griera and Anna Clot-Garrell

> For me yoga is one of the things that everyone should try in their life before dying. No one should miss out on the feeling of this connection that you have with yourself, because you work in a mental, physical and spiritual way. Yoga opens a door towards your inner self by moving away from the material and everything that is external. (Inmate)
> I want to show them [inmates] their potential as human beings so that they can construct their own reality. (Social worker)

## 9.1 Introduction[1]

In her book *Saving the Modern Soul* (2008), Eva Illouz states that ideas and meanings can become dominant when they fulfil three conditions. First, they have to help actors to make sense of their everyday social experiences. Second, they have to offer direction and patterns in uncertain or problematic societal spheres. And third, the carriers of such ideas and meanings must be able to take root and institutionalise those ideas and meanings within society. Taking Illouz's stance as a point of departure, this chapter explores the emergent and relevant presence of the holistic symbolic universe in prisons as an exercise framed within a cultural sociology

---

[1] We would like to thank Irene Becci and Marian Burchardt for their valuable comments and suggestions on the text. Marta Puig, Julia Martínez-Ariño and Gloria Garcíaa-Romeral for their help at the different stages of the research. Likewise, to all inmates and staff of the prison that have made possible the fieldwork.

M. Griera (✉) · A. Clot-Garrell
Sociology Department, Universitat Autònoma de Barcelona, Barcelona, Spain
e-mail: mariadelmar.griera@uab.cat

A. Clot-Garrell
e-mail: anna.clot@uab.cat

© Springer International Publishing Switzerland 2015                                        141
I. Becci, O. Roy (eds.), *Religious Diversity in European Prisons*,
DOI 10.1007/978-3-319-16778-7_9

perspective. We aim to engage with Illouz's interpretive conditions critically so as to examine the success of holistic activities in the Catalan penitentiary context—understanding "success" to mean the non-problematisation, acceptance and rapid diffusion of such ideas and practices.

With this approach the purpose of the chapter is twofold. First, it considers the role and significance of these holistic practices for inmates. Second, the conditions that have enabled their emergence, legitimacy and dissemination in the penitentiary sphere are explored. Along similar lines to Illouz, our principal argument is that the success of holistic activities within penitentiary institutions is mainly explained by their consonance with the two most important functions of a prison: discipline and rehabilitation. Holistic activities and therapies become symbolic resources through which inmates can make sense of their uncertain situation and (re)construct their self-image while also working as a "peace-making mechanism" that fits in with the institutional order. Prison staff—specifically social workers—plays a crucial role as carriers, in the Weberian sense of the term, of the ideas and values that underlie holistic activities. Without their initiative and support, these practices would hardly be present in the penitentiary context nowadays.

The research upon which this chapter is based is a result of serendipity and continuous sociological questioning. In September 2011, we began a research project that aimed to explore the role of religion in Spanish public institutions by focusing on Catholicism and religious minorities. While carrying out this study, we visited several prisons in Catalonia and Andalusia. During some of our fieldwork, we came across signs of what has been called the "holistic milieu" (Heelas et al. 2005). To our surprise, this presence was usually normalised, even unnoticed, by prison staff and management, in contrast to "problematic" religious issues with Muslims or Evangelicals. Holistic expressions manifested as a self-evident aspect of the everyday educational and leisure activities in prison that had no specific scientific interest for our interlocutors. This initial evidence, particularly regular yoga activities, attracted our sociological attention. A more careful and attentive subsequent exploration of this apparently trivial and irrelevant presence of the holistic milieu in prison revealed the existence of a complex and diverse entanglement of holistic practices and techniques—from yoga to Reiki, Qigong or transpersonal meditation—in the Catalan penitentiary setting.

Recent studies have documented the remarkable rise of holistic expressions in the Spanish religious environment (Cornejo 2012; Prat et al. 2012; Griera and Urgell 2002) in parallel with the results of other research in European contexts and elsewhere (Roof 1999; Heelas and Woodhead 2005; Aupers and Houtman 2006; Dawson 2007; Fedele 2013). However, little attention has been drawn to the presence of holistic expressions in public institutional domains. While the study of the holistic milieu has been developed by looking mainly at the popularisation of "alternative" spiritualities through market and/or personal networks, social scientists concerned with the interface of religion and the public sphere have basically focused on traditional religion in their analyses. This is certainly true of research performed specifically on religion in public institutions such as prisons, where interest has focused mainly on visible and institutionalised forms of religion (Beckford and Gilliat-Ray 1998; Martínez-Ariño et al. 2015; Furseth and Aa Kühle 2011; Becci

2012) while omitting, in many cases, other less explicit layers of the increasingly religiously diverse reality in prisons. Once noted, the growing significance of holistic practices in Spanish penitentiary settings provides clues to this fact and leads us to a more careful examination of this rarely explored reality. In this attempt to analyse the success of the holistic milieu in prison, we adopt a social constructivist approach (Beckford 2003) in order to examine the *emic* taken-for-granted separations of what is considered religious and non-religious in the penitentiary environment. The emergent presence of holistic activities challenges these limits. Accordingly, from the perspective of Beckford's conception of religion as "a social construct that varies in meaning across time and place" rather than as a fixed category and immutable expression (2003, p. 7), we look at the unmistakable boundaries that our informants establish when talking about the division between religion and spirituality. Along a similar line to Fedele and Knibbe (2013), we consider these terms analytically as complexly interrelated and situated within the same continuum rather than diametrically opposed.

The results presented and discussed in this chapter are derived from qualitative research divided into two phases. First, an exploratory phase was developed as part of the GEDIVER-IN project[2]. This included eight prisons (six in Catalonia and two in Andalusia) where we conducted interviews with institutional actors and prison staff along with observations in communal spaces, religious activities and, occasionally, holistic activities[3]. Second, a subsequent phase centred on two prisons in Catalonia that were selected as case studies in order to examine the presence of holistic activities in depth. This second part of the fieldwork consisted of participant observations in a yoga quarantine regularly performed in a prison (from July–August 2013) and an intensive yoga course in a preventive prison (three days per week during June and July 2014). Both participant observations were complemented by surveys of all participants and semi-structured interviews with a group of selected inmates, holistic actors, social workers and other professionals involved in the development of yoga activities in prison[4].

## 9.2  New Therapeutic-Spiritual Geographies in Prison

Over the last few years, yoga has become more common in Catalan prisons. A good illustration of this growing phenomenon is the agreement, signed in 2011, between the Justice Department of the Catalan government and a yoga organisation

---

[2] The Project entitled "GEDIVER-IN: The governance of religious diversity in prisons and hospitals in Spain" was funded by the Spanish National Research Program (2010–2014), reference number CSO2010-21248.

[3] This fieldwork stage was performed together with Julia Martínez-Ariño, Gloria Garcia-Romeral and occasional assistance was by Marc Sant, Laia Vidal and Gerard Tomàs. See Martínez-Ariño et al. (2015) or Griera et al. (2015).

[4] In this second phase, the research was funded by a grant from the Juridical Studies Center of the Catalan government and done in collaboration with Marta Puig, a criminologist and also a yoga teacher.

presented as "a non-profit and independent organisation centred on disinterestedly providing yoga benefits to disadvantaged groups". The purpose of this accord was to regulate yoga activities in prison through the following: "organisation of yoga practice, comfort to inmates, collaboration in treatment teams and participation in cultural weeks and other activities". What is remarkable about this arrangement is not the activities themselves, but the fact that the formalisation of this agreement represents official institutional recognition of the practice of yoga in prison. Yoga is a voluntary activity that has been practiced in different Catalan prisons since approximately 2000 and is gradually gaining prominence. In some penitentiary centres, yoga is coordinated as part of the formal agreement between the government and the aforementioned yoga organisation but, in other cases, some local yoga teachers offer voluntary classes to inmates without being formally affiliated with any yoga organisation or having any institutional agreement.

However, it is worth noting that yoga is not an isolated activity but rather the tip of the iceberg of a broad, complex and multilayered holistic reality. Diverse practices from Reiki to Sophrology, along with meditation or positive thinking courses, currently exist in Catalan prisons. These are conducted by either individual volunteers of different ages and backgrounds or more organised groups such as Brahma Kumaris, Reiki organisations or even Catholic volunteer groups. According to our findings, social workers play a key role in fostering these activities,we will discuss it in further detail in the fourth section, though sometimes the impetus comes from particular individuals and non-profit associations who attempt to gain access to a prison to propose this type of activity. In all cases, whether it be yoga, Reiki or meditation, they are generally considered by prison staff as suitable activities for inmates. They are commonly perceived as practices halfway between psychology or emotional education and physical exercise that can indirectly help to rehabilitate inmates or to support the programs specifically designed with this aim in mind.

The growth of these holistic expressions that we have observed in Catalan prisons is not an isolated phenomenon but rather one that is widespread in other European contexts, as Becci and Knobel have demonstrated (2014). These scholars have analysed the emergence of what they call the "grey zones", which they identify as those practices situated between spirituality and religion that are gaining grounds within penitentiary centres. They note the growing presence of actors related to "New Age" milieus that have training in yoga and other holistic techniques and highlight the fact that "while these actors define themselves as spiritual practitioners, they are never considered as religious actors by the penitentiary institution" (2013). We have found similar patterns in the Catalan penitentiary context, where holistic practices are incorporated in educational and leisure programmes and neither these activities nor their volunteers are considered or regulated as a spiritual–religious in nature. As a social worker commented concerning yoga: "We have to guarantee neutrality, it is not a religious activity despite its spiritual dimension. These are two separate things". This is representative of an oft-repeated answer of prison staff when asked about the spiritual-religious dimension of yoga. They usually downplay this aspect and regard it as secondary.

Nonetheless, the boundaries are vague. The fact that some holistic activities are conducted by groups which are registered as religious by the Spanish Justice

Ministry, for instance Brahma Kumaris, or that in some sessions religious leaders such as Buddhist Lamas are invited, is proof of these blurred boundaries. The inmates themselves also acknowledge the subtle conflation of the religious, spiritual and leisure components. In this regard, one of the regular attendants said, "although I am Evangelical, I have enjoyed the course", while another inmate told us that some Muslim or Pentecostal inmates refused to participate in the course due to the perception of its incompatibility with their faith. Needless to say that if these activities were labeled as religious, the regulations and bureaucratic control would be much stricter (Griera and Clot 2015). However, as most of these activities occur during less structured periods, such as weekends or leisure time, they receive less institutional attention and remain formally unnoticed. This, in turn, translates into less oversight over the contents taught, although the prisons' minimum levels of supervision still apply. In any case, despite their relative invisibility, the presence of holistic practices has had a positive reception among inmates while also fulfilling important institutional functions, as we will show in the next two sections.

## 9.3   The Participants: Narration, Meaning and Transcendence

It is ten in the morning and the yoga class is ready to start. The group of inmates make a lively little crowd while waiting in front of the theatre where the yoga classes usually take place. Matías[5], the head of the social workers, opens the door and everybody goes in and waits for his turn to take his mat from a large box that one of the inmates brings from a room next to the main hall. Meanwhile, the arts teacher lights several sticks of incense and places them in the corners of the large room. Ruben, the Friday yoga teacher, turns up his iPod and the sound of mantras fills the air. The arts teacher and Maria, a social worker, also lay out their own mats, take off their shoes and prepare themselves for the start of the session. Two minutes later, everyone is silent and in place. The hall's door is closed and Ruben smiles, offers a greeting and starts the class. He is a demanding teacher and the session will not be easy: "Today we are working on our will, the will that lies inside us, forgetting our environment, bringing the mind to the breath and holding the asana", he says loudly while asking the twenty-seven attendees of the session to hold an uncomfortable posture for more than three minutes. Most of the inmates take up the challenge and follow Ruben's class with a combination of devotion, concentration, intensity and intent. They sweat. In fact, some of them sweat a lot. During the class, Ruben intersperses his physical instructions with some existential comments, such as "Prepare to take a new path, open your mind to new endeavours and forgive yourself". Ten or fifteen minutes before ending the session, an inmate turns off the lights and the relaxation–meditation time begins. Ruben's strong voice guides the meditation and, as on some special Fridays, the voice of Violeta, a slender yoga singer, accompanies

---

[5] All the names used in this paper have been changed in order to protect and respect the anonymity of the informants.

him together with a group of musicians who play the didgeridoo and other instruments. About that moment one of the inmates remarked: "They [the yoga teacher and the musicians] turn the old, dirty and decadent theatre into a paradise, into a space of peace and take us into a floating state". When the meditation ends, the lights are turned on again and everyone returns to the ordinary reality of everyday life in prison.

### 9.3.1   The Centrality of the Body

This ethnographic episode took place in a specific preventive prison but it could have occurred in most of the voluntary yoga courses offered in Catalan prisons. We will not analyse this particular interaction in detail but it does serve to give a general feel for the practice of holistic activities in prison. As aforementioned, yoga, along with other holistic practices, is becoming more prominent in penitentiary settings and a very popular practice among inmates. In the course of this research, the participant observation that we have done in prison yoga classes has helped us to grasp the reasons behind the appeal of holistic practices to inmates. Their oral as well as written narratives have provided us with new insights. The goal has been to understand the specificity of these practices compared with other leisure and educational ones carried out in prison and the meanings that inmates attach to them.

At first sight, the fact that prisons are close to Goffman's ideal type of "total institution" (1961) has clear implications on how these holistic practices are experienced and rendered meaningful in this context seems obvious. In his work *Asylums* (1961), Goffman describes in great detail what entering a total institution signifies. For individuals, it involves being gradually divested of all that socially identifies one's self when the institution starts to activate different procedures of "self-mortification". He refers to these processes in terms of isolation from the external world, limitation of autonomy, depersonalisation and, particularly, the loss of control of the territories of the self (Goffman 1961; Nizet and Rigaux 2005). In the penitentiary space, these territories are constantly questioned and violated as well as open to "contaminating exposure to people, objects and activities that one would rather avoid" (Scott 2010, p. 216). The institution regulates these territories and imposes their rules upon them. Within a total institution, individuals lose their own autonomy over spaces, objects and even over the possibility to narrate their own lives. Inmates' own self-narration is constructed and imposed on them by others—judges, psychologists, social workers and other professionals—which clearly affects their self-image, self-esteem and agency.

Part of the popularity of holistic activities among inmates is that to some extent they enable inmates to counteract these impositions and offer room to recover the sense of the self. The most evident element, which is frequently emphasised by the inmates themselves, is that these practices create spaces of calm and quietude in the midst of the chaotic, noisy and cluttered penitentiary environment. The time dedicated to relaxation and meditation is one of the most valued moments as it offers an opportunity for introspection. Finding "safe" and silent contexts where one can feel intimacy with oneself is not easy in prison. In a way, through yoga, participants regain control over their private space and a way to access what is perceived and defined as the "inner self" or "authentic self".

The particular scenography of the yoga class—with the music, incense, mats laid out around the room and lights turned partially off—also aids inmates in crossing the threshold of the everyday reality of prison. The setting, the "scenic parts of expressive equipment" according to Goffman (1959, p. 23), plays a decisive role in facilitating or disturbing actors' performances and experiences. In the case of the yoga sessions observed, the specific disposition of the class and the sensory elements, like the sounds, the fragrances, the light or the touch, perform a crucial ritual function as symbolic transgressions of the penitentiary order and norms. They acquire a fundamental meaning and symbolic weight due to the context of the total institution where they take place (Goffman 1961). A good illustration of this aspect is the inmates' magnified perception of the touching that yoga teachers do (or not) to correct asanas during the classes. The importance of these touching gestures appears to be so important for inmates that they even clearly distinguish between the teachers that "touch" and do not touch, with those that do being more valued than the others. This recalls Becci when stating that "in a total institution, a space of freedom means a space of humanity" (2012, p. 112). In a certain way, this physical contact is considered as "humanising" and has the ability to momentarily dissolve the boundary between the internal and external prison world. What is more, through these touches yoga teachers themselves break the unwritten rule that there should be no physical contact between insiders and outsiders. Actually, holistic activities are often experienced as occasional and unnoticed episodes of transgression of the prison's prescribed order by inmates but, also, sometimes by the staff. The account of Maria, a social worker who is also a holistic practitioner and teacher, of the ritual celebration with the attendees of a prison Reiki course for St. John's Eve is highly illustrative of this point:

> This was the first time a ritual like this had been done in prison. We are not used to holding people's hands, everyone has their roles here. In prison we are very strict. [...] We lit a candle and each expressed their wishes, we formed a circle and clasped hands and each asked for his stuff and [...] we were all very happy after the ritual, we were hugging tightly. It was the first time, I think, that I hugged an inmate. And there was a beautiful sensation that something important had occurred.

Holding hands, hugging and lighting sticks of incense or candles are elements that clearly and symbolically challenge the "normal" interaction in prison. All of these elements contribute to building a new emotional and sensory context conducive to experiences of transcendence. In the vein of Schütz's phenomenological approach, we could argue that the practice of yoga permits inmates to enter into a particular "finite province of meaning" of a different nature to the "paramount reality" of everyday life in prison. Those inmates, who become seriously involved in yoga and master enough of the postures to be able to experience a "flow", in the Csikszentmihalyian sense of the term[6], are the ones who have a greater chance of transcend-

---

[6] A flow is defined as a process "[...] in which action follows upon action according to an internal logic which seems to need no conscious intervention on our part. We experience it as a unified

ing the prison walls and entering a finite province of meaning. According to our observations and interviews, not all inmates show such deep involvement in yoga sessions but most of those who regularly participate in them have expressed that they experience feelings of flowing at some point during the class. Nonetheless, the important aspect here is the centrality of the body in facilitating the experience of transcendence. To some extent, the body works as a trigger to develop a sense of spiritual awareness, fluidity and connection between body, mind and soul. As McIlwain and Sutton state, "yoga [...] promotes an increasingly subtle interpenetration of thought and movement" (2014, p. 655). Along these lines, the interviews with inmates show that they do positively correlate the performance of yoga's body movements with psychological, cognitive or emotional changes. Some of them expressed that "through the motions we regulate our interior", "yoga helps me to feel more agile and above all at peace with yourself" or "yoga helps me stretch my body and makes me feel very peaceful". To gain control over the body is often the first step to an inner transformative journey of self-discovery, self-reflection and agency by inmates, as the social workers also underlined.

## 9.3.2   The Spiritual Dimension

Inmate surveys and interviews show that those who are more committed to the yoga courses overtly recognise its spiritual side. Even more, the popularity of yoga in prison is specifically attributed to the connection between the physical and spiritual domains. The singularity of yoga, compared with the other physical activities offered, such as basketball or muscle-building exercises, is that it is not only a bodily exercise. Yoga classes are accompanied by small talks and comments by the yoga teachers that endow a spiritual and philosophical meaning to the practice. In some cases, the yoga teachers also offer some texts about the philosophy of yoga to inmates—at the beginning of a new course or as optional material for committed attendees in regular courses—as well as recommend books, films or music. Therefore, the spiritual-therapeutic narrative is transmitted little by little but this is not an obstacle for the construction of a coherent and meaningful spiritual universe by the inmates themselves. However, yoga's uniqueness also lies in its ability to go beyond the "talking cure". Most interviewees refer to the physical exercise as a precondition for the apprehension of the spiritual side of the practice. To some extent, the relief of the penitentiary stress that the physical exercise produces, together with the self-confidence gained when the inmates are able to master their own body, is what offers opportunities for experiencing transcendence. In this case, the body becomes a vehicle for starting a spiritual path at the same time that the physical and psychological effects of the practice help to authenticate and validate the spiritual journey that has been undertaken.

---

flowing from one moment to the next, in which we feel in control of our actions, and in which there is little distinction between self and environment, between stimulus and response, or between past, present and future" (Csikszentmihalyi 1975: 43). The specific differences between flow, finite provinces of meaning and religious experiences are interestingly addressed by Spickard and Neitz (1990) and also by Bloch (2000).

In a certain way, according to inmates' perceptions, the practise of yoga enables them to activate self-reflexivity and spiritual awareness. As one inmate attested, "yoga has lit a flame within me, now I know myself better in a physical, spiritual and emotional sense". But even more important than this space of reflexivity is the fact that holistic activities provide a vocabulary and a narrative through which to rethink and reconstruct the autobiographical narrative. The holistic environment introduces inmates to a therapeutic and spiritual language that enables them to acquire new concepts such as "power", "karma", "reincarnation" and "synchronicity" that are then incorporated in their "stock of knowledge" (Schütz 1945), and used to give meaning to their suffering, and their past and present moments. As stated by Goffmann in *Asylums*, one of the most devastating feelings of being confined in a total institution is the feeling of completely wasting one's time. In certain cases, the interviewees have shown that holistic narratives help to give meaning to the prison experience by portraying it as a period of personal and spiritual growth.

In this task, the self-help books or spiritual novels—such as those by Paulo Coelho—play a crucial role in offering metaphors, stories and concepts to complement the knowledge acquired in the holistic activities. All of the social workers have emphasised the popularity of these books in prison, especially among the participants in such activities, as well as in inmate meetings to share these materials. In this regard, it is important to acknowledge that the path undertaken by these inmates is an individual one though it also has a strong collective dimension. When not in class, some of them gather to exchange books, other materials or even to practice yoga. Thus, holistic activities serve the dual function of "supplying" and "confirming" meaning. While they generate meaning by new "knowledge repertoires", they also create spaces where interpersonal meanings can be expressed, shared and mutually validated (Hervieu-Léger 2001, p. 167).

Before finishing this section it is worth noting that, as already mentioned, not everyone experiences holistic activities with the same intensity or commitment. For some of them, the holistic world shapes the "raw" material from which to build a new social identity that in some cases will lead them to be trainers themselves or acknowledged "experts" in relation to other inmates. For some others, the practice of yoga is only a "pass-time" with no other commitment. In the middle, there is a wide range of involvement and commitment to the bodily and spiritual dimensions of holistic activities. However, in any case, the holistic universe has become an available resource at hand for inmates to help in coping with the confined prison existence.

## 9.4   The Penitentiary Institution: Affinities, Discipline and Rehabilitation

After resolving some bureaucratic issues we received permission to interview the prison staff. Today, there is a session with Natalia, one of the social workers who is in charge of supervising yoga activities. Later on comes Matías, another social worker, and then the last is Maribel, an arts education teacher. Several common aspects emerge in this intensive fieldwork day, which recur in further interviews. Natalia recounts, among other impressions, her amazement concerning some inmates' interest in and commitment to yoga. Throughout the interview, she uses the word "self-control" several times. She gives the example of an inmate that reacted in a very different way than usual, not aggressively or violently, when another inmate provoked him and she attributes these changes to his regular yoga practice. She uses this example to underline how yoga helps inmates to be relaxed and physically and mentally disciplined, which promotes general cohabitation. Matías, along these lines, underscores that yoga is low-cost and high-benefit for the institution and is an optional activity to the educational treatment programs with rehabilitation aims. He has been working in the same prison for almost 30 years. He tells us that in the last 5–7 years he has observed "an evolution in the rehabilitation treatments". Increasingly, they talk more in terms of "self-knowledge" and yoga fits into this scheme perfectly. They, the social workers, are the ones who propose educational activities and yoga was their idea. He emphasises that in proposing any activity to prison management, apart from fulfilling the institutional criteria of "opportunity, control and security", the interest and personal disposition of the social workers carries significant weight. In this regard, in the last interview, Maribel shares with us her personal training in holistic techniques. She gives the regular educational artistic workshops in prison and explains how she introduces her holistic experience in her job, for instance by having inmates do stretching exercises based on her background in Qigong, NLP (Neuro-linguistic programming), yoga or Reiki before her workshops. She tells us that sometimes she has prepared these stretching exercises on the basis of a Reiki symbol or has encouraged inmates to "do this yoga thing of rubbing their hands and after putting their hands on the eyes in order to make them feel the heat, that is, the energy generated by their bodies".

These examples from the prison staff interviews point to the second objective of this chapter, which is the analysis of the conditions that explain the emergence and increasingly legitimised presence of holistic practices in the institutional prison order. According to our findings, we hypothesise that to disentangle this "success" in the particular penitentiary context, the convergence and combination of three particular factors must be accounted for: the role of prison staff as carriers of these holistic practices, the contribution that these practices have in the maintenance of the institutional order and the affinity of these practices with new rehabilitation models.

### 9.4.1 The Prison Staff

As the empirical illustrations above indicate, the first factor that must be considered is the role that prison staff plays as carriers, in the Weberian sense, of holistic practices. Social workers in particular, but also pedagogues and some psychologists, are the promoters of these therapies within penitentiary institutions and their support is crucial in order to comprehend the introduction, acceptance and non-problematic development of such activities in the prison setting. We have demonstrated that this support is intimately related to a mimetic process that occurs between social workers and holistic volunteers on two levels. On the surface, social workers and holistic actors share an urban middle-class background and the possession of cultural capital, a fact previously noted by Becci and Knobel (2014). This common background is translated into a similar *habitus* (Bourdieu 1979), which is visible in affinities in aesthetics, language usage and corporal disposition. All of these similarities enable a quiet and friendly relationship between prison workers and holistic actors which is evident in everyday occurrences, such as having breakfast together in the prison canteen, exchanging personal e-mail and mobile phone contacts, informal conversations before and after yoga activities or even sharing impressions, and occasionally confidential information, about inmates.

At a deeper level, this mimesis also results from the fact that in many cases social workers and socio-educative teachers in the prison are themselves practitioners—and even teachers—of such holistic techniques. Actually, as one of the previously mentioned interviewees showed, some prison staff who work directly with prisoners more or less indirectly apply holistic techniques to everyday routines and activities with inmates. The narrative among the prison workers interviewed when explaining their experience within the holistic universe is similar. They all relate the discovery of one or various holistic practices in particular life situations and, exhibiting the typical pragmatism of new-era discourses (Dawson 2007, p. 99), they all claim that as these techniques have worked on a personal level, they wanted to apply them also at work. Furthermore, insofar as some prison workers are familiar with holistic language, they also play a bridging role between holistic volunteers and the institution, specifically by making these activities suitable to the eyes of prison managers, who are more concerned with the macro and security aspects of prison dynamics. According to some of our interviewees, these prison workers, who are "supporters" of holistic activities, are not isolated cases but rather part of a wave of mid-level professionals, particularly social workers and socio-educative teachers, who are increasingly sympathetic towards these matters. In summary, the crucial dual component that gives rise to these activities is exactly this: the affinity between staff and volunteers and the promotional agency of prison staff.

### 9.4.2 The Institutional Order

A second factor necessary to comprehend the "success" of these holistic practices in the penitentiary domain is that they are perceived as instruments that help to control, discipline and maintain prison order. Although yoga is introduced in prisons with philanthropic objectives, as our holistic interlocutors emphasised, one of the unexpected consequences of these activities' incorporation is that rather than sometimes empowering inmates, they become tools adapted for reinforcing and maintaining institutional order.

According to our interviews with prison staff, holistic activities encourage quietness and smooth relationships between inmates. The social workers in particular all constantly emphasise that these practices help inmates to calm down and offer tools to learn self-control and manage impulsiveness in a prison context where, as pointed out by Goffman, "staying out of trouble is likely to require persistent conscious effort" (1961, p. 43). As an example of this, one of the inmates reflected, "Now, I think twice before getting aggressive. When someone annoys me, first I take a deep breath and then I reply". Another one explained that after participating in the intensive yoga course "I react to people in a different way, with more compassion". As a result, holistic activities facilitate a nonviolent environment and, thus, fulfil the institution's essential aims of security and control. This is one of the crucial aspects in prison managers' perception of holistic activities as positive.

However, along with the adaptability of holistic practices to security requirements, there is another related aspect that is essential in order to explain the success of these spiritualities in the penitentiary order, the fact that they fill the time. As Becci states, "the temporal dimension plays a significant role in prison" (2012, p. 103). As an illustration of this point, in Catalonia of an inmate population of 9818 only 3884 participate in productive labour (CIRE 2013; Alós et al. 2009). The rest are occupied in training or rehabilitation programs but there are still many hours to fill (Martos García et al. 2009). In fact, as already noted by Goffman, "the rationales for mortifying the self are very often merely rationalisations, generated by efforts to manage the daily activity of a large number of persons in a restricted space with a small expenditure of resources" (1961, pp. 46–47). Consequently, the pressing need to fill inmates' time, together with the existence of volunteers ready to offer their own time for altruistic motives, provide the conditions to give momentum to these practices within a context of economic crisis, cuts and reductions in formal programs. Again referring to Goffman, we could argue that "the sense of dead and heavy-hanging time probably explains the premium placed on what might be called removal activities", such as holistic practices, which, rather than the ordinary ones that "can be said to torture time, these [removal] activities mercifully kill it" for inmates (1961, p. 69). This is an important issue for institutional order due to the fact that, as underlined by Martos García et al., "boredom can become the worst of the punishments for inmates and a source of problems concerning cohabitation within the institution" (2009, p. 393)[7]. For this reason, if, ultimately, holistic activities fill inmates' time at a low cost, support the institution's aims and have the support of the prison workers who implement them, it is difficult for prison management to actively oppose them.

Nevertheless, the existence of a substantial number of holistic volunteers willing to donate their time to teach yoga or other holistic activities to inmates is not enough to explain the success of these techniques. A second crucial aspect to consider is that these holistic actors are not viewed with suspicion as, for instance, the proselytism of some Evangelicals. The aforementioned affinities with social workers along with the vague boundaries between the spiritual and educational dimension of holistic

---

7 Authors' translation

activities open the doors wider for all holistic groups and volunteers. However, at the first sign that yoga, Reiki or any holistic activity runs counter to the disciplinary order, it will be automatically suppressed, whatever the supposed benefit is for inmates. As argued by Martos García et al., "the regime wins over treatment […]. When an educational activity involves any kind of risk to or calls into question the formal organisation, it is simply eliminated" (2009, p. 409)[8]. Limits in the prison context are designed to be clear and holistic volunteers know that some things cannot be said or done. As one social worker, who carefully supervises the organisation of activities in one prison, stated: "We cannot take the risk of allowing anyone to enter, someone who can send a very different message (from the one that we propagate) to inmates". The line between what is allowed and forbidden, what represents the "apparent normality" in Goffman's terms (1961), seems invisible, but when crossed becomes completely evident (Foucault 1977). While Reiki and yoga volunteers are generally perceived as trustworthy and fully accepted by prison staff, some "alternative" groups such as Wicca or Pagan have seen their entrance as volunteers very limited because, according to the experience of the social worker mentioned above, some Wicca discourses concerning spirits could contradict and alter the treatment of inmates in mental health units. To some extent, while the spiritual dimension of yoga or Reiki can easily be conflated with the language of therapy or psychology, some of the statements of Wicca or Pagan groups more openly engage with a spiritual or religious realm that is perceived to be inappropriate in penitentiary settings—or at least, unsuitable to be offered to all inmates as an educational or leisure activity.

### 9.4.3   The Rehabilitation Models

Finally, we have discovered a third factor for an understanding of the success of holistic therapies in the penitentiary sphere: the affinity between the increasing presence of holistic activities and the emergence of a new approach to and meaning of rehabilitation. The aforementioned evidence that holistic practices contribute to recreate intimacy in a prison context is related to the fact that these "therapeutic narratives" through which inmates learn to narrate themselves are based on a language usage that has gradually gained more institutional recognition, both within prison and in society at large (Illouz 2008). We argue that the rise in the significance of yoga and other holistic activities in Catalan prisons reflects a gradual transformation of traditional rehabilitation models more concerned with external proof for evaluating the degree of a prisoner's reintegration, such as having a job or cell cleanliness, towards an emergent, more self-centred model. Garreaud and Malventi (2008) are among those who have noted the construction of a new therapeutic-penal space which goes hand in hand with "emotional capitalist" dynamics, where "the

---

8 Authors' translation.

therapeutic self" becomes important as a new hegemonic paradigm (Illouz 2008; Füredi 2004).

The fieldwork has revealed that the silent takeover of this new rehabilitation model is happening at the level of daily treatment through professionals' practices and the language of Catalan prisons rather than at the more institutional level of formal structures and programs. The responses of our mid-range professionals' interviews have repeatedly referred to the interface of yoga and rehabilitation benefits in terms of "personal transformation", "self-responsibility", "self-management of individual behaviour" or of how "yoga goes beyond sporting activities in terms of self-knowledge and self-control, because in sporting activities these abilities are less explicit". Evincing the normalisation of this terminology as well as the latent shift towards a therapeutic-penal model, an increasing number of prison staff conceives of their commitment towards inmates' rehabilitation in line with how one social worker—also a holistic practitioner—expressed her approach to her job: "I focus on potentialities rather than looking at what inmates lack, encouraging their positive abilities".

However, this shift towards a new rehabilitation model that apparently encourages inmates' empowerment also entails new forms of power (Garreaud and Malventi 2008), signaling a move away from authoritarian surveillance and mass routines to "soft-power" and "self-regulation" (Crewe 2011, p. 528). The existence of holistic practices in prison is, in this sense, both a cause and a result of this shift. Echoing Garreaud and Malventi, who observe how in this new form of power "the regressive time of penitentiary experience is substituted by a progressive (productive) time of the therapeutic one, where prisoners become self-administrators of their own space of punishment and reform" (2008, p. 8), a social worker who is part of a treatment team explained how active productive use of prison time by an inmate is a key variable in receiving a positive evaluation from the treatment team—that is, a sign of their assisting the rehabilitation process. He added how the social workers, recommend and encourage inmates to get involved in yoga activities not only to fill the time but also as an activity that "offers tools that inmates could apply individually in their everyday life without our supervision". In this more demanding prison environment, holistic activities seem to fill empty schedules with the logics, demands and imperatives of this new therapeutic-penal order due to its nature and content. Our fieldwork shows that the presence of holistic therapies, therefore, indicates a new trend in prison governance based on a growing conception of "the subjectivisation of punishment and the individualisation of the prison sentence" (Garreaud and Malventi 2008, p. 9).

## 9.5 Conclusion

We have taken Illouz (2008) as a starting point in order to examine the emergent growth and silent success of holistic spiritual activities in prisons. A careful engagement with Illouz's explanatory conditions regarding the success of therapeutic ideas has helped us to make clear that the expansion and popularity of yoga, Reiki and other holistic activities among staff and inmates in Catalan prisons is neither an isolated nor random case.

As we have tried to demonstrate, the new language verbally and corporally transmitted in these holistic practices enables inmates to construct new narratives through which they can make sense of their past, current situation and future prospects. As Garrett observes:

> Reiki, meditation and yoga do try to change people for their own good and for the good of their society, and they do aim for some kind of liberation (at least freedom from suffering and, ultimately, freedom from ego). Some of their practitioners call them "spiritual" while others describe them more prosaically as "working on myself" but both these descriptions refer to the transformative potential of ritual, to take people beyond their current selves and towards a differently imagined future. This "other" space is what we call the sacred and we often experience as magical the means we use to reach it. (2001, p. 335)

However, what is important is that these transformative narratives are in consonance with therapeutic languages that are gaining ground and legitimacy in the institutional structures of prison. The analysis of this case has shown that "therapeutic narrative" is gradually becoming the basic self-schemata expected to organise autobiographical discourses, as Illouz pointed out with respect to modern western societies at large (2008).

Nonetheless, as much as to show these relationships within broader therapeutic culture (Füredi 2004) and the important role played by prison staff in order to legitimise and promote such activities, we have demonstrated that a decisive aspect for understanding the success of holistic activities is their consonance with prison's apparently opposed function. On one hand: punishment and the maintenance of order at minimum cost. On the other: the offer of opportunities for reintegration—that is, education and treatment. As Rodríguez Cesped (2010) argues:

> Regarding the material organisation [prison] is a hard segmented system. However, it is crossed by flexible functions. In this sense, prison is like an institution of punishment, discipline and control that sometimes refers to specific closure, segments and discontinuities; while in other circumstances it communicates through an abstract flexibility, with vagueness and fluidity. (2010, p. 150)

In a new therapeutic-penal space governed by novel forms of power (Garreaud and Malventi 2008; Crewe 2011), holistic activities transcend and converge through these different and ambivalent penitentiary fields, from discipline and control to education and health. This is without doubt another important ingredient of their success.

Overall, our fieldwork points towards the camouflaged but increasingly prominent presence of holistic practices in the penitentiary context, a sign which adds complexity and encourages further examination. Drawing on our case studies, we consider that the relatively rapid incorporation of holistic practices in the prison setting with little institutional resistance is not only a clear indicator of transformations in institutional penitentiary structures but also a significant evidence of the increasing popularity, legitimacy and hegemony that the holistic milieu is acquiring in contemporary western societies.

# References

Alós Moner, R., Martín Artiles, A., Miguélez Lobo, F., & Gibert Badia, F. (2009). Sirve el trabajo penitenciario para la reinserción? Un estudio a partir de las opiniones de los presos de las cárceles de Cataluña. *Revista Espanola de Investigaciones Sociologicas, 127,* 11–23.

Aupers, S., & Houtman, D. (2006). Beyond the spiritual supermarket: The social and public significance of new age spirituality. *Journal of contemporary Religion, 21*(2), 201–222.

Becci, I. (2012). *Imprisioned religion. Transformtions of religion during and after imprisionement in Eastern Germany.* Farnham: Ashgate.

Becci, I., & Knobel, B. (2014). La diversité religieuse en prison: entre modeles de regulation et emergence de zones grises (Suisse, Italie et Allemagne). In A. S. Lamine & N. Luca (eds), *Quand le religieux fait conflit. Désaccords, négociations ou arrangements* (pp. 109–122). Paris: La Découverte.

Beckford, J. A., & Gilliat-Ray, S. (1998). *Religion in prison: Equal rites in a multi-faith society.* Cambridge: Cambridge University Press.

Beckford, J. A. (2003). *Social theory and religion.* Cambridge: Cambridge University Press.

Bloch, C. (2000). Flow: beyond fluidity and rigidity. *Human Studies, 23*(1), 43–61.

Bourdieu, P. (1979). *La distinction: critique sociale du jugement.* Paris: Éditions du Minuit.

Centre d'Iniciatives per a la Reinserció (CIRE) Departament de Justícia, Generalitat de Catalunya. http://justicia.gencat.cat/ca/departament/Estadistiques/cire/. Accessed 15 October 2014.

Cornejo, M. (2012). Religión y espiritualidad: Dos modelos enfrentados? Trayectorias poscatólicas entre budistas Soka Gakkai. *Revista International de Sociologia, 70*(2), 327–346.

Crewe, B. (2011). Soft power in prison: Implications for staff–prisoner relationships, liberty and legitimacy. *European Journal of Criminology, 8*(6), 455–468.

Csikszentmihalyi, M. (1975). *Beyond boredom and anxiety.* San Francisco: Josey–Bass.

Dawson, A. (2007). *New era, new religions: Religious transformation in contemporary Brazil.* Aldershot: Ashgate.

Fedele, A. (2013). *Looking for Mary Magdalene: Alternative pilgrimage and ritual creativity at catholic shrines in France.* New York: Oxford University Press.

Fedele, A., & Knibbe, K. (Eds). (2013). *Gender and power in contemporary spirituality: Ethnographic approaches.* New York: Routledge.

Foucault, M. (1977). *Discipline and punish: The birth of the prison.* London: Random House LLC.

Füredi, F. (2004). *Therapy culture: Cultivating vulnerability in an uncertain age.* London: Psychology Press.

Furseth, I, & van der Aa Kühle, L. M. (2011). Prison chaplaincy from a scandinavian perspective. *Archive des sciences sociales des religions, N.153,* 123–141.

Garrett, C. (2001). Transcendental meditation, reiki and yoga: Suffering, ritual and self-transformation. *Journal of Contemporary Religion, 16*(3), 329–342.

Goffman, E. (1959). *The presentation of self in everyday life.* New York: Anchor.

Goffman, E. (1961). *Asylums: Essays on the social situation of mental patients and other inmates.* New York: Doubleday.

Griera, M., & Urgell, F. (2002). *Consumiendo religión: un análisis del consumo de productos con connotaciones espirituales entre la población juvenil.* Barcelona: Fundació La Caixa. ISBN: 84-7664-795-6.

Griera, M., & Clot, A. (2015). Banal is not trivial. Visibility, recognition and inequalities between religious groups in prison. *Journal of Contemporayry Religion, 30*(1), 23–27.

Griera, M., Martínez-Ariño, J., & Clot, A. (2015) Religión e instituciones públicas en España. Hospitales y prisiones en perspectiva comparada. *Revista Espanola de Investigaciones Sociologicas.*

Heelas, P., Woodhead, L., Seel, B., Szerszynski, B., & Tusting, K. (2005). *The spiritual revolution: Why religion is giving way to spirituality.* London: Blackwell.

Heelas, P., & Woodhead, L. (2005). *The spiritual revolution. Why religion is giving way to spirituality.* Oxford, Blackwell.

Hervieu-Léger, D. (2001). Individualism, the validation of faith, and the social nature of religion in modernity. In: K. R. Fenn (Ed), *The blackwell companion to sociology of religion* (pp. 161–175). Oxford: Blackwell.

Illouz, E. (2008). *Saving the modern soul: Therapy, emotions, and the culture of self-help.* California: University of California Press.

Malventi, D., & Garreaud, A. (2008). Curar y reinsertar. El fenómeno de la deslocalización terapéutica en el engranaje penitenciario. In: Revista de Espai en Blanc. Available via Espai en Blanc: http://www.espaienblanc.net/Curar-y-reinsertar.html. Accessed 10 Oct 2014.

Martínez-Ariño, J., Garcia-Romeral, G., Ubasart, G., & Griera, M. (2015) Demonopolization and dislocation: (re-) negotiating the place and role of religion in Spanish prisons. *Social Compass.*

Martos García, D., Devís Devís, J., & Sparkes, A. C. (2009) Deporte entre rejas? Algo más que control social? *Revista Internacional de Sociología, 67*(2), 391–412.

McIlwain, D., & Sutton, J. Yoga from the mat up: How words alight on bodies. *Educational Philosophy and Theory, 46*(6), 655–673.

Neitz, M. J., & Spickard, J. V. (1990). Steps toward a sociology of religious experience: The theories of Mihaly Csikszentmihalyi and Alfred Schutz. *Sociology of Religion, 51*(1), 15–33.

Nizet, J., & Rigaux, N. (2005). *La sociologie de Erving Goffman.* Paris: La Découverte.

Prat, J. (Eds). (2012). *Els nous imaginaris culturals: espiritualitats orientals, teràpies i sabers esotèrics.* Tarragona: Universitat Rovira i Virgili.

Rodríguez, Céspedes Á. L. (2010). *El Gobierno terapéutico: subjetividad, cuerpo y resistencia en la prisión contemporánea.* Dissertation, Universitat de Barcelona.

Roof, W. C. (1999). *Spiritual marketplace. Baby boomers and the remaking of American religion.* Princenton: Princenton University Press.

Schütz, A. (1945). On multiple realities. *Philosophy and Phenomenological Research, 5*(4), 533–576.

Scott, S. (2010). Revisiting the total institution: Performative regulation in the reinventive institution. *Sociology, 44*(2), 213–231.

# Chapter 10
# Languages of Change in Prison: Thoughts About the Homologies Between Secular Rehabilitation, Religious Conversion, and Spiritual Quest

Irene Becci

## 10.1 Introduction[1]

In principle, in Western countries, rehabilitation is one of the core objectives of the criminal code since approximately the end of the World War II (WW II).[2] In this chapter, the focus will go on three European contexts, where I have been conducting fieldwork in prisons and with ex-prisoners: central Italy, Eastern Germany, and (Western) Switzerland.[3]

In Italy, the basic pillars of a rehabilitation process, that is education, work, religion, cultural activities, leisure and sports activities, and relationships with the family and with the external world, are defined in article 15 of the penal law of 1975 (Bagnoli 2008, p. 18). In Switzerland, rehabilitation is affirmed in particular in article 37 on community service and in article 75 of the criminal code which states that

---

[1] My gratitude for reading and constructively commenting on previous versions of this text goes to James Beckford and Mar Griera in particular. Furthermore, I thank Ana Clott, Muriel Bruttin, and Alexandre Grandjean for having pointed out some incongruities. All have hugely improved the quality of this chapter.

[2] The use of the notion of rehabilitation in this text refers to an organized process aimed at modifying the social attitudes of delinquent prisoners in order to eliminate or reduce the factors sustaining criminal actions, or to strengthen the conditions allowing for a civil integration into society (Dolicini quoted by Bagnoli 2008, p. 29). While the Swiss law refers to this process in terms of resocialization, I privilege here the notion of rehabilitation in order to avoid any confusion with the sociological idea of socialization.

[3] The data I rely on in this chapter come from my own empirical research projects: first between 2001 and 2005 in different prisons in Italy and Germany (Becci 2011), then on ex-inmates in Berlin and Brandenburg between 2006 and 2009, and finally in Switzerland between 2007 and 2010 (www.pnr58.ch/e_projekte_institutionen.cfm). I am regularly updpating my data through interviews and observations.

---

I. Becci (✉)
Institute for the Social Sciences of Contemporary Religions (ISSRC), University of Lausanne, Lausanne, Switzerland
e-mail: irene.becciterrier@unil.ch

© Springer International Publishing Switzerland 2015
I. Becci, O. Roy (eds.), *Religious Diversity in European Prisons,*
DOI 10.1007/978-3-319-16778-7_10

the "execution of sentences must encourage an improvement in the social behavior of the prison inmates, and in particular their ability to live their lives without offending again. The conditions under which sentences are executed must correspond as far as possible with those of normal life, guarantee the supervision of the prison inmates, counteract the harmful consequences of the deprivation of liberty and take appropriate account of the need to protect the general public, the institution's staff and other inmates."[4] Moreover, the criminal code insists that the "prison inmate must actively cooperate in resocialization efforts and the preparations for release."[5] The paragraphs referring to the management plan of prison sentences in the German Prison Act[6] are very similar. The third section on the prison regime states that:

> (1) Life in penal institutions should be approximated as far as possible to general living conditions.
> (2) Any detrimental effects of imprisonment shall be counteracted.
> (3) Imprisonment shall be so designed as to help the prisoner to reintegrate himself into civil life.

According to these regulations, the institution is supposed to offer the best conditions to "normalize" life in prison, that is, to shape daily life inside prison so that it resembles normal life as much as possible.[7] For decades, both the United Nations and the European Council have been affirming the need to individualize the treatment offered in prison. The plan managing the sentence is formulated as an individualized treatment, adapting a combination of given elements (such as work, education, etc.) to a person's intellectual and social capabilities. This objective is, however, subject to the principle of order (within a correction facility) and security (of the people for whom the offender could represent harm). The excessively high proportion of security agents vis-à-vis rehabilitation staff is a sign of one aim yielding to the other (Bagnoli 2008, p. 32). In the Italian case, studies reveal that more than 75 % of the prison population is actually considered to be impossible to rehabilitate (Bagnoli 2008, p. 31). Most of these are drug-addicted inmates, non-nationals, inmates in maximum security prisons or very young persons. Such a subjugation of rehabilitation to order and security creates a tense relation. Through a strictly scheduled daily institutional organization, which is one of the characteristics Erving Goffman (1961) sketched out in his study of total institutions, the two aims are supposed to be balanced.

---

[4] Source, last accessed 21.11.2014, http://www.admin.ch/ch/e/rs/311_0/a75.html.

[5] http://www.admin.ch/ch/e/rs/311_0/a75.html.

[6] That is, the act concerning the execution of prison sentences and measures of rehabilitation and prevention involving deprivation of liberty. Source: http://www.gesetze-im-internet.de/englisch_stvollzg/englisch_stvollzg.html last accessed 21.11.2014. Translation provided by the Language Service of the Federal Ministry of Justice and Consumer Protection.

[7] Such a "normalization" effort can, among other things, be seen when looking at the type of occupational activities prisons offer to men and women. In a women's prison in Switzerland, prisoners receive training in domestic economy, sewing, washing or packing, that is, they are prepared to have very lowly qualified domestic (reproductive) occupations. Imprisoned men have the opportunity to learn printing techniques to work in carpentry or bakery, that is, also lowly qualified occupations which are, however, oriented towards the labor (production) market.

In the studied countries, the prison treatment hence contains, besides disciplinary practices around one's body (the practices of eating, sleeping, moving or washing are determined by the institutions), a certain amount of work, education, sometimes therapy. The exact temporal and spatial organization of these activities varies according to whether the prisoner is at the beginning, the middle, or the end of his sentence. Formally, the structure of imprisonment is a system of stages, which is oriented towards less and less imprisonment. In a first stage, which ideally lasts only a few weeks, the prisoner is kept in single detention, no activities apart from religious services are offered to him and he or she is usually alone, although numerous prisons have a structural problem of overpopulation, and prisoners are in overcrowded cells. At a second stage, the prisoner spends less time in the cell, since work, treatment, vocational training, and leisure activities take most of his day. At the earliest after the first half of the sentence, if the prisoner is not considered to represent any risks of escaping or any threats to security and order, he can start a third stage in which he may work and live in a slightly freer way, having more responsibilities, such as preparing his own meals. Architecturally, the section where his cell is located is a separated unit of the prison. In the last part of the sentence, the inmate who receives a positive evaluation can be released on probation, possibly under legal custody.

Across these stages, the prison is supposed to encourage the positive value of work and of repentance, and to support inmates in reconstructing their relations with their relatives or support groups. Prisoners should not only receive psychological, medical, and social but also spiritual support, when passing through these stages. The way these different types of support interact varies.

In this chapter, I shall locate these principles of rehabilitation into the larger frame of the idea of change in prison. I shall first clarify some historical, theoretical, and methodological reflections on change in prison before presenting some of the results emerging from my empirical studies. I propose an analysis of the narratives used by prisoners about the change experienced in prison. Among prisoners' narratives of personal change, I distinguish between ways of framing the change as secular, religious, or spiritual. I shall also address the question of what the results of my analysis tell us about the larger context in which these languages emerge. Lastly, some elaborations shall connect these findings to the current context of the debates on the social function of prisons.

## 10.2 Change in Prison: Historical and Theoretical Considerations

At the center of the current organization of the sentence lies the idea of change, a belief that through the prison experience a person changes for the better. A quick look at the history of this idea in prison brings us back to the eighteenth century, at the very beginning of the notion that through the treatment offered in prison, inmates can improve themselves. This long history contains both secular and religious key arguments and actors.

Utilitarian and enlightened secular thinkers, such as Cesare Beccaria or Jeremy Bentham, and philanthropic and religious actors, such as John Howard or Elizabeth Fry (see Ignatieff 1978 and Santoro 1997), have promoted this notion from two different angles, where finally very similar ideas crystallized pragmatically in the penitentiary. The creation of a modern prison system, which was no longer dedicated to being a place where people are simply kept before being punished, but rather an organized space where punishment is measured with the unit of time in order to allow people to change through penitence, has been motivated historically by the belief that when put under certain conditions, criminals can be reformed and go back to society as different, improved persons who will not cause harm any longer. The Philadelphia penitentiary, founded by committed Quakers on a rigorous religious practice, is the historical example of such a model in the USA. Other examples are Pentonville prison near London or Regina Coeli in Rome. While at the time, religious practice was directly linked to the importance of discipline, in the last century, and more importantly with the introduction of religious freedom and freedom of conscience as a human right, religion has become a protected, private, and autonomous sphere. Prisoners' religious practices are today no longer subject to any disciplinary constraints. There is no obligation about religion, as the secular sentence is separated from any religious implication. In the secular total institution, as Goffman (1961, p. 24) pointed out, inmates undergo a "moral career" across roughly three phases. First, they pass through a "prepatient phase" when they become aware of what imprisonment all implies. As a matter of fact, when a sentence is pronounced, it mainly refers to its length in time while the experience of "abasements, degradations, humiliations, and profanations of self" is passed under silence. Goffman's analysis has also shown that the inmate's "self is systematically, if often unintentionally, mortified" (1961, p. 24). In the successive phase, the inpatient phase, the inmate is humiliated before being released in the last phase.

Rehabilitation has nowadays stopped to go hand in hand with change through religious practice and insight. Ironically, today, when it comes to minority religions, we often observe the opposite: the religious radicalization of inmates is commonly considered as dangerous—in the sense of disfunctional to the main social institutions. A widely known case is Malcolm X's conversion to the Nation of Islam (Marable 2011, p. 90). In more recent years, in the three studied countries, media attention has easily shifted to the high numbers of prisoners of Muslim origin and some observed processes of religious radicalization in prison. This is however not true for the traditional religious groups which were present since the birth of the penitentiary system. If the topic of change is inherently linked to the prison itself and a structural and representational pattern of it, the type of change still needs to be qualified in the concrete situation. Relying on Pierre Bourdieu's (1979 and 1997) framework, I shall draw the contours of the current structural context for the emergence of different ways to narrate the experienced change in prison. A recent critical elaboration of this framework by Bernhard Lahire (2011) points to the importance of considering a person's performance as the result of a particular mobilization of a variety of cultural resources according to concrete situations rather than as the repetition of a predetermined embodied socialization. In this revised framework, the language is neither the result simply of one person's dispositions nor of the person's full adaptation to the experienced context of a total institution, rather it is a combination of both giving place to a plurality of combinations. The coexistence of different frames of narratives of change has to be referred both to the prison's institutional context (as the concept of the total institution suggests) and the person's social and cultural profile, hence giving more space to the actor's agency. The analysis therefore needs to take into consideration both the precise context of action and the cultural dispositions of a person.

In my empirical studies carried out in various prisons in Germany, Italy, and Switzerland since 2003[8], I found a whole set of narratives alluding to change, positive as well as negative. Change can indeed also be a negative experience, when one's human condition is deteriorated through imprisonment. In what follows, I shall first make some conceptual clarifications about my empirical work, before presenting three different languages used to narrate a change experienced in prison: a secular, religious, or spiritual language. Different languages can coexist in the same institution and even be used by the same person; they refer, however, to different repertoires.

## 10.3   The Empirical Approach to Self-Narratives of Change in Prison

As a large body of studies has shown, self-narratives can be analyzed as "observable events" (Maruna et al. 2006, pp. 162–163). At the latest since the linguistic turn, sociologists know that "narratives tell researchers more about the individual's present construction of personal identity than they tell us about the past" (Snow and Machalek 1983). The situations in which the inmates, I shall quote, constructed their narratives was that of a face-to-face interview taking place mostly in a meeting room in prison. Instead of simply analyzing the content of the utterances on oneself, it is essential to reflect about their form, question the interruptions, and interpret the hesitations (Fournier 2009). Interviews with prison inmates request some additional epistemological considerations. When doing fieldwork in prisons, a researcher meets difficult conditions, not only materially but also relationally. As everyone, the researcher approaches the inmates with a series of preconceptions in mind, which are difficult to overcome. Despite the reflexive attitude I continuously used in my work to control my possible biases of interpretation, I only came to realize the strength of the preconceptions I held on this topic for the past 10 or so years I have been working on this topic when I recently talked to a prisoner. I was indeed

---

[8] I concentrate here mainly on the imprisoned and released men that were interviewed in a face-to-face meeting not under surveillance. Please refer to my previous publications for details on the methodology.

struck by the bad smell present in prison each time I entered one: it was a mixture of body sweat and iron, cleaning chemicals, and dirty clothes. Not hearing, however, anybody mentioning such an observation, I quite obviously thought that inmates no longer noticed that smell.[9] But in the summer of 2014, in a city in northern Italy, I spoke to an inmate who was spending a day outside the prison in preparation of his release. At some point, he started to talk about his disgust at the idea that he would be going back to prison at the end of the day and smell the prison.

> - You see, for me, prison has a particular smell.
> I—Hasn't it? It really has [surprised].
> - Freedom smells differently … It has a particular smell.
> I—My God, yes!
> Do you understand?… Inside there … inside … the air is really stale.
> I—Can you still smell it though?
> - Hem?
> I—I thought if one always lives in there/
> - No no no! I have been smelling it all my life
> I—… have you?
> - Yes, I have been smelling it all my life.

This interaction shows the asymmetrical character of the relationship between the researcher and the inmate. While in everyday interactions, one usually supposes that he shares the same type of sensory experience as his interlocutor, this cannot be taken for granted in prison. Such an asymmetry throws a shadow on certain parts of the narrative and probably directs too much light on others. Since I started my research with the intention to know more about the relation to religion[10] in prison, for a long time I actually passed over all other narratives of change. Although I asked rather open questions such as "could you tell me what your every day looks like in prison?", and I rarely mentioned notions such as religion directly; the whole interview situation was framed in terms of me doing research on the relation to religion in prison. In this analysis, my aim shall be to draw a picture of some of the major types of languages used to tell narratives of change—and the religious language is probably the most studied one. The purpose of this contribution is therefore to take a step back and theorize the types of narratives of change present in the prison context. Since I am operating a secondary analysis of my data, the results presented here have an exploratory status. This exploration has brought me to identify that most frequently the narratives of change in prison refer to a secular frame. A reference to religious change is less frequent, but contains a surprising coherence. I also identified a third type of narrative frame, which I will call spiritual. In order to illustrate the identified categories, I will offer quotes from the interviews.

---

[9] Quraishi (2008, p. 460) also mentions the smell as a further difficult condition of imprisonment.

[10] In my research, the notion of religion was inductively defined as generic and multidimensional. It resulted from the empirical findings of how actors inside and outside the prisons deal with questions of worldviews or beliefs, practices, and traditions of a symbolic or/and transcendental order.

## 10.4   Variations in Narrating Change in Prison: Current Languages

### 10.4.1   Change in a Secular Language

In their structural and architectural organization, the prisons in Eastern Germany and Switzerland were strongly secularized. A highly educated[11] Swiss inmate in his sixties expressed this in a conversation about religious life in the prison he was kept in:

> There is nothing here, it's really hyper secular, you see, it is absolutely a-religious, yes here it is a-religious. There are the chaplains, they pass by, they offer their service, yes … because that [such an assistance] could not be prohibited, that would go against the laws wouldn't it? But they don't encourage you, no inhibition, no pushing, there is nothing.

The different prison organizations provided a whole vocabulary, in their treatments, to express the change and the improvement of an inmate's behavior. The most plausible way for inmates—if their psychological and physical conditions were not hindering them—was to adopt the institution's language. One frequently observed way to do so was to talk about order. Indeed, when I asked the inmates how they would describe the change prison caused for them, some answered they now had "an ordered life." The two principles of order and rehabilitation were overlapping in these narratives. When interviewing inmates serving long-term sentences, I found that many referred to a positive change that imprisonment brought into their life. For a Swiss inmate,[12] the fact of being locked up, in itself, is experienced as a test, even as a chance to stay away from his criminal life:

> Well, for me prison is the material expression, reminding me every day, that I am going through a test. That's why for me, as I said, it's a chance, it puts me back on track. And it allowed me to work on myself, the prison, the fact of being imprisoned, I would never have made it if I had not been locked up.

The prison experience is not one single block, it is itself subdivided into several blocks of time to which different changes can correspond, as the following quote by a German inmate converted to Buddhism illustrates:

> I—Does that mean that the whole, at all, the interest in religion and all the thoughts, did they all come up in prison?
> - It all came up only in prison, and, now, actually during the last years, I mean not in the first 10 years not really, that I got interested in Buddhism, so extremely in religion. Since I am interested in Buddhism I also started to learn about Christianity …

---

[11] This father of four had received a protestant socialization. The interview took place in 2009.

[12] The interviews in Switzerland were made in the framework of our research financed by the Swiss National Science Foundation between 2007 and 2011. Besides myself, the empirical data were collected by Mallory Schneuwly Purdie, Brigitte Knobel, Claude Bovay, and Delphine Gex-Collet.

The interpretations of one's change are constantly under self-scrutiny, and the boundaries negotiated. For Carlos, a Brazilian Catholic inmate interviewed in a Swiss prison, and afflicted by multiple addictions, the treatment they had followed, in particular, therapies or sport, had a beneficial impact on him. This inmate in his late thirties, father of three, and convicted to a 10 years sentence, found a large repertoire in prison in order to change.

> I started to follow a—what's the name—a therapy in prison X. at the beginning I used to take a lot of medicine to remain calm and now ... I am doing a lot of sports. I really lost sixteen kilos ... Since I have been in prison, I have been changing a bit my behavior, I am not smoking any longer, I even quit cigarettes ... and it's tough ... I am no longer on drugs. I used to be a lot on drugs outside, really a lot. I won't say I am healed to one hundred percent but I am not far from that ... if I do no jogging three or four times a week, I am not fine. But I have learned that in prison.

Frequently, changes were described as coming along with culture or arts, in particular through reading, painting, or writing. The example of a Swiss inmate in his mid sixties is very telling in this regard. A divorced atheist, he had a sentence of 18 years. When he arrived in prison, he said, he

> fell into reading and writing actually. I had never been writing beforehand, I started to write in prison. And it took a lot of pain away from me.

In the interview, he described his love and fascination for books. While he was in jail, he took care of the library, although that was not his official job. He spontaneously made the link between imprisonment and reading:

> It was not my job but it was my aim in that library to try to push, to suggest to the guys to read as much as they could because I realized that reading is extremely important (.) in prison, because that's the only thing we can do. At the beginning, the first days, if you fall into a book that puzzles you at the beginning, you will lose a second day and then maybe a third day.

Closed up in a high security prison with a virtually endless sentence, he simply planned to read all the books, from A to Z, in order to gain some mastery over the notion of time which is completely in the hands of the total institution. He had arrived at B when he was interviewed. A Moroccan Muslim, in his late thirties, convicted for almost 5 years in his first sentence, was also interviewed in a Swiss prison and offered a similar reasoning:

> We have time, the problem is that here, we have the time, so we have to use it at best to read, to learn things because outside one does not have the time.

Prison libraries are particularly interesting places to study empirically. The type of books they have, and the relation inmates have to them, clearly reveal which languages circulate in prison and which are appropriated. According to the information gathered in various prison libraries visited, the most popular books among inmates were indeed novels and law books. A closer analysis shall follow in the next sections.

Besides reading, writing is also often mentioned by inmates as a coping strategy. One man I interviewed in 1998 in the same Swiss prison told me about his passion for writing and now, more than 15 years later, he is a locally well-known fiction

author. A young ex-inmate who recovered from alcoholism during his imprisonment and is, now released, active in the alcoholics anonymous association, stated in
an interview in Berlin in 2007.

> … two things I was unable to do earlier … because I could not write—I couldn't. not in a
> structured way … I still am no professional but I manage already to say write texts that are
> two or three pages long, coherent texts … that means a lot to me …

The correction facilities for men were very different—at an organizational and architectural level—to the setting I observed in a woman's prison in Switzerland.
Here, treatment was put at the center of the sentence plan even more. The percentage of rehabilitation personnel within the prison's staff is much higher than in prisons for men. A Swiss woman imprisoned for manslaughter told me in 2010 she used
the time that was given by the prison daily schedule to reflect on her crime, a crime
that brutally interrupted her brilliantly started career in the media business. She had
always held strong Christian beliefs and reflected on what the prison experience had
changed in that regard.

> I have always been very busy and in spite of my believing … I never listened to myself …
> to my inner self and my own needs … I mean I predominantly cared for others and now
> I realize that it is important to look after oneself and to listen to oneself, to how I feel and
> what is important to me. And my worldviews have changed in prison. My whole life has
> changed completely.

The change she described did not refer to religion but concerned secular values. All
the inmates using such a secular language had a certain level of cultural dispositions
they could mobilize in the context of prisons: they read a lot and were mostly following a clear educational program.

The secular offer of change was, however, not helpful to all inmates. The organization of the sentence plan is rarely applied as smoothly as it is theorized. Some
changes can actually be very harsh for prisoners, as the passage from presentence
jail to the penitentiary tends to be, and more generally, some changes are simply
negative. In an interview made in Saxony in 2003, one multi-recidivist inmate of
almost 50 years told me about failed alcohol therapies:

> I am just getting out of a therapy, I mean I had to interrupt it … it was an alcohol therapy,
> I mean I became a drunkard in the can, X [the chaplain] has witnessed it, I never drank
> outside, in the can I became a drunkard.

In particular, for inmates dealing with feelings of heavy guilt due to repeated violent
crimes, the secular frame had only a limited impact, since it was often interrupted
for security reasons. Religion sometimes came as a powerful alternative.

### 10.4.2   Change Through Religion and Conversions

I found most of the narratives of change referring to religion in the prisons in Italy
and Switzerland. In the highly secularized Eastern German context, a direct reference to religion was much less frequent. Usually inmates in the German prisons I

studied rather talked about their relation to the chaplains or other religious actors as persons. The collected religious narratives most frequently resembled the following one given by Umberto, a South American Catholic inmate imprisoned in Switzerland:

> Earlier, when I was outside, I did not know Jesus—I did not like praying because I never had any problems, I was fine: I had my family, some money, I had health. I did not need God to ask, to implore for something … I really know God and Jesus since I am in prison. It is since I am in prison that I started to pray and to put my problems in his hands and to resign all my life to him. It's in prison that I got to know God.

In Umberto's account—as in many other narratives of religious change in prison—a basic organization can easily be identified: when he was a criminal before entering prison, there was no religion in his life. His life outside is opposed to his life inside prison, marked by his religious involvement. The changes in individual identity overlap with institutional changes. I shall here consider a conversion, as suggested by Maruna et al. (2006), as a reinterpretation of "one's autobiography" or an experience of "change in subjectivity." More specifically, "prison conversion narratives [are] an example of narrative identity change … narrative redefinition and reflexivity are exaggerated for religious converts because they are constantly being asked and expected to "give witness" to their experience of how they have changed" (Maruna et al. 2006, p. 163). As I shall elaborate further on, in the contexts studied, a common framework to "provide the master story that allows individual to 'read' the world again" (Maruna et al. 2006, p. 167) was Christianity. For a Brazilian inmate in a Swiss prison, a change started with the sacrament of confession.

> It is here in prison that for the first time, I went to confess, the first time I confessed it was here. Now, I already did it twice. It was the first time that I took the bread and the wine. I never did that earlier, because I never confessed. And since I did not make my first communion, I could not confess. It is here in prison that I asked to talk with a priest, it is here that I stopped the drugs. I asked the chaplain … and I said: "I would like to make a confession … only with a priest" … He said: "I will talk to a priest and check if he can come to see you". And he came, and I confessed. And since then, I never touched drugs anymore.

There is no clear-cut distinction between religious conversions and "those changes that are not conversions" (Maruna et al. 2006, p. 166). In the narratives, a certain continuity emerged between secular activity and religious change. A young inmate imprisoned in Eastern Germany, for instance, came to religion through reading

> For me it came from inside. First through literature, through reading. I went to the library and had some thoughts and picked out a book, then I looked at it, I took it and only when I was reading it I realized that it actually had a religious background. That was like that with several books.

The social context in which a conversion takes place seems, in these cases, to be primordial. In the Italian prisons, the presence of Catholic chaplains was strongly anchored. I could find a surprisingly high number of conversions to Christianity during my research. Christianity should however not be taken as a universal notion. A Nigerian inmate in his thirties, despite being a Christian, was very confused with what he saw in terms of religious practice in Italy, where he was imprisoned. He explained to me that the understanding of Christianity and of religious practice in his village in Nigeria and in Italy diverged.

> There is something that is confusing me because … we Africans didn't believe—European before are taking it—at the beginning. You people have brought that God—Religion—Christianity to us because we had our own religion before but maybe it was not inspired in the Christianity. But in my own country and my village we did to Christianity to 100% … there my people don't even know that Italians don't go to Church but here is very hard you see youth going to Church. Very very hard—to see small 15, 16, 17, 18, 19 years old people going to Church. But in our society—in Africa if a person is a Christian—well has accepted all that … you go to Church … and read the bible.

For this inmate the secular context in Italy, where young persons do not attend religious services, was nearly incomprehensible. The experience of prison shakes all certainties of one's personal identity. In this context, a conversion to the Christian local model can offer the narrative of "a clear and socially acceptable path out of this state of identity crisis" (Maruna et al. 2006, p. 174). When Hans, an ex-inmate converted to Baptism whom I interviewed in Berlin in 2007, talked about his life, which included a number of extreme ruptures, with his family after his homicide, with the community through alcoholism, and with society through imprisonment, he managed to give it a certain unity through the narrative of his religious quest and finally conversion. Religious change seemed to need very few personal predispositions, but the context played a crucial role.

The narrative of a Swiss inmate in his late thirties with serious psychic troubles was also organized as mentioned above. To us of the research team, this inmate appeared as somewhat confused from the beginning. He mixed fiction and real life in his narratives, giving very incoherent accounts. We asked ourselves whether we had to include his point of view in the analysis. It is indeed challenging, but since we are not taking any of the assertions at face value, it seemed logical to us to include his narrative as one of those circulating in a prison.

> I have a huge faith now. I believe a lot, a lot of things. What has changed is that I am much more dynamic.

The faith he talked about was directed at a series of divinities such as "Mary, Buddha, God, Athena, Jesus, Eve." We met him indeed at some ritual celebrations of the chaplaincy, where he showed a high degree of involvement, playing his musical instrument. Just talking about his faith seemed to put him in a euphoric state. Emotionality is often mentioned as the starting point towards a change framed in religious terms. The commonality of different cases in this category is that the new religious belonging represented for inmates the possibility to leave previous deviant identities behind and adopt a new one. While numerous interviewed inmates and ex-inmates affirmed they had experienced a change regarding religion in prison, only a few respondents had converted formally—as for instance a Baptist, a Protestant Lutheran, some Catholics, and one person who joined the Salvation Army. The converted persons now prayed or read the Holy Scriptures regularly, but more important for them was the fact that they had chosen a religious community to belong to. This community did not seem to be chosen at random, as it often had a strong presence in prison through the chaplaincy and volunteers.

One of the narratives of the increased religious involvement of prisoners stresses the creation of a religious need in the situation of deprivation (Sykes 1958). In many of them, religion comes as an answer to needs expressed in terms of identity deprivations. Scholarly work, in particular in the Anglo-Saxon world, shows that the relationship between religion and rehabilitation is equivocal. It seems that religion can, but does not necessarily increase a prisoner's ability to cope with his situation of deprivation. Rachel Sarg in France, for instance, shows that a regular religious practice is experienced as beneficial in prison. In her article written with Anne-Sophie Lamine (2011), she stresses the time structuring effect of religious practices, which allows inmates to appropriate an existential dimension that imprisonment had taken away from them.[13] Religion in prison can, however, also be experienced as one additional deprivation to deal with. One long-term imprisoned man, who has been interviewed during the team research in a Swiss prison in 2009, expressed it this way:

> In prison, so many things are already imposed on you, but I don't want to be told: you will feel better as soon as you will have repeated fifty times the same sentence ... So prison is a permanent punishment ... because ... one is free in the mind but that's all.

In addition, staff members happen to be skeptical about religious conversions of inmates, in particular, conversions outside of Christianity. Prison staff would find the conversion beneficial only if the conversion influenced the inmate's behavior according to the expected program of change, only, in other words, if a sort of homology between the structure of the secular prison program and the religious practice came up. This was more likely to be so if the new religious practice would not clash with the temporal, administrative, and spatial organization of a prison, which would be considered as a threat to order and security. This observation brought me to analyze the situation in terms of the result of a structural homology. The idea of structural homologies, correspondences between power structures and mental structures, has emerged with Bourdieu's work (Bourdieu 1971, p. 299) on the religious field. In the current secularized institutional context, religion is no longer powerful enough to function as a symbolic medium to impose a model structure on people's consciousness, but some symbolic systems can be strengthened by the structural context, and they still do contribute to giving social conditions an apparently natural order. According to such a view, there is an overlap between the mainstream religious values and symbolic underpinnings of a society, which is reflected in its institutions. The success of religious narratives of change therefore depends on its closeness to what is considered "natural" in the prison's institutional narrative.

### 10.4.3  Change Told in the Language of Spirituality

Recent investigations on religious diversity, such as those of Wade Clark Roof (1999), or more recently, Wendy Cadge (2012), have proposed a multiplicity of

---

[13] On this structuring effect, see also Rostaing, Galembert, and Béraud in this book.

categories that go beyond the mere distinction between secular and religion. These authors distinguish indeed whether persons use languages of religion, of the secular (Cadge 2012), or of spirituality. Also the results of the European Value Survey[14] documents the increasing number of persons in Western societies defining themselves as "spiritual more than religious" since the 1990s, and the decrease in beliefs in a personal God. In addition, the well-known expression of the "Spiritual revolution" (Woodhead and Heelas 2005) confirms this trend by showing that, since the 1990, the offer in terms of new spirituality has grown by 300%, where it now touches more than 10% of the population. Through the enlargement of the notion of spirituality, we can observe what Hubert Knoblauch (2009) has qualified as the popularization of religion. According to this author, some "New Age" practices, such as the use of stones or crystals, concentration techniques focusing on "energies," etc. are so widely known nowadays that they have become an obvious part of popular culture. The following analysis aims to show that this development can also be observed in prisons.

A third language to tell the narrative of change comes indeed as an opposition to both the secular and the religious languages. A Swiss inmate in his seventh sentence of over 2 years drew on his double socialization as a protestant and a Hindu to formulate his in-between, *spiritual*, position:

> God is something that shows us the path, energy. I don't call that God, because it's not God, it's not God as it's written in the Bible. It's not that at all. But, one shows us the path and religion is there to help us see that path.

I also interviewed East German inmate in his thirties who had been locked up in youth homes because of smaller felonies committed as a minor. He was spending a long sentence for two homicides when I interviewed him. In prison, he had converted to Buddhism. His narrative is a good illustration of this third language. He explained the ups and downs he went through in his search for a way to cope with his feelings of guilt.

> I ended up attempting suicide several times. […] Then I followed a therapy for two years, which helped me to some extent […] it helped me see that my crimes were not something separate from me, that I had to take them on like a stone, I could reconcile them with who I am, put them into my life-story. After this therapy I could say, "OK, I know the causes, I know how it came to these excesses." And I could conceive them as part of myself, a small part, a dark part, but a part of me. I managed to do that thanks to the therapy. But the therapy could not help me deal with my guilt, only Buddhism did that to some extent, so that today I can carry my guilt without it eating me up.

Certainly, the new reference to Buddhism clearly gave him a new orientation, some direction, and future perspective in his life going beyond his release. He said that at his release:

> First I will lead an ordered life outside. I plan firmly, after my release, that eight years afterward, I manage to move into a monastery, yes. I will probably already move there five years after my release, if my life plan works, to monasticism as a lay practitioner, as do most Buddhists, I will get closer to monasticism and … when I become a monk, I mean I will then

---

[14] cf. among others the analysis of Aupers and Houtman (2012).

make my vows and the highest priority in Buddhism is—well at least in that Buddhism I study, that is the north Vajrayana Buddhism—there the highest aim of being a Buddhist is, that is, I only exist in order to help others out of their painful conditions.

This inmate had a clear idea of how Buddhist philosophy was helping him to deal with his feelings of guilt towards having done irreparable damage:

That certainly has lot to do with the law of Karma, that is, the law of cause and effect and with this different aspects of Buddhist philosophy … that one recognizes the meaning of things, that is of life. I always thought—before I started to think about that—I have killed someone, that is an irreparable story, I used to do much other bullshit, I have been a dealer, a thief, I have been punching people and much more but somewhere this could be healed and with money, and it all became reparable, but that was a story that is not reparable. And through Buddhism I received the possibility that I certainly could not repair the idea but somehow I can improve it, the whole story. Yes, by becoming a better person by training myself to set me free of negative emotions and that this goes beyond my life. I can put my existence in the service of other persons. I can lead an altruistic existence and so this is for me a sort of compensation.

While secular therapies could help him to stop his self-destructive impulses, a Buddhist narrative of change helped him out of his guilt. The analysis of the long narrative of this inmate points to the link established between the long-term sentence of incarceration and his change. It indeed took him a long time to find the answers he was looking for; Buddhism, came as a response for him to cope with the deep crisis he experienced in his long-term imprisonment. He had to invest a significant amount of energy and time into this process. I consider this a spiritual change because of this inmate's insistence on this Buddhist philosophy as something different from religion and secular philosophy. The following quote indicates this clearly:

I started to be interested in religion because I have recognized some truths. First in general for religion, I compared them and … then I found my philosophy that somewhere suited me. And it is for me anchored in Buddhism.

Buddhism was an alternative worldview compared to traditional secular as well as religious ones and it emerges from the quotations that the boundaries between the categories of spiritual, religious, and secular are actually porous. This multirecidivist, who basically spent all his adult life in prison, came to Buddhism after reading numerous books. In all of the three national contexts, the library contained numerous books in the realm of religion and spirituality. In a Tuscan prison, aside from the sacred texts such as the Bible, the Gospel, and the Qur'an, I also noticed the Biography of Malcolm X, books of Ellen White, a lot of science fiction and novels, and psychology. In Germany, I observed a big section of books by esoteric authors. It was in a Swiss prison that the most exhaustive material could be collected.[15] Of all the books that the library counted in 2009, less than 2% were classed in a RELIGION section and were mainly about the history of Christianity and important Christian biographies, with few books on Islam, Dalai Lama, or on Jewish Kabbalah. Only four books of this category were borrowed by inmates. Interestingly, about 2.5% of the books were classed in the ESOTERISM/ORIENTALISM

---

[15] I thank in particular Brigitte Knobel for having first explored the data collected in this library.

section. Some of these concerned occultism, spiritism, theosophy, parapsychology, healing, mediums, hypnosis, reincarnation, anthroposophy, or prophecies. The section ASTROLOGY contained less than 1 % of the books. The books in these latter two sections were more popular among inmates than those in RELIGION, but still less than those in the PSYCHOLOGY or CARTOONS sections. Most of the books were offered to the library, but the library did not accept everything. According to the inmate who was in charge of the organization of the library, Bibles coming from Jehovah's Witnesses or books of the Scientology movement were refused.

Other emblematic cases of spiritual change I observed were the inmates implicated in the discussions of the anonymous groups. Drawing on Hubert Knoblauch's (1995) reflections about the religious background of the alcoholic anonymous groups, one can consider that joining an anonymous group is like a change framed by a popularized form of religion, a spiritual language. The 12 steps of the program put a self at the center to encourage a personal change. The narrative of the anonymous groups puts spirituality as an alternative to secularity and to institutional religion. An elderly ex-convict interviewed in Berlin narrated his change during the prison experience he had had when he was young.

> I knew a doctor—he could proof that therapeutic measures have a success rate of at least 50 % within 5 years after release—I tried that out with a social-therapeutic unit in prison— then I attended a unit for schooling that was of course my luck, and my enlightenment actually came through the anonymous alcoholics because I knew, if I get out the bender starts again whether I say ten times "I don't drink" there is no alternative for me … the anonymous alcoholics opened my eyes.

In my fieldwork in Berlin, I found the spiritual frame of change in the discourses of inmates' relatives. The following quote comes from an interview I had with a woman who had paid attention to the changes that occurred to her imprisoned brother and her husband. She told me the conclusion to which she came to while attending, together with her husband who was close to release, a rehabilitation program organized by the charity service of the Berlin Protestant church. For her, spirituality entered the picture in opposition to religion, in terms of blind belief in God. We were talking about the recent turn to fundamentalist Islamic practices observed among some Muslim prisoners when she gave her opinion about the efficacy of the different means for the treatment she observed:

> I think these yoga classes and ehm these therapies—ehm—the sort of [therapeutic] games we played, are more useful than bringing in God [as a solution] all the time …

This woman refers to yoga classes and indeed, in Switzerland, out of the 16 prisons we have contacted, 5 were proposing yoga classes or meditation on a regular basis.[16] For the interviewed woman, the recourse to religion, more precisely to a God, for coping, is seen as an easy solution, while spirituality obliges the person to look inside herself, which interestingly is considered as much more challenging than in the context outside of prison. What homology can be observed here? Griera and Clott give some first possible answers to this question in their chapter in this book. They suggest that some holistic activities in prison are increasingly used in a therapeutic

---

[16] In some prisons these activities take place in an appropriate room, in others on the prison floors.

way and enforce institutional order through the construction of a pacified self. This development comes close to what Philipp Rieff (1966, p. 98) had already called the "triumph of the therapeutic" even within the sphere of religion.

## 10.5   Conclusion

From the daily experience as a security agent or as an inmate in prison to the sentences expressed in court and even to political discourses referring to prisons in public debates, the injunction of change swings between rehabilitation and pure punishment to reestablish "order." Often, the immediacy of the success of clearly rehabilitating actions proves to be difficult. In the political arena, the idea of rehabilitation as such is often questioned, in particular when offenders relapse and commit violent crimes that provoke strong emotional public reactions. As a matter of fact, it is particularly difficult, if not impossible, to make general claims about the failures or successes of rehabilitation programs. Although there are laws and general indications about rehabilitation, programs can indeed be very different from one correctional facility to another. Due to overcrowding or management dysfunctions, it often happens that offenders spend years in the jails where they were supposed to stay only a few months before their conviction was pronounced, and which are not organized towards the aim of rehabilitation. In this somehow confused carceral world, a place is made for religion and spirituality. On the one hand, there are historical and currently working chaplaincies, and on the other, there are alternative types of spiritual offers in prison, for instance yoga practice or reading. Institutional dynamics are at work to bring both of these in line with the institution's aims.

The languages offered by the prison to narrate change are secular. Change can however also be articulated in a religious or a spiritual language. Religious languages offer a belief in rehabilitation, in radical change, despite structurally fragile social conditions. Spiritual languages enter the discourses in a more subtle way and request more resources on the part of inmates. Religious and spiritual languages nowadays favor rehabilitation rather than punishment. While a couple of decades ago, spiritual languages were rare, they are gaining increasing legitimacy nowadays. At an analytical level, this notion of spirituality transgresses the boundaries between religion and nonreligion, making the boundaries of the religious field more porous. Being spiritual no longer refers to following a given set of religious laws and prescriptions, it has entered mainstream culture and broken out of the institutional religions, even becoming a sphere opposed to them.

If the social importance of the so-called spiritual or "holistic milieu" is increasing, this also has ethical consequences. As the holistic message mainly orients persons towards the quest for the accomplishment of their "self" and uniqueness, it seems to locate the experience of spirituality at a strongly individualized and particularized level. Through practices such as yoga, reiki, reflexology, tai chi, homeopathy, or shamanistic practices among others, a large panoply of choice is offered to individuals who want to enroll in a process of self-monitored improvement. Change, in this perspective, goes hand in hand with the quest for the "true self" while following no dogma or standardized solutions. One of the core features of the successful new spirituality in contemporary society is their holistic character, that is, their emphasis on well-being achieved by focusing, at the same time, on "body, mind, and spirit." These three elements are held together by the reference to the individual rather than to the concept of a personal God. This focus on the individual self perfectly suits the penal institution's discourse that centers rehabilitation less and less on community and increasingly on the individual. Focusing on the centrality of the self in this context opens up the foucauldian (1978) question about governing subjectivity.

On this basis, future research on prisons and religion really needs to work on mediating processes, such as change, while using an extended notion of religion, one that includes spirituality, within its own specificity.

# References

Aupers, S., & Houtman, D. (2012). The spiritual turn and the decline of tradition: The spread of post-Christian spirituality in 14 Western countries, 1981–2000. In: P. Heelas (Ed.), *Spirituality in the Modern World* (Vol. 1, pp. 390–412). London: Routledge.

Bagnoli, V. (2008). *Subcultura penitenziaria e trattamento rieducativo*. Doctoral thesis, Law Department, University of Milan.

Becci, I. (2011). Religion's multiple locations in prisons. *Archives de sciences sociales des religions, 153,* 65–84.

Bourdieu, P. (1971). Genèse et structure du champ religieux *Revue Française de sociologie, XII*(2), 295–334.

Bourdieu, P. (1979). *La distinction: Critique sociale du jugement*. Paris: Minuit.

Bourdieu, P. (1997). *Méditations pascaliennes*. Paris: Le Seuil.

Cadge, W. (2012). *Paging God: Religion in the halls of medicine*. Chicago: University of Chicago Press.

Foucault, M. (1978). La gouvernementalité. Cours au collège de France, année 1977–1978: "sécurité, territoire, population", 4e leçon, 1er février 1978. Aut-Aut, n° 167–168, septembre-octobre: 12–29. In Michel Foucault, Correspondance Dits et Ecrits: tome III, texte n° 239. Paris: Gallimard.

Fournier, C.-A. (2009). Le récit de soi, la dimension religieuse et le dévoilement de l'identité. In P.-Y. Brandt & C.-A. Fournier (Eds.), *La conversion religieuse. Analyses psychologiques, anthropologiques et sociologiques* (pp. 101–123). Genève: Labor et Fides.

Goffman, E. (1961). *Asylums: Essays on the social situation of mental patients and other inmates*. New York: Doubleday.

Ignatieff, M. (1978). *A just measure of pain: The penitentiary in the industrial revolution, 1750–1850*. New York: Pantheon Books.

Knoblauch, H. (1995). *Kommunikationskultur. Die kommunikative Konstruktion kultureller Kontexte*. Berlin: de Gruyter.

Knoblauch, H. (2009). *Populäre Religion. Auf dem Weg in eine spirituelle Gesellschaft. Cover: Populäre Religion*. Campus, Frankfurt a. M.

Lahire, B. (2011). The *plural actor*. Cambridge: Polity Press.

Marable, M. (2011). *Malcolm X: A life of reinvention*. New York: Viking.

Maruna, S., Wilson, L., & Curran, K. (2006). Why God is found behind bars? Prison conversions and the crisis of self-narrative. *Research in Human Development, 3*(2&3), 161–184.

Quraishi, M. (2008). Researching Muslim prisoners. *International Journal of Social Research Methodology, 11*(5), 453–467. (Taylor & Francis).

Rieff, P. (1966). *The triumph of the therapeutic*. New York: Harper & Row.

Roof, W. C. (1999). *Spiritual marketplace: Baby boomers and the remaking of American religion*. Princeton: Princeton University Press.

Santoro, E. (1997). *Carcere e societÃ liberale*. Turin: G. Giappichelli Editore.

Sarg, R., & Lamine, A-S. (2011). La religion en prison. Norme structurante, réhabilitation de soi, stratégie de résistance, *Archives de Sciences Sociales des Religions, n° 153*, 85–104.

Snow, D. A., & Machalek, R. (1983). The convert as a social type. *Sociological Theory, 1*, 259–289.

Sykes, G. M. (1958). *The society of captives: A study of a maximum security prison*. Princeton: Princeton University Press.

Woodhead, L., & Heelas, P. (2005). *The spiritual revolution. Why religion is giving way to spirituality*. Oxford: Blackwell.

# Chapter 11
# Restorative Justice: Asserted Benefits and Existing Obstacles in France

Frédéric Rognon

## 11.1 Introduction

It is well known that the concept of "Restorative Justice" stems from Mennonite communities in the USA, and was particularly developed by Howard Zehr[1] (1990) in the 1970s, who was inspired both by evangelical principles and indigenous traditions, including those of native American and Maori. For the past two or three decades, it has been incorporated into the legislation of a number of Anglo-Saxon countries and, in the French-speaking world, for the past 15 years in Québec and 10 years in Belgium (where it is obviously never imposed but systematically offered). France has just recently incorporated some provisions into its new criminal law under the heading of "the individualisation of sentences and strengthening of the effectiveness of criminal sanctions", submitted to Parliament by the Minister of Justice, Christiane Taubira, adopted on the 17th of July and enacted on the 15th of August 2014.

In France, after many terms were considered, the choice seems to have been made for the neologism "*Justice restaurative*", which is a literal translation of the English term "*Restorative Justice*". Quebeckers opted for the term of "*Justice réparatrice*" (Jaccoud 2003; Jacquot and Charpenel 2012), and a number of French researchers followed suit, while others, concerned by linguistic correctness, pleaded in favour of the expression "*Justice restauratrice*" (Gailly 2011). Prison chaplaincies seem to have won the day by preferring to use the term "*Justice restaurative*" in French. This is because, on one hand, they found that it was not a question of "repairing" something that very often cannot be repaired (human relations are not like cars for which one can simply replace parts); and, on the other hand, because a neologism

---

[1] The criminologist Howard Zehr is also a photographer deeply inspired by Mennonite communities.

F. Rognon (✉)
Faculty of Protestant Theology, University of Strasbourg, Strasbourg, France
e-mail: rognonfr@yahoo.fr

© Springer International Publishing Switzerland 2015
I. Becci, O. Roy (eds.), *Religious Diversity in European Prisons,*
DOI 10.1007/978-3-319-16778-7_11

produces its own semantic associations and can therefore express something other than the connotations pertaining to the French noun of *"restauration"*. "Restorative Justice" consists in "restoring" each person implicated in an offence, in their dignity as speaking subjects, with needs and relationships. The same applies to the French term of *"infracteur"*, which a neologism translated from the English *"offender"* that enables us to introduce a new concept, divorced from the connotations linked to the terms "author", "delinquent", and *a fortiori* "criminal".

In order to evaluate the benefits of "Restorative Justice" and the obstacles that have yet to be overcome, we will follow three stages: Firstly, we will talk about the conceptual benefits of this notion, after which we will analyse the success of experiments already conducted in French-speaking countries, before mentioning the obstacles to its full recognition and broad implementation.

## 11.2   Conceptual Benefits

"Restorative Justice" (RJ) is, therefore, aimed at each person involved in an offence, that is to say the offender, victim (or the victim's close ones if he or she is no longer alive), and the "community" (i.e. the neighbourhood, village, and immediate surroundings affected by the breach of the common rule). The application of RJ is divided into three levels:

a. Pre-sentence deliberations (prior to the trial) aimed at reaching an agreement between the offender and the victim on the nature of the sentence;
b. Post-sentence meetings, rigorously prepared and supervised, between the offender and the victim during the execution of the sentence, in order to recognise the other's dignity as a speaking subject with needs and relationships;
c. Finally, the establishment of a "support and solidarity group" during the term of the sentence, with a view to reintegration and the prevention of repeated offending.

On the basis of these three practices, the conceptual benefits of RJ can be divided into seven axes that I would break down as follows:

1. RJ follows a *holistic anthropology* whereas criminal law proves to be highly reductive, considering the offence as a violation of the law and a breach against the State, at the risk of depriving the offender and the victim (for whom the stakes of the trial, with all its rituals, largely remain unfathomable) of any say, RJ considers each person as a human being with needs and relationships, as historical subjects, as beings with affections, emotions and passions, and above all as speaking and listening subjects. This latter decisive element appears in particular in the post-sentence meetings between offenders and victims. It is this pluri-dimensional anthropology[2] which restores each person's dignity, since each indi-

---

[2] By "anthropology" here I mean a discourse on man (anthropo-logos), so to say a certain representation and conception of a human being.

vidual is treated as an end in themselves, and not just as a means, according to the famous Kantian definition of dignity (thus neither the offender nor the victim are instrumentalized in the defence of the law or the State).

2. This holistic anthropology enables the *re-humanisation of the protagonists* concerned by the offence: By distinguishing the offender from his or her past actions, but also the victim from his or her past traumas, RJ symbolically reintegrates the offender, but also the victim, in the human condition. Once again it is here that the post-sentence restorative meetings provide the best examples of this conversion in one's perception of one's self and others. This mingling of perceptions provides alternative perspectives, the founding potential of which cannot be overestimated. To state it briefly: "I'm not a monster and the other person is not an object of pulsion", or: "I'm not an object and the other person is not a monster". The person's humanity is therefore revealed beyond all phantasmagoria: One's fantasy images of the other and one's self, which are fundamentally reductive and products of the imagination, are erased behind what precisely makes a human being a human being, that is, sensitivity, history, wounds, weaknesses and the ability to open up.

3. The re-humanisation of each person infuses *pertinence into the very heart of justice*: Because RJ, in fact, breaks the vicious circle in which the offender victimises his or herself and the victim feels guilty, particularly in the case of sexual delinquency. On the contrary, it initiates, through each party's access to language, a virtuous circle for the de-victimisation of the offender and the deculpabilization of the victim, by placing each in his right place: The offender is identified as guilty and the victim as victim, which is a condition for overcoming these two statuses. Is RJ, therefore, a "just" justice, according to the two meanings of the ambivalent qualifying adjective *"juste"* in French? In French, in fact, it covers two elements, which are equity and aptness.

4. This establishment of aptness is based on the *heuristics and hermeneutics of shame*: The shame of the offender, in fact, is the remorse felt for the suffering that has been inflicted, makes it possible to shed light on the truth of the offence and to interpret it in its proper context. The re-integrative virtues of repentance should not be underestimated. Far from being a mortifying guilt that keeps them locked in the past, the shame experienced by offenders during their imprisonment or when meeting their victims, offers them a future.

5. This future entails adopting *a new position with the assumption of responsibility*: RJ, in fact, promotes responsibility that not only consists in "accounting" in dialogues but also "being accountable", that is, to assume responsibility for the consequences of one's actions through one's current and future behaviour. "Being accountable" for the offender means making the material and symbolic reparations related to the offence, but also restoring affected or broken relationships. Nevertheless, responsibility intervenes both upstream and downstream in post-sentence meetings: upstream, on one hand, during mediation discussions or family group meetings, since it is the offender, victim and community who discuss the actual modalities of reparation and restoration; and downstream, on the other hand, when the support and responsibility groups are set up, because at

the end of their prison sentences, the released person, when faced with the temptation to "relapse", will find him or herself facing their responsibilities, with the choice of either relapsing or asking the support group for help. An empowering position if ever there was one.

6. By making each of the protagonists responsible, RJ *relies more on the human investment rather than the purely technical one*: Beyond high-security prisons and electronic surveillance tools, RJ chooses to favour acts of conscience and trusting attitudes that create bonds. The example of support and responsibility groups is emblematic of this approach, which involves human beings, as well as the community, called into question by the offence and the presence of an ex-offender in their midst. It is this investment in fertile human ground which eventually enables both the offender and victim to emancipate themselves with regard to their respective statuses as "offender" and "victim", which are only transitory statuses that are destined to be overcome and superseded.

7. Finally, this returns to the only permanent status, which is that of being a human being, expresses the fundamental logic of RJ, which is to *demand a change in focus*. To quote the title of a work by Howard Zehr, *Changing Lenses* (1990), RJ invites us to shift our perspective, to alter our viewpoint to a "wide angle" view and broaden our vision to embrace the offender, the victim and the community, as well as individual needs. It is only at this price that RJ can be a resilient vector for the victim, enable the offender to give a meaning to his/her sentence and give the community a major role in the restoration of the social bond. Henceforth, everyone will be capable of regaining control over their own lives.

Having presented these conceptual benefits, let us now mention the empiric and experimental successes of RJ in French speaking countries.

## 11.3 Successful Experiments

a. The first level in the practice of RJ, *Pre-sentence deliberations (prior to the trial)* aimed at reaching an agreement between the offender and the victim on the nature of the sentence; this has never been experimented in French-speaking countries. It seems to be more suited to the countries that take aboriginal laws into account, such as New Zealand where, in an endeavour to highlight the traditional rights of the Maori population, 40% of cases follow this type of procedure.

b. The second level of practice, i.e. post-sentence meetings between the offender and victim, has been experimented with great success at the Maison Centrale de Poissy prison (which houses inmates serving long sentences) in the region of Paris: The manner in which committed or suffered criminal acts are perceived, and the suffering that has been inflicted or endured have been transformed for both offenders and victims alike. In a report on past experiences, François Goetz, the director of the Maison Centrale de Poissy prison, expressed it in these terms:

In the provisions for meetings between inmates and victims, suffering is at the heart of a process of mutual reparation, which one could almost call mechanical; in the absence of any judicial issues, these meetings bring two sufferings face to face. The suffering of the victim reveals that of the author [i.e. the offender] and establishes his or her humanity by evoking the inhuman act.

The author becomes fully aware of the suffering inflicted on the victim by his or her actions, and this suffering refers him back to his own suffering and disordered history. The victim obtains answers for the reasons why an action was taken and how, what goes on inside the author's head and his thought processes.

This process, which is particularly intense from an emotional and human point of view, only offers some element of liberation and healing, of course, but it is nevertheless an element, which is already very important. Victims often talk about relief and liberation, feelings which are also to be found in the authors [the offenders], which leads one to believe that suffering takes no sides. (Goetz 2012, p. 96)

Therefore one notes the awakening of an awareness on both sides of a suffering that is, no doubt, uneven, but at least shared.

The most unexpected phenomenon is that the victims or their families are not the last to want these meetings. This explains why victim associations, such as IN-AVEM (National Institute for aid to victims and mediation), have become involved in RJ programmes. Marie-José Boulay, whose daughter was murdered and who has participated in post-sentence meetings between offenders and victims at the prison of Poissy, bears witness as follows:

I drew some personal benefits from this experience that I wasn't expecting at all. For twenty-two years, I dealt with outstanding questions on my own which would regularly come back to me, triggered by some news item or other. Through these meetings, I realised that the convicts themselves can't provide all the answers, which enabled me to accept that there are some questions that remain forever unanswered. And this acceptance brings a certain peace.

I also became aware of the reality of prison. None of the inmates tried to excuse their actions, they were always taking responsibility. They refused to complain. But I was able to discover their own suffering and the damage caused in their families.

I was also struck when one of the convicts told us that he needed the long years of detention (about ten years) to assume responsibility for his actions, to no longer consider himself as a victim and to accept doing some work on himself. I would have understood him more if he had complained about the weight of his sentence.

In prison, we were told, they have to show themselves to be hard and strong in order to survive. They can't show themselves as they are, betray moments of weakness, have true friends. I wonder what one can be like, after playing the role of the "tough guy" for ten, twenty years in prison (Boulay 2012, pp. 103–104).

Thus both offenders and victims saw this experience as a shift in focus, as a liberation from the mortifying seclusion of suffering and as a restoration of one's own humanity just as much as the other's. The most striking point is perhaps an implicit benefit: The recognition that certain questions can never be answered and the therapeutic and cathartic effect of that realisation.

c. But the third level of RJ practice is perhaps the most promising. It concerns the establishment of a "support and solidarity group" for after the sentence has been served. Over the past 15 years, Québec has increased initiatives of this kind, and, as a result, recidivism rates have dropped dramatically. The principle of "support and solidarity groups" consists in this: While serving his/her sentence, the offender gets to know a dozen people who come to visit him/her and make a commitment towards him. Upon leaving prison, offenders who have served their sentences are taken on by this support group, which is reinforced by a second and larger group, not only to facilitate their integration, but above all to avoid a "relapse". The released person knows that at any time of the day or night, if they should feel tempted to commit another breach (including an offence or sexual crime, following an impulse or fantasy), they can phone a member of the group (who, like doctors on call, are available at certain times, for example from 3 to 7 in the morning) and who will come immediately to talk to them and calm them down. The person concerned is therefore placed in a position of responsibility, since they have the choice between giving into their impulses or calling for help. This procedure highlights the solidarity role of the community, whether it be a community based on spatial, religious or elective affinity considerations. The French Minister of Justice, Christiane Taubira, who up until now viewed RJ with a benevolent eye, but as something purely theoretical, travelled to Canada in the spring of 2014 and returned convinced by what she had seen: Investing in the human dimension rather than in a repressive logic yielded considerable results. She, therefore, proposed amendments in that direction in her own bill, when none of the other approached members of parliament dared to do so.

d. Experiments with RJ were therefore, to some extent, vindicated by the law of 15 August 2014, which paves the way for new practices. The article devoted to RJ is worded as follows:

> During an entire criminal procedure and at all stages of a procedure, including during the execution of a sentence, the victim and author of an offence may be offered some measure of RJ, provided the facts have been recognised.
> A measure of RJ is to be considered as any measure which will enable the victim, as well as the author of an offence, to actively participate in the resolution of difficulties caused by the offence and particularly the mending of any kind or prejudice by the commission of the offence. This measure can only be taken after the victim and author of the offence have been completely informed on the subject and have expressly consented to participate in it. It is implemented by an independent third party established for this purpose, under the supervision of the judiciary authority or at the request of the prison administration. It is confidential, unless the parties have agreed otherwise, except in cases where an overriding interest linked to the need to prevent or rectify offences justifies information relating to how the measure is proceeding be made known to the Public Prosecutor[3].

While reading this article, one notices that its wording leaves some scope for interpretation and therefore implementation ("the resolution of difficulties caused by the offence") by favouring post-sentence meetings ("during the execution of a sentence"), but without limiting itself to them ("at every stage of the procedure"). However, despite this undeniable progress made thanks to its eruption onto the

---

[3] *Law for the Individualisation of Sentencing and Reinforcing the Efficacy of Penal Sanctions* (enacted on 15 August 2014), Chapter II a ("Provisions regarding restorative justice"), article 7 d, subheading II ("Restorative justice"), article 10–1.

legislative stage and therefore consecration, the implementation of RJ in France faces a number of obstacles, which should now be listed.

## 11.4 Obstacles as Conclusions

The analysis of the situation led me to identify four major obstacles:

1. The first obstacle is circumstantial, but nevertheless crippling: that is the political obstacle. When the new criminal law, which incorporated elements of RJ, was adopted, the popularity of the French president was at a record low and there were manifest tensions between the Prime Minister and the Minister of Justice. The latter was to suffer at the hands of the populist opposition, which relentlessly attacked her for her supposed laxity; her name is attached to the "marriage for all" bill (marriage for same-sex couples), the voting on which provoked massive protests from the right, extreme right and Catholic church (Stains 2013; Hoffner 2012). It is therefore not certain that the law, even if enacted, will be easily implemented and, above all, proves to be long lasting. This obstacle poses a question about the strategy of the promoters of RJ, who have rallied together under a "Platform for restorative Justice" initiated by the protestant chaplaincy for prisons: Should they favour a top-down approach through legislative decisions, at the risk of being at the mercy of the political whims of the moment (a law can always replace another) and reclamations through the penal system; or make progress from the bottom up, by increasing the number of satisfactory experiments for all the actors concerned, by therefore remaining the masters of the procedures, but run the high risk of being condemned to impotence or insignificance? The two strategies can probably be combined.
2. The second and more fundamental obstacle concerns resistance, particularly in France (and, to a lesser extent, Switzerland), to the idea of taking into account the notion of "community" in restorative procedures, because of its communitarian connotations. The republican model which prevails in France only recognises individual citizens as equal in the eyes of the State. The introduction of intermediary bodies is traditionally viewed in a negative light, particularly in the case of ethnic or religious communities. Nevertheless, the mention of "community" in the RJ approach enables one to break out of the victim/offender polarisation, because an offence does not just affect the immediate victim, but also his or her family, neighbourhood and village. Without neglecting the hazards involved in how they function, including their inflammatory and potentially conflictual nature in contemporary societies, these "micro-communities" could participate in the RJ process in such a way that the offender will one day be able to return to live in their midst, under certain conditions negotiated between the three poles involved in the dialogue. Similarly, the "support and solidarity groups" make it possible to jointly seek solutions that suit everyone. On this point it is important to distinguish two levels of "community" in RJ: the "community" as one

of the three poles affected by the offence and the "community" as a "support and solidarity group". These two aspects need to be distinguished in order to be better articulated. A way out of the semantic deadlock pertaining to the notion of "community" might be to, in a similar way to the neologisms of "RJ" and "offender" in French, create a new expression, divorced from any troublesome connotations: The term of "civil community", based on the model of "civil society", might be proposed. It provides the double benefit of staying linked to the notion of "community", while at the same time questioning the listener through its novelty and its implicit reference to the classic tension, which harkens back to Ferdinand Tönnies, between "community" and "society" (Tönnies 1957), which it proposes to supersede.

3. Finally, the third obstacle is without any doubt the most formidable and counter-productive regarding open prospects for RJ. It concerns the so-called unthought cultural-religious elements of judiciary and penitentiary practices (the term "penitentiary" speaks for itself) in Latin countries with a Catholic tradition, and in particular France. RJ radically distinguishes itself from the principle of redemption through suffering by refusing the fatal trappings of statuses and roles, focusing on the capacity to amend and enable a person to assume responsibility, and opening up to the possibility of forgiveness and reconciliation (even though these may not be their ultimate goals). In this regard, RJ entails elective affinities with the protestant tradition and it has managed to flourish in countries with Lutheran or Reformed cultures. This presents a double handicap and challenge for secular France: RJ will only be accepted and legalised if its theological grounds will be secularized, but also some lucid work on the unthought aspects of its legal model and prison system. RJ has to stand for what it is: A parallel and not alternative proposal to criminal law, which is capable of renewing our classical approaches to the meaning of a sentence[4]. Could the "u-topia" of RJ therefore one day find its place in France as well?

Some authors have started that debate recently and invite to more elaborate reflections.[5]

---

[4] I shall point out that the new criminal law on "the prevention of recidivism and on the individualisation of sentences", is not in any way centred on RJ, but it introduces the notion of "penal constraint", which, exercised in an open environment, is called upon to become the reference sentence, as an alternative to prison: Incarceration will no longer be at the core of the provision, but rather will be a specific kind of sentence. This represents a real shift in the paradigm of how we think about the meaning of a sentence. Even though retribution remains the decisive accepted meaning of a sentence, restoration can more easily be combined and articulated with retribution within the framework of "penal constraint" than in systematic imprisonment.

[5] Cf. Cario and Mbanzoulou (2010) and Rognon and Deymié (2014), p. 96.

# References

Boulay M.-J. (2012). Rencontres détenus-victimes: quels intérêts pour les victimes? In R. Cario (dir.), *Les rencontres détenus-victimes. L'humanité retrouvée* (pp. 99-104). Paris: L'Harmattan.

Cario R., & Mbanzoulou P. (dir.) (2010). *La Justice restaurative: une utopie qui marche?* Paris: L'Harmattan.

Gailly P. (2011). *La justice restauratrice*. Bruxelles: Éditions Larcier.

Goetz, F. (2012). Les rencontres détenus-victimes: quels intérêts pour les auteurs, quels bénéfices pour la société? In R. Cario (dir.) (Eds.), *Les rencontres détenus-victimes. L'humanité retrouvée* (pp. 93-97). Paris: L'Harmattan.

Hoffner, A-B. (2012). La "manif pour tous" rassemble une foule festive et familiale, in *La Croix*, 17 November.

Jaccoud, M. (dir.) (2003). *Justice réparatrice et médiation pénale. Convergences ou divergences?* Paris: L'Harmattan.

Jacquot S., Charpenel Y. (2012). *La justice réparatrice. Quand victimes et coupables échangent pour limiter la récidive*. Paris: L'Harmattan.

Rognon, F., & Deymié, B. (dir.) (2014). *Punir, restaurer, guérir. Regards croisés sur la justice restaurative*, Paris: L'Harmattan.

Stains R. (2013). Famille: La grande mobilisation, in *Le Figaro Magazine*, n° 1681, 12 January, pp. 28–29.

Tönnies F. (1957). *Community and society* (trans. C. P. Loomis). East Lansing: The Michigan State University Press.

Zehr H. (1990). *Changing lenses. A new focus for crime and justice*. Scottdale (Pennsylvania)/ Waterloo (Ontario): Herald Press.

# Chapter 12
# Conclusion and Perspectives

## The Diversification of Chaplaincy in European Jails: Providing Spiritual Support for New Inmates or Countering Radicalism?

Olivier Roy

The institution of prison chaplaincy reflects the church/state relationship specific to each of the European countries, hence the great diversity of both the institutional forms it can take and the functions it is intended to perform. Is the *raison d'être* of chaplaincy to be part of a process of redemption and reintroduction into society, or is it just a way to provide a social service: to care for the spiritual needs of individual inmates? Who controls the chaplaincy: the state or the different church institutions? In other words, should chaplaincy be subcontracted to a given religion and church (Italy) or should it be a service provided by the state (France)?

The first answer to these questions is to be found in history. Chaplaincy has everywhere been shaped according to the specific history of the state/religion relationship, or more exactly in Europe, state/church relations. For instance, in France, chaplains should only provide spiritual support to people who ask for it (even if they do not belong to the same faith community); there is no right to proselytize or to distribute Bibles or Qurans to people who do not ask for them, or even to meet inmates who have not put themselves on the list of those requesting assistance; worshipping rooms are multifaith. In Italy, the Catholic chaplain is expected to play a larger role of spiritual and social support for all inmates, he may meet inmates at his own will and there is usually a church or chapel inside the prison compound. There is no symmetry in Italy between the Catholic chaplains and the representatives of other faiths, who come from outside and are only entitled to meet their coreligionists.

Such specific configurations not only mirror the state/church relations but also the place of religion in a given society more generally. Prisons reflect society, a fact that might explain why chaplaincy has rarely been a political issue; they were seen as a subset of the larger society (even though, from a sociological point of view, this has never been true because the social backgrounds of inmates never match the society outside).

O. Roy (✉)
Robert Schuman Centre for Advanced Studies, European University Institute,
Via delle Fontanelle 19, San Domenico di Fiesole, 50014 Florence, Italy
e-mail: Olivier.Roy@EUI.eu

© Springer International Publishing Switzerland 2015  187
I. Becci, O. Roy (eds.), *Religious Diversity in European Prisons,*
DOI 10.1007/978-3-319-16778-7_12

However, the situation has gradually evolved since the end of the twentieth century for two reasons. First, inside European societies, newcomers—namely Islam and the new religious movements (Jehovah witnesses for instance)—are challenging the quasi monopoly of the dominant church(es). Second, the population in prison does not reflect, in terms of religious affiliation, the external society: in France, Great Britain, Germany, the Netherlands and Belgium, among others, a major group among prison inmates is made up of young males with a Muslim background (at least as far as short- and medium-term prison sentences are concerned). Certainly, two other elements play a role in this overrepresentation: the criminalization of clandestine immigration also brings to prison a population that is more often Muslim or Evangelical than Catholic or mainstream Protestant. Moreover, prisons are a place of proselytizing and conversions, strengthening the new fundamentalist trends in both Islam (Salafism) and Protestantism (Evangelicalism). Therefore, the religions that flourish in prison do not necessarily consider themselves to be part of the "national pact" that defines the place of religions in the public sphere.

Prison authorities did not respond swiftly to the sociological changes among inmates. Either out of sheer inertia or because of their commitment to the old "order", they have been reluctant to open and extend the ranks of chaplaincy to newcomers. In countries with a dominant and more or less established religion (Italy), neither the state nor the church has been eager to deprive the Catholic church of its dominant position in the chaplaincy, and to acknowledge that the country has a growing Muslim population. The same prejudice is shared in the outside society: municipalities and local bishops are quite reluctant to let mosques be built in town centres. In France, many prison governors put forward the concept of *laïcité*, on the one hand to restrict religious practices among Muslims, and on the other hand for fear of "cults", for instance to forbid Jehovah's Witnesses from participating in chaplaincy activities. The same reluctance is to be found outside the prison system: schools forbid religious "visibility" (veils, prayers), and the Parliament has set up a special commission (MIVILUDE) to monitor and curb what they called "cults" (*sectes*), among them Jehovah's Witnesses (even though the courts recently concluded that the law does not and cannot make a distinction between a "religion" and a "cult", the Jehovah's Witness movement has been granted tax exemption by the *Conseil d'Etat* on religious grounds). In a word, the reluctance to open up chaplaincy reflects the dominant prejudices of societies.

Nevertheless, a growing phenomenon is pushing prison authorities in many countries to adopt a more proactive approach to chaplaincy: the religious radicalization among young Muslim inmates, which eventually leads to an increasing political radicalism. For instance, the role of prison radicalization has been documented in the case of the cell that murdered 17 journalists, Jews and police officers in France on 7 January 2014. All three of the terrorists were radicalized in prison through the influence of a member of Al Qaeda, Jamel Beghal. They had previously been arrested for petty delinquency and met seasoned militants in prison. Incidentally, this is a recurrent pattern among jailed political militants (like the ultra-left in France, Italy and Spain during the seventies): when state authorities are reluctant to grant them the status of political prisoners, they share their cells with petty delinquents whom they may contribute to politically educating and grooming.

The issue is complicated by the fact that in Sunni Islam it is easy to play the role of an imam (leading the prayer) because it does not depend on any diploma or accreditation from a religious institution, but relies only on the consensus of the local community, who, wrongly or rightly, attribute knowledge and charisma to the self-proclaimed leader. By making use of loopholes in prison regulations or playing on the authorities' fear of incidents, they have been able to organize prayers and training sessions among young inmates in search of spiritual support and socialization. They provide them with a paradoxical redemption: they shun delinquency, drugs and alcohol and turn into rigorous *salafis*. Local Muslim circles in prison may also play the role of protection against other inmates. Conversions to Islam of non-Muslims and to strict practice of Muslims who previously were only nominally so have become a current pattern that has alarmed prison authorities. Because it provides a set of clear and explicit norms, well adapted to inmates who lack culture and religious education, the dominant religious school of thought that spreads among Muslim inmates is "*salafism*", a strict scriptural and fundamentalist form of Islam that promotes "secession" from the "unbelievers"; petty delinquency can thus be legitimized as long as it only concerns "unbelievers", and allows inmates to reconcile faith and social marginalization.

Therefore, the first motive for prison authorities to develop a Muslim chaplaincy is to counter the radicalization of young Muslim inmates. This entails two main difficulties, first that of promoting, and hence defining, moderate Islam, and second of bestowing legitimacy on a category of "moderate imams" who are as much self-proclaimed as the so-called "radical imams" for a very good reason: no institution in Europe is in charge of training "moderate imams" or any kind of imams at all, while the very definition of "moderate Islam" is still under debate.

Thus, the state is confronted with two totally new tasks: instead of just recognizing a new religion, it has to "choose" the practitioners and set up, if not define, some criteria for what can be accepted as a moderate Islam. In both cases, the state has to depart from its traditional constitutional role: the separation of church and state and subcontracting the appointment of chaplains to churches.

The issue for Islam is not so much a lack of volunteers for chaplaincy, but the selection and the status bestowed on chaplains. The lack of clerical institutions in Islam blurs the line between a Muslim social worker and a religious practitioner. While Christian clerics who are employed by their church or faith community might go into prisons without any payment from the prison administration, there is no religious organization that can provide Muslim chaplains with a salary, or at least take care of their expenses.

The consequence of the new policy of promoting moderate Islam in prison by appointing "moderate" imams is that the European states are embroiled in a process of "formatting" Islam along the familiar patterns of Christian churches: professional clerics, providing a specific and clearly defined range of social and spiritual services to individuals. Such a position simply does not exist in traditional Muslim societies (there are no "Muslim chaplains" in the jails or defence forces of Middle Eastern countries). It is interesting to note that most Western prison administrations do not speak of "prison imams" but of "prison Muslim chaplains", using a Christian term and it is not such a surprise to find that, to my knowledge, most of the Muslim religious practitioners who accept the job do not protest against the use of a Christian term for their new occupation, they understand very clearly that the function is not that of an "imam" but is specific to the Western context of the relation between state and religion. The Western "Muslim chaplain" is not what an imam is in the usual Sunni tradition, where any pious Muslim can lead the prayer. An imam does not have a personal clerical status, but his duty is just to manage a mosque, lead the prayers and occasionally preach from the pulpit. The Muslim chaplain in a Western prison has no mosque, does not preach, and does not necessarily lead prayers, but he is expected to teach the inmates "true" Islam. He is thus not necessarily the most pious among his peers, but needs to have specific knowledge and training from a legitimate institution. In this sense, Islam is pushed to conform to the Christian-based definition of what a religion is. Chaplaincy is formatted as a mix between spiritual assistance, performance of rites and social service.

But beyond the establishment of a "Muslim chaplaincy", another issue is looming: how to define a "moderate" Islam? Everywhere in Europe, states are prevented from interfering with the theological debate: the good old times of "Gallicanism" and "Josefism", when the French and Austrian monarchies in the seventeenth and eighteenth centuries allowed themselves to interfere with the fixing of church theological tenets, are gone. The way a "Muslim chaplaincy" is being set up questions the very tenets of the definition of secularism in Europe.

Having said all this, a last issue is whether the "Muslim chaplaincy" project will be enough to "saturate" the religious field by depriving individual inmates of the capacity to proselytize. Chaplains are forbidden from proselytizing and so may not reach out to people who are looking for a new or different form of faith. They may also miss contemporary forms of religious practices which are highly individualized and not linked with any given faith community. Chaplaincy is part of a policy of "institutionalizing" religions which might miss the real spiritual expectations and religious practices of inmates, who may look towards religion not for solace and penance but for protest and revolt.

There is a price in building an institution like "Muslim chaplaincy" in prison out of strictly security concerns instead of taking into consideration the real spiritual needs and demands of inmates.

# Index

© Springer International Publishing Switzerland 2015
I. Becci, O. Roy (eds.), *Religious Diversity in European Prisons,*
DOI 10.1007/978-3-319-16778-7